FAMILY CIRCLE

EAT WHAT YOU LOVE & LOSE

FAMILY CIRCLE

EAT WHAT YOU LOVE & LOSE

Quick and Easy Diet Recipes from Our Test Kitchen

PEGGY KATALINICH

Diet Developed by SUSAN McQUILLAN, M.S., R.D.

ReganBooks

An Imprint of HarperCollinsPublishers

This book is not intended to replace medical advice or to be a substitute for a physician. Always seek the advice of a doctor before beginning any diet and/or exercise program.

The author and the publisher expressly disclaim responsibility for any adverse effects arising from following the diet or exercise program in this book without appropriate medical supervision.

Photography Credits

Black-and-White Photographs
Scott Jones: pp. xi, xiii, xiv, 243; Ross Whitaker: pp. 4 (both), 5 (both), 7 (both), 8 (both), 10 (both), 11 (both), 236 (both), 237 (both), 238 (both); Brian Hagiwara: pp. 30, 100, 110, 132, 155, 164, 167, 212; Mark Ferri: pp. 35, 38, 50, 62, 70, 86, 93, 103, 114, 123, 135, 136, 145, 151, 181, 195, 214; Steve Cohen: pp. 45, 81, 200, 218; Dasha Wright-Ewing: p. 67; Mark Thomas: pp. 78, 188, 203; Beatriz Da Costa: p. 161; Katrina De Leon: p. 196.

Color Photographs
Mark Ferri: 1, 3, 5, 6, 9; Brian Hagiwara: 2, 4, 7, 8, 10, 12, 13, 15; Steve Cohen: 11; Mark Thomas: 12, 14; Steve Mark Needham: 16.

FIRST EDITION

Designed by Joel Avirom and Jason Snyder
Design Assistant: Meghan Day Healey

Printed on acid-free paper

Library of Congress Cataloging-in-Publication Data has been applied for.

ISBN 0-06-056462-8

03 04 05 06 07 QW 10 9 8 7 6 5 4 3 2 1

Dedicated to all of you who love food as much as we do.
You can *eat what you love and lose.*

CONTENTS

PREFACE

· · · · · · · · · · · · ·

YOU CAN HAVE YOUR CAKE AND LOSE WEIGHT TOO!

Imagine for a moment that you work here at *Family Circle* magazine. As you walk down the halls of our offices, you can't help but smell tempting aromas from our test kitchen: one day it's pasta, another chocolate desserts, and another an entire menu of barbecue options. The editors and I love producing food stories, but we also pride ourselves on dreaming up great diet and fitness articles. Yes, life is full of temptation and paradox!

Indeed, our dream story would be titled "The No-Calorie Chocolate Cake That Burns Fat Fast." Now that may never be possible, but our food director, Peggy Katalinich, and her crew, including nutritionist Susan McQuillan, have come close. They've designed a weight-loss strategy—backed up with more than 250 recipes—that is a dieter's wish come true. The diet works because you can have your cake and drop pounds too.

When Peggy pitched the idea of our food department staff teaming up to take off pounds, I knew it would be a terrific story—if they could win the battle of the bulge. After all, they are paid to eat! But their camaraderie and commitment was motivation to us all. In fact, as their waists got thinner, many of us joked that ours were getting thicker, since we were now dining on leftovers from the test kitchens.

Susan McQuillan, Susan Ungaro, and Peggy Katalinich in the test kitchen.

So now it's our turn—and yours. With the publication of this diet cookbook, we are also launching the *Family Circle* Eat What You Love & Lose Diet America Challenge. There's no doubt that the friendship factor can make the difference in diet and fitness success. Read our tips and tricks and then check out our website at familycircle.com for more details—and a little more help from your friends at *Family Circle*.

Susan Ungaro
Editor in Chief, Family Circle

INTRODUCTION

. . . .

WHEN PEGGY KATALINICH ASKED ME to meet with her to talk about a group weight-loss program for *Family Circle*'s food department, I thought, "What a great idea!" And what a great opportunity for me to help prove that one easy plan can work equally well for six very different people with one thing in common: they love to eat. In fact, they love it so much, they've made a career of it.

As a former *Family Circle* "foodie," I worked as a staffer and freelancer in the magazine's test kitchens for the better part of twelve years. I know how much fun it is to sample recipes and I also know how easy it is for weight to pile on as the years go by. I, too, eventually got a fifteen-pound "bonus" for all my good work. Of course for me it wasn't just a physical burden, there was the added embarrassment of being a weight-loss expert who had gained too much weight. The time had come for me to practice what I preach. Although I never went on a structured diet, I shed the pounds and I did it pretty much the same way Peggy and her team did. I went back to eating sensibly (most of the time), I started walking farther, and more often, and I never, ever, deprived myself of favorite foods. I simply learned to eat less of them. And therein lies the key to the *Eat What You Love & Lose* plan.

Although a shared work situation was a big reason that the *FC* food department gained weight, each member also has his or her own personal relationship with food. As individuals, they eat for varying reasons, follow very different schedules, and have distinct food preferences. To cover their differences and make sure this program worked, I had to give them a plan they could adapt to their specific lifestyles, menus they could switch around to fit their own particular needs. They quickly learned to make the necessary adjustments. And that's why it worked.

Because they started losing weight right from the beginning and continued to drop pounds with each passing week, the entire team was motivated to stick with the plan until each of them reached his or her goal. Then they said "What now?" The only sensible answer I could give them was, "Keep doing what you're doing." And because what they did made them feel so good, and wasn't difficult, they're still doing it.

Years of scientific research and hundreds of fad diets have proven only one thing—when it comes to losing weight and keeping it off, there's no substitute for a balanced diet with lots of choices coupled with regular exercise. Weight control is *not* about cutting carbohydrates unless you're eating too many, and it's not about increasing protein, unless you're not getting enough. It's not about eating low-fat foods or high-fiber foods. The formula for maintaining a healthy weight is this: Calories consumed = calories burned. Ideally, the calories you consume come from something that resembles a nutritionally balanced diet. That never changes, no matter what the latest pop diet suggests. When you need to lose weight, you don't need gimmicks. What you need is a permanent plan for healthy eating. Lucky you! You're holding that plan in your hands.

Susan McQuillan, M.S., R.D.
New York City

1 WE DID IT AND YOU CAN TOO!

IT'S A DELICIOUSLY DIRTY JOB, but somebody has to do it: triple-testing—and triple-tasting—the upwards of twenty-five recipes that appear in each issue of *Family Circle*. That's hundreds of sweet and savory dishes each year! As this national magazine's food director, I am often asked how I manage not to triple my waistline in the process.

Well, I thought I had a handle on the situation, and so did several other members of *FC*'s test-kitchen crew, including Diane Mogelever, Julie Miltenberger, Donna Meadow, Michael Tyrrell, and Althea Needham. After all, we are food professionals. We knew what went into each bite and had the nutritional background to make smart substitutions. If anyone could accommodate a little excess here and there, it was us, right?

Gradually, though, those daily forkfuls of pasta and nibbles of brownies began putting a strain on our chef's shirts. Julie no longer felt svelte in her favorite pair of suede pants. Diane realized it had been ages since she could tuck her blouses into her skirts. I found myself hitting the clothes racks for larger sizes. One day as we were sitting around the test kitchen trying various versions of pizza, Michael muttered that if he kept this up he'd need to create new holes in his belt. That comment prompted us all to admit that we'd been piling on extra pounds. So we decided to collaborate on our biggest project ever: slimming down while still developing the same quality recipes that have made *Family Circle* famous.

Think about it. We spend at least eight hours a day, five days a week, cooking, sampling, thinking, and writing about food. How could we get through those testings and tastings—sometimes ten a day!—and still lose weight?

Yet we did it! Together we dropped a total of 146 pounds in less than four months on the *Eat What You Love & Lose* plan designed by nutritionist Susan McQuillan. Each of us not only met our original get-trim goal, but a few even exceeded it. And we did it the healthy way, averaging a weekly 1- to 2-pound loss.

During those fifteen weeks, we faced the same challenges that tempt all of you—and then some. The very first day of the diet, for instance, we started a feature story on that most tempting of desserts, cheesecake. Outside the test kitchen, we had to learn to navigate weddings, vacations, family feasts, even a press trip to Italy. The staff at some local restaurants know what I do for a living, and often the kitchen would send me tidbits to try things I did not order. Sounds great, you say? But then the choice becomes: Please the chef or stay on the diet. Happily, I discovered I could do both, by taking one bite and passing the rest on to my tablemates. (How my family didn't balloon up during this time, I'll never know.)

More important, if we could do it, so can you! Like you, we were among the majority of Americans who want to lose anywhere from 10 to 30 pounds. Like you, we lead very busy lives. Each of us holds down a full-time job, some of us are parents, juggling our kids' needs along with our own, and others are singles with very hectic schedules. Like many of you, we're at an age where we no longer burn up extra calories the way we used to. And like everyone else out there, we had specific, even quirky, eating habits and agendas. A very early riser, Diane is awake at five o'clock each morning. How could she survive the seven hours till we all broke for lunch? Donna confessed she was an evening grazer who often stayed up until 1 A.M. What could she do to keep from noshing nonstop between dinner and bedtime?

That's what is so wonderful about the *Eat What You Love & Lose* program, set out for you in the next chapter: One size fits all! It is flexible enough to adapt to various lifestyles, food preferences, and body clocks. Since the plan allows two daily treats, up to 150 calories each, we substituted our kitchen samplings for those snacks on the days we had recipe taste-testings.

It doesn't hurt that the suggested meals and recipes pile on the flavor. As foodies, we wouldn't have been content with plain broiled chicken every day, so we've given you plenty of taste sensations in the chapters that follow. Working within the plan's guidelines, we came up with a bounty of breakfast ideas; savory sandwiches, salads, and soups for lunchtime; palate-pleasing pasta, seafood, poultry, and meat main meals; and, yes, desserts to die for. Many are make-ahead, freeze-able, and otherwise convenient for preplanning your weekly menus. And as with all our family-friendly *Family Circle* recipes, these dishes get you out of the kitchen fast!

THE DREAM TEAM

We can't underestimate how much it meant that we were all in this together. The group support—nagging as well as cheerleading—really took us over the finish line. We confess that this also added a certain element of competition to the camaraderie. The rest of our *Family Circle* colleagues were cheering us on too, offering kudos and compliments. (Of course, they also appreciated that we brought them the leftovers when each test-kitchen sampling was over.)

So our advice to you: Join forces with a group of office mates, friends, neighbors, or family, and get losing! You can even try collective cooking, with everyone contributing part of the meal.

In the end, though, we all had to come up with very personal game plans. Here are our stories and strategies. Hopefully, our experiences can guide you as you join us in taking control of the scale with the *Eat What You Love & Lose* diet.

Peggy Katalinich

*Food director, married,
mother of two teens who like to eat*

ORIGINAL GOAL: 20 pounds
TOTAL LOSS: 28 pounds

Biggest temptation: French fries
How she coped: Peggy bought all the available brands of reduced-fat and baked potato chips and stuck to the portion size. They met her need for salty crunch with fewer calories, less fat.
Favorite new recipe: "Fried" Chicken & Potatoes (page 112)
Tip: Flavor club soda with a teaspoon of creme de cassis for a festive drink at parties or at restaurants.

Peggy admits that the first day on the diet, she felt she couldn't do it. "Here I was, the food director, the one who urged everyone else to join in this venture: I looked at my plate of Sausage and Peppers with Spaghetti, and thought, I'm going to starve. The portion size was so much smaller than usual that I was dumbfounded."

But she reminded herself that since coming to *Family Circle* in 1994 she'd gained two pounds a year. At 5-foot-7, she could get away with a lot more than if she were 5-foot-2, but the extra weight didn't feel good. "My 'comfortable' clothes were no longer comfortable and the next step would be a larger wardrobe. So I ate all of the sausage and peppers, savoring each mouthful, and actually licked the plate of Grilled Chicken Salad that I brought home for dinner. I woke up feeling lighter—not to mention very virtuous—the next morning."

As the days passed, Peggy was surprised at how satisfied she was with smaller servings. And she discovered her own appetite-appeaser: roasted peppers! "I love them for adding body, flavor, and texture to my sandwiches," raves Peggy. (In chapter 10, you'll find a quick way to roast your own.) "In crunch situations, I brought my own pre-portioned snacks, even sneaking air-popped or low-fat popcorn into the movie theater. Most important, I realized that if I can just hold out for 20 minutes, a craving will pass."

To spur her progress, Peggy went running whenever possible. "One Saturday, I even took over the lawn-mowing—sweating like crazy because I didn't know the machine had an 'easy-push' feature. A great workout, though. And it all paid off," she states proudly. "I knew the diet had succeeded when I dragged most of my wardrobe to Luigi, the tailor. He kept pulling at my waistbands in amazement. He had to take in my skirts two full sizes!"

In fact, at the group's last weigh-in, Peggy measured nine pounds lighter than she was at her wedding. What an anniversary gift!

Diane Mogelever

Senior food editor, married, mother of two grown children

WEIGHT-LOSS GOAL: 10 pounds
TOTAL LOSS: 16 pounds

Biggest temptation: Vanilla ice cream with hot fudge sauce
How she coped: Diane turned to prepared rice pudding and snacked on a third of a cup (for about 100 calories) whenever she thought of her favorite dessert.
Favorite new recipe: Strawberry Parfait (page 166)
Tip: Instead of dollops of butter or oil, sprinkle balsamic vinegar over vegetables—and salads, too—to maximize flavors without adding fat.

Diane never gave dieting a thought until she could no longer tuck her blouses into her skirts. "I used to be able to eat whatever I wanted," sighs *FC*'s longtime senior food editor.

"I think much of my recent weight gain was a slowdown of metabolism due to age." But surely the kitchen's frequent dessert testings were another factor. "A recipe would be so wonderful that I would want to eat it, instead of just taste it."

The *Eat What You Love & Lose* menus were a revelation. "It was easy to stick to the plan, and I learned new eating patterns in the process," Diane says. "When eating out, I chose low-fat items, yet I still walked away from the table totally satisfied."

Peer pressure helped curb her urges at afternoon tastings. "With everyone standing there and everyone thinking 'diet,' I didn't dare take a second bite unless I absolutely needed to determine a flavor," laughs Diane.

Mornings were a little trickier. An early riser, Diane needed to keep hunger pangs at bay between her 5 A.M. wake-up time and our 12:30 office lunch. She came up with the perfect solution: splitting up breakfast. "I have a little cereal with my coffee when I first get up, then around 9:30 I have the rest of my cup of cereal and some fruit. I wound up doing this even on the weekends."

Diane always walks the twenty blocks to and from work. But when a mid-diet plateau threatened to discourage her, she turned to her stationary cross-country ski machine, pumping up her routine to three 10-minute sessions a day. She added some light weight-lifting and was soon back on a losing streak.

Diane's formerly tight waistbands are now so loose that her skirts keep twisting around from back to front. "I've even lost weight in my feet—I keep stepping out of my shoes!" she laughs.

Julie Miltenberger

Senior food editor, single

WEIGHT LOSS GOAL: 20 pounds
TOTAL LOSS: 24 pounds

Biggest temptation: Crusty french bread slathered with salted butter
How she coped: Julie coated flavored flatbreads with a yogurt-butter spread to mimic her favorite flavors.
Favorite new recipe: French Bread BBQ Pork Melts (page 212)
Tip: Keep no-fat popcorn on hand. It's easy to measure out for portion control and gives crunchy, salty satisfaction.

Julie suspected the reason she was having trouble zipping up her beloved suede pants. "I was a white-food kid—pasta, rice, bread, milk," she reports. The *Eat What You Love & Lose* plan helped her cut down on the white stuff. "In the past, I would just guess at those portions. But I will now use a cup measure to serve my starches."

She also takes an ultra-practical approach to special occasions. At parties, she positioned herself far from easy-to-grab snacks. For Thanksgiving, she decided that no particular food was taboo. "I just didn't have second helpings." On Week Two of the diet she went off on a cruise. Since she had lost nearly five pounds the first week, she decided to hold steady rather than put pressure on herself to drop more. By keeping active and being mindful of portion sizes at the buffets, she gained nothing but a healthy tan.

But Julie did need a slight adjustment to her body clock. Because she usually hits the gym after work, she had fallen into the habit of not eating dinner until 8 or 9 P.M. Ravenous one Saturday at 5 P.M. and afraid she'd give in to an overwhelming passion for a burger and fries, she made a panicked 911 call to test-kitchen pal Michael Tyrrell. "I'd just walked past a diner and

smelled all the fried food," Julie recalls. "But simply talking to Michael about my urge to binge helped me get over it." Still, she realized that waiting so long between meals was sabotaging her willpower. "These days I try to have supper no later than 7:30."

She's made an A.M. change as well. "I eat a little more breakfast than I used to. That keeps me satiated until lunchtime."

Losing nearly five inches in her waist means Julie is now swimming in those suede pants. "I need to have them taken in. But that's a good problem!"

Donna Meadow

Food department associate, married, mother of two

WEIGHT LOSS GOAL: 25 pounds
TOTAL LOSS: 30 pounds

Biggest temptation: Chocolate layer cake with chocolate frosting
How she coped: Donna munched on chocolate-mint meringue cookies—a sweet hit of cocoa that helped stave off the craving.
Favorite new recipe: Choco-Mocha Angel Food Cake (page 182)

Tip: Starving in the afternoon? Slice up a large dill pickle—very flavorful, very filling, and very low in calories. Also, find a way to work walking into your routine; it will make all the difference.

For Donna, diet had always meant deprivation. "Whenever I tried to lose weight before, I would never dare eat pasta, potatoes, bread." So she was thrilled that our plan included these staples.

Donna had also been depriving herself of breakfast. "I skipped it, then I would make it up with the tastings, but ultimately those were not satisfying. A bite here and there throughout the day didn't make me feel like I'd eaten a real meal—even though the calories added up." Now, sitting down each morning to a blueberry muffin or a scrambled egg and hash browns keeps her from oversampling in *FC*'s kitchen.

As with many busy working moms, Donna stayed up late doing chores—often until 1 or 2 A.M.—and munching to keep her energy up. "I would make my kids' lunches then and pick at the food, even eating the crusts I cut off their sandwiches." To stop her grazing, she set her snack curfew at 9 P.M., and made an effort to go to bed sooner and wake up earlier, tackling tasks when she is less tired and tempted to nibble.

Last but not least, Donna knew she had to incorporate some aerobic activity into her life. She thought she had no time to work out, but Susan McQuillan suggested she simply walk from her home to the train station and then to the office. The half hour of exercise five days a week did wonders for Donna. "That small change in my routine really helped the weight drop off."

Not long after reaching her 30-pound goal, Donna found photographs of herself taken over the summer. "I couldn't believe that used to be me! Those pictures will be my inspiration to keep on going."

Michael Tyrrell

Food department associate, single

ORIGINAL GOAL: 15 pounds
TOTAL LOSS: 18 pounds

Biggest temptation: Cheese pizza
How he coped: When the craving hit, Michael gave in, but limited his consumption to a single slice or baked up the fixings on half a pita.
Favorite new recipe: Spicy Sausage Pizza (page 159)
Tip: Keep individual boxes of pretzel sticks around—they're only 100 calories each and fill you up.

In the previous eight months, Michael had lost fifteen pounds on a diet of his own devising. But by the end of the summer, his weight loss had slowed and he was finding his low-low-fat diet boring-boring. He was also frustrated with going it alone. "The group support really helped, especially on Monday mornings. After our weigh-ins, we would have a diet powwow and talk about what worked for us during the week and what hadn't."

Michael used his culinary flair to jazz up "freebie" veggies: He roasted zucchini slices with oregano, lemon pepper, and a spritz of cooking-oil spray and tossed cucumber slices with nonfat plain yogurt and garlic. Not content with canned low-fat soups, he came up with many of the great-tasting spoonable meals featured in chapter 5.

On the job, he and Julie found that "by 3 or 4 each afternoon, we would both hit the wall." So they reserved their snacks for this slump time, sitting down together for pretzel sticks, a fat-free cookie, or popcorn and a cup of tea.

On the weekends, Michael saved his "snack allowance" for a glass of wine or other treat. And when he found himself dying for a cheeseburger, he indulged without guilt. "I wound up not eating the bun—it was nothing special and wasn't worth the calories. But I got the burger out of my system, and the next day, I went back on the plan."

His waist now three inches trimmer, Michael credits our test kitchen diet with reminding him to eat at regular times and to include all the food groups. He's also more realistic about portion sizes. "I have a better feeling for what 'moderation' really is: not eating three pieces of bread and butter instead of six, but having one piece instead of three."

Althea Needham

Test kitchen assistant,
single mother of two

WEIGHT LOSS GOAL: 30 pounds
TOTAL LOSS: 30 pounds

Biggest temptation: Coconut cream pie
How she coped: Althea discovered reduced-calorie frozen fudge pops that satisfied her sweet tooth.
Favorite new recipe: Coconut Dream Pie (page 172)
Tip: Try low-fat yogurt with a little granola for breakfast to really set you up for the day.

"Sweets are my weakness," admits Althea. Her love of pies, cakes, and other tantalizing treats didn't catch up with *FC*'s test kitchen assistant in her native Jamaica, where she was a track-and-field star. But in New York City, after eleven years of hopping subways

instead of running to wherever she needed to go, Althea began to feel weighed down. Before starting the group diet, she had lost 34 pounds, mainly through rigorous gym sessions three or four times a week. But she wanted to go further and jumped at the chance to shape up her diet too.

Althea resolved to keep her usual temptations out of her house, and we helped her stick to only one sampling during dessert tastings. "No more double dippings!" she reports. And the *Eat What You Love & Lose* plan introduced her to a new treat. "I never liked yogurt before, but now I'm hooked on low-fat vanilla," she says. "Sometimes I'll just have that for dinner, with sliced strawberries and a little granola on top." She also lowers the fat when cooking her home island favorites, like brown-stew chicken. She seasons the sauté pan with a teaspoon of oil, quickly browns skinless cutlets, then wipes out the pan and adds a little water to cook the chicken through before she puts in the rest of the ingredients. Meals are filled in with salads, and her water bottle is always close at hand.

If she does indulge, she adds an extra hour on the treadmill, knowing that will burn off another 700 calories. "I'm solid muscle, so it was harder for me to lose," notes Althea, who can now slip into size-8 slacks. "Even my upper arms are thinner. I'm on the right track, and I'm going to keep going."

THAT EXTRA STEP

Even though we all found our own ways to deal with our personal diet traps, it wasn't gravy (no pun intended). We were definitely cranky those first two weeks, as we battled our natural impulses, adjusted ourselves to a new way of eating, and contended with the inevitable tummy rumblings. But those were the moments we reached out to each other. Then we saw the results: losses from 2½ to 7 pounds (that was Donna) in the first seven days alone! At our weekly weigh-ins, we shared high-fives and invaluable insight that kept us motivated.

It wasn't long before our new way of eating became a part of our lives. Our losses came so steadily that Donna began to wonder if she had misread her scale and Julie double-checked her food diary to be sure she hadn't skimped on portions. We all had times when we felt too full to snack, then worried if we had done something wrong. But no. We just weren't hungry. Our sleeker bodies had simply adjusted to getting the right amount of fuel.

Retraining our appetites had an unexpected benefit: Our households are in better shape, too! "Instead of snacking at night and on weekends, I hung pictures on the walls, and gathered paperbacks to donate to the library," reports Julie. Michael reorganized his cutlery drawers. Donna and I straightened out our linen closets. Althea scrubbed her bathroom so hard it literally sparkled. And we probably burned off a few extra calories in the process.

And that was another key component of our success: added activity. It sped up our metabolism and eased us past plateaus, not to mention boosted energy and toned muscles. Each of us found a way to bring more exercise into our lives. Those of us who had worked out regularly before found other ways to sneak in an extra session. The best fat-burner also turned out to be the simplest: walking. We all made a point, whenever possible, to take the stairs, forgo public transportation, and plan a post-tasting stroll around the block.

Find a fitness routine that works for you, too. Learn a new sport, sign up for yoga, play soccer with the kids. Or simply be open to moving around a little more than you usually do: Pace while you're waiting for the bus, do biceps curls with a soup can as you talk on the phone, fill your laundry basket only halfway, then make two trips upstairs to put clean clothes away. As we proved, every extra step counts!

Before you go to the next chapter for the details on how to bring the *Eat What You Love & Lose* plan into your life, turn the page and take our quizzes.

ARE YOU READY?

You've unearthed the treadmill from underneath the mound of laundry and stocked the fridge with all the right foods. But losing weight and keeping it off involves more than getting portions under control and exercising regularly. Before you can successfully take off pounds, you need to identify and address the issues that could sabotage your dieting efforts.

1. How much weight do you expect to lose in the first month of your diet?

    A. 7 pounds or less

    B. 8 to 12 pounds

    C. 13 pounds or more

2. When do you eat?

    A. only when you are hungry

    B. when you are upset or stressed out

    C. when you are happy, sad, and everything in between

3. Why do you want to lose weight?

    A. You know it will make you feel happier and healthier.

    B. Family and friends nag you continually about your weight.

    C. You know all your problems would be solved if you had Jennifer Aniston's body.

4. The stress level in your life most resembles which TV show?

    A. *Seventh Heaven*

    B. *Everybody Loves Raymond*

    C. *Survivor*

5. You've had a long, bad day. You finally have some time to yourself. You...

    A. go for a 20-minute spin on your exercise bike

    B. veg out in front of the TV

    C. finish the leftovers from dinner

6. *As part of your weight-loss program, you...*

    A. plan to get up a half an hour early to go for a power walk four days a week

    B. plan to work out to an exercise video every day, although you don't have a specific time reserved for it

    C. don't plan to exercise because you're too busy and it'll just make you hungrier

7. *You intend to have a healthy dinner every night. At 6 P.M. you are ...*

    A. putting out the low-fat chicken dish you prepared on Sunday

    B. at the supermarket, buying frozen lasagna and a premixed salad

    C. pulling up at the fast-food drive-through window

8. *When you go out to dinner in a restaurant, what do you usually do?*

    A. You are satisfied with the salad and piece of fish you ordered, since you filled up on a bowl of vegetable soup before you arrived.

    B. You eat four pieces of bread while waiting for your salad and chicken to arrive.

    C. You have potato skins and pork chops, then polish off whatever crème brûlée your family didn't finish. After all, who can diet in a restaurant?

. . . .

Key

Tally up your score. If most of your answers were. . .

A's: Congratulations. You know you need to do this for yourself, have realistic expectations of how much you can lose, and will block out the time necessary to exercise and prepare healthy meals. With nothing to stop you, check out the diet and strategies in this book to find your path to success.

B's: Be careful. There are obstacles that may prevent you from acheiving the weight loss you desire. Maybe your goals are unrealistic or you need to think about ways to find the time to fix healthy food and to exercise. Reevaluate what you want and what you'll do to get it.

C's: This is probably not the right moment to take on a big, time-consuming project like a diet. You may be going through a tense period that drains you of the time, energy, and motivation necessary to be successful. Instead, try making small, healthy changes in your lifestyle, such as eating more fruits and vegetables and taking occasional walks, even something as simple as switching from whole milk to skim. The advice in this book can help you to resolve impediments you're facing. When your crisis passes, you'll have a leg up on pursuing a diet.

. . . .

WHAT'S YOUR FITNESS STYLE?

Are you more apt to find success at a health club, with a customized plan, or doing it on your own? Take our quiz to find out. The section you answer "yes" to the most is likely to be your best bet.

- Do you enjoy exercise's social aspects?

- Do you like a variety of fitness options and aids?

- Is it easy for you to eat healthfully?

Try a health club. You'll have tons of exercise alternatives and machines—as well as the opportunity to meet new people which might give you needed motivation. Clubs also offer access to the pros.

- Do you find structured diets difficult to stick to?

- Do you find it hard to stay motivated?

- Is personal attention an incentive to keep you going?

A one-on-one approach, with a personal trainer, may fit the bill if cost isn't a concern. You're likely to see faster progress because you'll learn new skills more quickly and will have personal support whenever you need it. If cost is a factor, consider joining a health club and set up sessions with one of their trainers on a regular basis.

- Are you motivated and disciplined?

- Do you like to do things your way?

- Are you willing to do research?

Developing your own plan may be the best thing for you. This tactic lets you devise an approach that fits your schedule and psyche.

If your answers don't fall into one category, consider signing up—and paying in advance—for a series of exercise classes. Local YMCAs, high schools, and adult centers as well as certain workplaces and gyms frequently offer these. This way you'll still have freedom, but can benefit from professional leadership. How you choose to interact with others in the class is entirely up to you!

2 IT'S ALL ABOUT THE CALORIES

. . . .

TO MAKE OUR DIET DREAMS A REALITY, we first turned to Susan McQuillan, a registered dietitian, food and nutrition consultant, and *Family Circle* test-kitchen veteran. We were sure that only someone who had joined us in the trenches, shoulder to shoulder and ladle to ladle, would know what we were up against.

Of course, we were also hoping that Susan might share some insider strategy, some pound-paring preparation that would make it all effortless. Tactics like drinking a special tea before each meal, perhaps. Or eating only one food group at a time. Or even walking while we ate to burn up calories instantly. After listening to our concerns and sifting through the latest medical research, Susan revealed to us the magic formula: "It's all about the calories."

"But isn't that so old-fashioned?" we protested. "Shouldn't we combine this food with that food, swear off certain ingredients altogether, or simply drink water every 30 minutes?"

Susan repeated, "It's all about the calories."

And so it is. Even though there are hundreds of diet studies every year and research constantly turns up new information, the fundamental truth is this: Take in 3,500 more calories than you use up in the activities of your daily life, and you gain a pound. Eliminate or burn up 3,500 calories, and you lose a pound. That mathematical equation has not changed despite other leaps in scientific knowledge. The body needs fuel, and when it gets more than it needs, it stores it—on our hips, on our thighs, and around our waists. A very efficient, though often discouraging, system.

So the next step was to put this system to work for us, instead of against us. This meant forgetting all those "tricks" for losing weight that have become part of diet folklore and accepting that only nutritious, well-balanced eating would get us where we wanted to go and, what's more, keep us in that healthy place for the rest of our lives.

THE STARTING LINE

The *Eat What You Love & Lose* diet kicks off with the two-week menu plan shown on the following pages. Once we were comfortable with the flow of these meals, Susan said, we could mix and match—have dinner for lunch if that was more suitable or switch around meals from different days—as well as substitute comparable dishes based on the recipes in this book. We could even repeat certain menus as often as we liked. Michael, for instance, loves Day 14 and uses it often; Peggy religiously sticks with the breakfasts on Days 3 and 5. In keeping with current health guidelines, the daily menus each tally in at less than 30 percent of calories from fat. And Susan kept the total average daily calorie count just under an easy-to-live-with, but still-get-slim 1,500.

As anyone who's ever dieted knows, when you're eating less, every bite has to taste fabulous or you won't stick to it. So Susan channeled all her nutrition and cooking knowledge into developing super-tasty meals. And even with an extremely critical audience like us, she passed the test. Says Peggy: "Penne with Cherry Tomatoes, Smoked Mozzarella & Basil (Week 1) makes me feel like I'm in Italy in the summertime." And Diane gave two thumbs-up to Spicy Beef in Lettuce Rolls (Week 2). "The tang of the beef and the crunch of the lettuce is incredible!" So, with dishes like these—hearty and healthy and loaded with flavor—we still felt satisfied and energized.

But tempting and tasty as they were, two weeks of menus is probably not enough. So we called on our own test-kitchen know-how to expand our choices. We logged into our database and pulled out lower-fat, lower-calorie, plus quick and easy recipes. We also revisited many of our favorite dishes and tweaked them, reducing the calorie count while bumping up the flavor, to fit the guidelines. We were pleasantly surprised at how easy that was to do. We added oomph with herbs, spices, and other low-cal extras: Tarragon, shallots, and scallions perked up a simple crab salad; green peas and sautéed scallions brightened plain rice; fennel seeds and mushrooms smartened up a sausage sauce. You can do the same, adjusting for your and your family's tastes.

So in addition to the menus in this chapter, there are more than 250 recipes that work with the plan. We've given you omelets and sandwiches, Caesar salads and stir-fries, international and all-American main dishes. And for dessert, we've whipped up sensational sweets under 200 calories that you can trade in for one or two snacks depending on the particular calorie count. Along the way, we also offer some quick-prep tips and cook-slim secrets.

Begin with the basic two weeks' worth of menus; each listing represents one serving. For more ideas, check out the twelve Lighter Lunch suggestions. Enjoy the snacks given for each day, or pick two daily from our Snack Attacks list.

We mentioned before that the daily calorie totals average around 1,500. If you are a veteran dieter, this may seem high. But Susan explained that this is a healthy, realistic calculation to guarantee a steady weight loss as well as assure easy maintenance. You'll find that by staying within these limits, you'll lose without feeling famished. (Remember, we did; indeed, several of us exceeded our goals!) If you hit a slowdown for more than two weeks, you can eliminate a snack. But the much better tactic would be to increase your exercise.

As a general guideline, and when planning your menus beyond the two weeks, keep in mind the number of portions of each of the essential food groups you'll be eating each day.

THE BALANCING ACT

As Susan outlined the *Eat What You Love & Lose* plan, we saw that it was flexible and sensible. It doesn't skim off all the fat, or fill out our plates with mega-fiber foods that taste like pencil shavings. It doesn't exclude any particular food or any food group. It isn't high or low in anything. Instead, control is the watchword and moderation the mantra: Prepare nutritious dishes in real-life portions (no supersizing!), don't deprive yourself of anything, and take it one day at a time. Two snacks were built into each day, not the usual boring fruit cup either, but chips and salsa, jelly beans, even chocolate! Susan also gave us fast-food and restaurant options—pizza! a sub-shop sandwich!—for those days when we weren't in the test kitchen or had to grab a meal on the go.

So there we were, armed with an easy-to-follow menu plan, plenty of healthy and delicious choices, and the recipes to make it all work.

WEEK 1

1 Sunday

BREAKFAST

Potato-Bacon Frittata (page 203)

1 cup low-fat milk

1 orange

LUNCH

Grilled Chicken Salad: Grilled boneless, skinless chicken breast half, sliced and tossed with ¼ avocado, chopped, ½ cup salsa, 1 cup shredded romaine, ½ cup plain low-fat yogurt

1 cup tomato soup made with milk

DINNER

Baked Turkey Sausage and Peppers with Fennel (page 135)

1 cup cooked spaghetti or one 4-inch piece of toasted Italian bread

SNACKS

1 reduced-fat ice cream sandwich

1 ounce baked tortilla chips and ½ cup salsa

2 Monday

BREAKFAST

2 whole-grain frozen waffles

2 tablespoons maple syrup

½ cup reduced-fat milk

½ cup orange juice

LUNCH

Meatball Minestrone (page 80)

2 pieces garlic-flavored flatbread

DINNER

Stir-Fried Scallops and Snow Peas (page 104)

½ cup cooked white rice

1 cup salad of sliced cucumber, water chestnuts, and radishes sprinkled with salt and rice vinegar

SNACKS

1 apple and 1 large Dutch-style pretzel

2 fat-free devil's food cookie cakes with ½ cup low-fat (1%) milk

3 Tuesday

BREAKFAST

Tropical Fruit Salad: Combine ½ cup mango cubes, ½ cup pineapple chunks (if canned, use pineapple in juice, drained), ½ banana, sliced, 1 kiwi, peeled and sliced, and 2 tablespoons chopped walnuts

1 cup low-fat (1%) milk or 1 cup low-fat plain yogurt

LUNCH

Crabmeat Salad: ½ cup crabmeat (or shrimp), chopped, mixed with 2 tablespoons light mayo, ½ teaspoon tarragon, ½ teaspoon rice vinegar

1 large pita round

1 cup cantaloupe cubes

DINNER

Picadillo with Rice (page 147), *at left*

2 cups torn romaine lettuce topped with ½ cup orange sections

SNACKS

5 Hershey's Kisses

1 cup fruit juice with 5 Triscuits

BREAKFAST

Cheese Grits:
Prepare ½ cup
packaged quick grits,
topped with 1 ounce
grated reduced-fat
cheddar cheese

½ grapefruit

½ cup juice

LUNCH

1 reduced-fat,
low-calorie fast-food
sub sandwich

½ cup fresh fruit salad

1 cup low-fat (1%) milk

DINNER

Honey-Mustard
Chicken and Veggies
(page 113)

SNACKS

1 apple and 1½ ounces
reduced-fat cheddar
cheese

¼ cup raisins

BREAKFAST

1 cup low-fat vanilla
yogurt topped with
½ cup strawberries,
sliced, ½ banana,
sliced, ¼ cup low-fat
granola

LUNCH

Egg Salad:
2 hard-cooked eggs,
chopped, mixed with
2 tablespoons light
mayonnaise,
1 teaspoon Dijon
mustard, and
1 teaspoon pickle
relish

2 slices reduced-
calorie bread

2 cups tossed salad

2 tablespoons fat-free
salad dressing

DINNER

Penne with Cherry
Tomatoes, Smoked
Mozzarella, and Basil
(page 52), *at left*

2 cups salad greens

1 tablespoon low-fat
dressing

SNACKS

3 cups 40% reduced-fat
cheddar-flavored
popcorn

¼ cup chopped dried
fruit with 1 cup low-fat
(1%) milk

BREAKFAST

1 medium orange

½ toasted cinnamon
bagel topped with
1 tablespoon all-fruit
spread and ½ cup
part-skim ricotta

LUNCH

Ham 'n' Cheese
Sandwich: 1 ounce
thinly sliced baked
ham, 1 ounce thinly
sliced reduced-fat
Swiss cheese, 1
tablespoon Russian
dressing on 2 slices
reduced-calorie bread

10 baby carrots

1 banana

DINNER

Crispy Fish 'n' Chips
(page 94)

1 cup steamed
asparagus tossed with
sprinkling lemon juice
or balsamic vinegar
and oregano

SNACKS

1-ounce box pretzel
sticks with ½ cup low-
fat (1%) milk

1 small frozen yogurt
cone and ½ cup
strawberries

BREAKFAST

Banana-Berry
Smoothie: 1 cup low-fat
(1%) milk whirled in
blender with ½ banana
and ½ cup strawberry
slices, fresh or frozen

1 small bran or oat
bran muffin

LUNCH

Black Bean and Corn
Soup (page 72)

½ ounce baked tortilla
chips with ⅓ cup
guacamole

DINNER

Warm Chicken and
Roast Vegetable Salad
(page 38), *above*

1 slice Italian bread or
2 breadsticks (to equal
100 calories)

1 cup pineapple chunks

SNACKS

1 frozen fruit bar

4 graham crackers with
1 cup low-fat (1%) milk

WEEK 2

BREAKFAST

2 Blueberry Cottage Cheese Pancakes (page 204)

2 tablespoons maple syrup

½ cup low-fat (1%) milk

LUNCH

Creamy Mushroom-Barley Soup (page 75)

2 thin slices Italian bread

2 cups tossed green salad

2 tablespoons fat-free salad dressing

DINNER

Pork Adobo (page 150)

½ cup cooked brown rice

1 cup steamed spinach with finely chopped scallions and garlic

½ roasted red pepper

1 slice pineapple

SNACKS

1 cup low-fat (1%) milk with 1 oatmeal-raisin cookie

1 cup low-sodium vegetable juice and 8 thin pretzel twists

BREAKFAST

1 cup cantaloupe cubes

1 cup oatmeal, topped with 2 teaspoons cinnamon-sugar and 2 tablespoons chopped walnuts

1 cup low-fat (1%) milk

LUNCH

Cheese Sandwich: 2 slices whole grain reduced-calorie bread, 2 ounces reduced-fat Swiss cheese, 1 tablespoon spicy or grainy mustard, 1 slice tomato, romaine lettuce leaves, ½ roasted pepper

1 apple

DINNER

Lemon Chicken (page 114), *at left*

1 cup steamed green beans

½ cup linguine tossed with 6 cherry tomatoes, halved, and 1 teaspoon olive oil

SNACKS

½ ounce baked tortilla chips with ¼ cup bean dip

½ cup chocolate sorbet with ½ banana, sliced

BREAKFAST

½ cup orange juice

1 cup raisin bran cereal

1 cup low-fat (1%) milk

2 cups honeydew melon cubes

LUNCH

1 slice purchased cheese pizza

2 cups tossed green salad

2 tablespoons fat-free dressing

DINNER

1 cup beef broth simmered with ½ cup noodles, ¼ cup sliced mushrooms, 2 tablespoons chopped scallions, and pinch ground ginger and cayenne

Spicy Beef in Lettuce Rolls (page 145)

SNACKS

½ cup lower-fat rice pudding

1 ounce baked tortilla chips with ½ cup salsa

BREAKFAST

1 frozen oat bran waffle

1 tablespoon maple syrup

½ cup blueberries

¼ cup vanilla yogurt

1 cup low-fat (1%) milk

LUNCH

Tex-Mex Tuna: 3 ounces canned light tuna packed in water, mixed with 2 tablespoons chopped red pepper, 1 tablespoon corn kernels, 1 tablespoon minced scallion, 1 tablespoon each salsa and fat-free sour cream

2 slices reduced-calorie bread

½ banana

DINNER

Ravioli with Sausage Sauce (page 62)

2 cups tossed green salad

2 tablespoons fat-free salad dressing

SNACKS

1 brownie (2-inch square)

4 saltine crackers and 1 ounce reduced-fat cheddar cheese

BREAKFAST

1 small blueberry muffin

1 cup low-fat (1%) milk

½ pink grapefruit sprinkled with 1 tablespoon light brown sugar

LUNCH

1½ cups chicken noodle soup

1 slice rye bread

½ cup jarred three-bean salad over 2 cups spinach leaves

1 apple

DINNER

Teriyaki Turkey Burger (page 134), *bottom left*

½ cup steamed snow peas

½ cup angel hair pasta tossed with chopped scallions, fresh ginger, and 1 teaspoon dark Asian sesame oil

½ cup mandarin orange slices

SNACKS

½ toasted bagel, with 1 ounce reduced-fat Swiss cheese

⅓ cup nonfat ricotta cheese sweetened with 1 tablespoon sugar and topped with ¼ cup sliced strawberries

BREAKFAST

1 small bagel

1 tablespoon light cream cheese

1 cup orange juice

LUNCH

1 regular fast-food cheeseburger

2 cups tossed green salad

2 tablespoons fat-free salad dressing

DINNER

Tandoori Salmon (page 92), *above*

½ cup cooked basmati rice mixed with ¼ cup green peas

8 cherry tomatoes, halved and sautéed with minced shallot in 1 teaspoon vegetable oil

SNACKS

½ cup lower-fat chocolate pudding topped with ¼ cup raspberries

1 apple and 1½ ounces reduced-fat Swiss cheese

BREAKFAST

½ cup orange juice

1 scrambled egg

½ cup hash brown potatoes

1 slice reduced-calorie whole wheat toast

1 teaspoon butter or margarine

LUNCH

Salsa Fish Soup (page 75)

4 saltine crackers

½ ripe tomato, diced, and tossed with ½ cup corn kernels, chopped fresh cilantro, and 1 tablespoon lime juice

DINNER

Chicken Parmesan Pita Pizza (page 122)

2 cups tossed green salad

2 tablespoons fat-free salad dressing

SNACKS

1 cup low-fat (1%) milk with 1 tablespoon chocolate syrup

½ ripe pear and ½ ounce blue cheese and 10 thin pretzel sticks

After looking at the menu plans and sampling the food, we all started exclaiming about what a great diet this was and how readers would love it. Michael gave Susan a high-five, Julie burst out with wonderful ideas about garnishes, Peggy wanted to open a bottle of wine for a toast. Then reality hit. We had to do this. This diet was our diet, and we had to follow it for the next four months or so. Our personal, and professional, lives were on the line. We had to commit. And we had to do it right now. Suddenly, the conversation turned serious, and we started bombarding Susan with questions.

Do we really have to count calories?

Please don't! You'll just drive yourself crazy, and will be less likely to stick with the plan. Instead, follow the amounts listed for the portion and serving sizes in each recipe and menu, and you'll be within range. The math has been done for you: Each meal weighs in at around 400 calories. The two daily snacks average 150 calories each. You can even swap a lunch from Tuesday for a dinner on Thursday. But do aim for variety. We get different nutrients from different foods, and the more, the healthier.

What about beverages?

All no-calorie drinks are "free": seltzer, coffee, water, tea, diet sodas. It's best if they're decaffeinated. (Caffeine stimulates your nervous system—and your appetite.) If you do choose a calorie-dense drink, including wine or other alcoholic beverage, just eliminate one daily snack per drink. Do try to get in at least eight 8-ounce glasses of water a day. Not that H_2O will help speed your weight loss, but it does flush out excess salt in your system, which would otherwise cause bloating and can make a difference at your weigh-in. It also aids digestion, refreshes your skin, and makes everything else run smoothly!

What if we don't like something on the food plan?

Substitute within the same food group. For instance, if you don't like peppers, give yourself an equal amount of another vegetable. If you turn up your nose at yogurt, switch it for a cup of milk or an ounce of cheese. Make a pork recipe with chicken. The idea is to hold steady to the nutritional value and portion sizes, not to force you to eat something that makes you gag! You should be enjoying every bite.

Most of us wind up in a restaurant at least once a week. How can we handle eating out?

No problem! Order a meal that is similar in content to whatever is planned for that day or any other day. Just be assertive about how it's prepared: Ask for your meat grilled, sauces on the side, vegetables without butter. Remember, you're paying for the meal and should get what you want. (When in doubt, eat only half and save the rest for another meal.) On the other hand, if you know you'll want to order something off the plan, eat lightly the rest of the day so you can have that extra glass of wine, say, or taste a fabulous dessert. (See more tips in chapter 11.)

Guilt does more to undo a dieter's willpower than any brownie. So if you choose to indulge on occasion, at least enjoy it. Just be sure to go back to eating right the next day.

We can't carry the test-kitchen food scale with us everywhere. How can we be sure we're not eating too much?

You have everything you need on hand: A three-ounce supper-size portion of cooked fish, poultry, or meat, for instance, is about the size of your palm (no fingers!). One thumb measures an ounce of cheese or meat. One tablespoon is the size and depth of just the tip of your thumb, and you'll find 1 teaspoon at your index fingertip. Your cupped hand fits 1 to 2 ounces of pretzels. And make a fist to determine 1 cup of anything: milk or yogurt, pasta or beans, fruit or veggies. But whenever possible, pull out your measuring cups and spoons. Guesstimating too often can add up to extra calories and unwanted pounds.

Some of the recipes call for low-sodium ingredients. Why?

High- and low-sodium foods were balanced to stay within the healthful limits recommended by the National Academy of Science, which is between 1,100 to 3,300 milligrams a day. (One teaspoon of table salt contains 2,300 mg.) However, unless you have high blood pressure or another medical condition that requires a reduced-salt diet, you can use regular products without worry or interfering with your weight loss.

KEEP IN MIND

No diet, no matter how well designed, can cover 100 percent of your daily requirement for every nutrient, every day. If you're eating the varied meals recommended on this plan, you won't need a daily multivitamin and -mineral supplement. However, you might want to take one, with no more than 100 percent of the Recommended Dietary Allowance (RDA) for any nutrient, three or four times a week for insurance. To boost your calcium intake without adding more calories or more dairy items, choose calcium-fortified products such as juices and cold cereals. In addition, you might want to consider a calcium supplement with magnesium, particularly if you skimp on milk or other dairy products. For teenagers, pregnant women, and those breast-feeding, the RDA is 1,200 mg per day. The National Institutes of Health has made separate recommendations of 1,000 mg of calcium per day for premenopausal women and postmenopausal women taking estrogen, and 1,500 mg for postmenopausal women not taking estrogen and all women over sixty-five. Check with your doctor before beginning this or any new weight-loss plan.

Portion Options

Feel like a bagel instead of cereal? Rather have pasta instead of rice? Here's a handy checklist of the foods suggested in the plan that keep your diet nutritionally balanced and within the calorie count. Check the nutrition labels on foods you use to be sure they fit or make adjustments in serving size if they don't.

CARBOHYDRATES
On average, a portion of bread, cereals, grains, legumes, and starchy vegetables contains about 80 to 100 calories. Options include:

1 slice bread (1 ounce)

½ small bagel (1 ounce)

½ 6-inch pita (1 ounce)

1 4-inch pancake

1 6-inch flour tortilla

½ cup cold, unsweetened cereal

½ cup cooked cereal

½ cup granola cereal

½ cup cooked pasta

½ cup cooked brown or white rice

½ cup legumes including any of the following: black beans, black-eyed beans, kidney beans, lentils, split peas

½ cup corn kernels

½ cup green peas

½ cup mashed potatoes

1 small baked potato (3 ounces)

FRUIT

Fruit contains 60 to 80 calories per portion. A substitute portion of fruit juice is about ½ cup. Alternatives include:

1 apple	15 grapes
4 fresh apricots	1 kiwi
7 dried apricot halves	½ mango
½ cup applesauce	¾ cup cubed pineapple
½ large banana	2 plums
¾ cup blueberries or blackberries	2 tablespoons raisins
⅓ of a cantaloupe or 1 cup cubes	1 cup raspberries
½ grapefruit	1¼ cups strawberries

VEGETABLES

A portion of nonstarchy vegetables contains about 25 calories. Suggestions are:

½ cup cooked asparagus	½ cup cooked eggplant
½ cup cooked broccoli	½ cup cooked sugar snap peas
½ cup cooked carrots	1 cup cut-up raw sweet pepper
½ cup cooked cauliflower	1 cup sliced fresh tomato

DAIRY PRODUCTS

As in any healthful diet, choose low-fat dairy products. A portion contains between 75 and 120 calories. Choices are:

1 cup low-fat or skim milk or buttermilk	1 ounce part-skim mozzarella
1 cup low-fat or nonfat yogurt	2 tablespoons grated Parmesan
1 ounce regular or reduced-fat cheese	

MEAT, POULTRY, AND FISH

A portion of lean meat contains about 50 to 75 calories. Picks include:

1 ounce beef round, sirloin, flank, or tenderloin	2 ounces fresh fish
1 ounce pork tenderloin, loin, fresh, cured, or boiled ham	¼ cup canned salmon or tuna in water
1 ounce lamb chops, leg or roast, trimmed	2 ounces shellfish such as shrimp, crab, lobster, scallops, and clams
1 ounce skinless chicken, turkey, or skinless duck	1 ounce reduced-fat cold cuts
1 large egg	4 ounces tofu
3 large egg whites	

LIGHTER LUNCHES

Mix up your midday meal with these choices. You'll appreciate that some can come from the coffee shop, pizza parlor, or fast-food drive-through.

1

1 cup low-sodium split pea soup

4 saltine crackers

½ ripe tomato, diced and tossed with ½ cup corn kernels and 1 tablespoon lemon juice

2 canned peach halves

2

1 regular fast-food grilled chicken sandwhich

2 cups tossed green salad

2 tablespoons fat-free salad dressing

3

Tuna Sandwich: 3 ounces light tuna in water mixed with 1 tablespoon light mayonnaise on 2 slices whole-grain bread

½ roasted red pepper

½ banana

4

1 fast-food spring mix salad

2 tablespoons fat-free dressing

4 reduced-calorie crackers

1 apple

5

BLT Salad: 2 cups torn romaine lettuce; 1 tomato, chopped; 1 ounce reduced-fat Monterey Jack cheese, cubed; 1 slice cooked bacon, crumbled; ½ cup croutons; 3 tablespoons low-fat Ranch salad dressing

½ cup German potato salad

1 pear

6

1 cup reduced-sodium tomato soup made with milk

2 thin slices Italian bread

2 cups tossed green salad

2 tablespoons fat-free salad dressing

7

Turkey-Cheddar Melt: 2 slices whole-grain bread, 2 ounces sliced turkey, 1 ounce reduced-fat cheddar cheese, 1 jarred roasted red pepper, 2 teaspoons Dijon mustard

1 apple

8

Sliced skinless cooked chicken breast (3 ounces)

Tex-Mex Treat: ¼ avocado, ½ cup salsa, 1 cup shredded romaine, and ½ cup low-fat plain yogurt

9

1 cup ready-to-serve chicken-rice soup

2 thin slices Italian bread

¾ cup celery and carrot sticks

1 cup mandarin orange slices

10

Cold Pasta Salad: 1 cup cooked pasta, ⅓ cup diced provolone cheese, ¼ cup raw chopped broccoli, ¼ cup red pepper, and 2 tablespoons light mayo or salad dressing

10 baby carrots

1 banana

11

Seafood Salad Pita: ½ cup crabmeat or shrimp mixed with 2 tablespoons light mayo in large pita round

1 cup cantaloupe cubes

12

Italian Chicken Salad: strips skinless cooked chicken breast (3 ounces), ½ cup cooked green beans, ½ cup halved cherry tomatoes, 2 cups mixed salad greens

2 tablespoons fat-free Italian dressing

1 tablespoon sliced almonds, toasted

½ cup pineapple chunks

SNACK ATTACKS

When the urge hits, you can reach for any two of these treats, each 150 calories or less!

37 jelly beans

18 Quaker caramel-corn mini rice cakes

7 gherkin pickles

8 Triscuits

¼ cup raisins or chopped dried fruits

7 Social Tea biscuits

3 Snackwell's devil's-food cookie cakes

4 cups (unbuttered) air-popped popcorn

1 non-premium ice cream sandwich

½ cup Häagen-Dazs frozen yogurt

6-ounce container Dannon Light 'n Fit nonfat yogurt

5 graham cracker squares

65 small, thin pretzel sticks

4 pretzel rods

SURPRISING SECRETS WE LEARNED

We borrowed some tricks of the trade from Mindy Hermann, R.D., that helped us keep on track during the diet. Here are our favorites:

- Dim the lights. Soft lighting has a calming effect and can slow down the rate at which you eat so you wind up eating less. Can't dim the lights in your home? Shut them off completely and dine by candle-light instead.

- Remember the 10-minute rule. Feel the desperate need to indulge in a treat? Stall for 10 minutes and the urge may pass, especially if you weren't that hungry in the first place.

- Sit down for every meal. Eating on the run can invite disaster and the tendency to grab anything to kill the appetite. A sit-down meal automatically forces you to pay attention to what and how much you eat.

- Learn to say no. Politely turn down family and friends who encourage you to eat more than you'd like.

3

SPEEDY SUPER SALADS

. . . .

THAT SALADS PLAY A STRONG ROLE in our weight loss plan won't come as a surprise. Salads, after all, are a diet mainstay. What is unexpected, however, is how satisfying they can be. And how tasty. Right from the get-go we were determined to create main dish salads that emphasized robust food—items like chicken, pasta, pork, even beef—rather than relying on a variety of different greens. We craved substance, crunch, gusto; we wanted to walk away from the table feeling as if we enjoyed a meal, not a side dish.

All these recipes passed the test. Some, in fact, like the splendid Steak and Roquefort Salad (page 44), are impressive enough to serve to company. Others are simply delicious. Imagine juicy pork tenderloin, redolent with rosemary, served with pears over Madeira-dressed greens (page 48). Or, curried turkey laced with cashews and apples, cunningly tucked into a zucchini shell (page 43). If chicken's your thing, we have several choices, including a Buffalo Chicken version (page 41) that we swear will satiate your urge for those calorie-laden wings. And who could resist our Mexican-inspired Shrimp Taco Salad (page 34), with beans, tortilla chips, and cheddar cheese, appetizing warm or chilled.

If you have your own salad favorite, feel free to include it in your diet menu. Just remember to top it with one of our Delicious Diet Dressings (page 39).

Lemon-Tarragon Shrimp Salad (page 32).
. . . .

Grilled Scallop
and Pasta Caesar

MAKES: 4 servings
PREP: 5 minutes
COOK: 10 minutes

Salad:

 ½ pound farfalle (bow ties)

 1¼ pounds sea scallops

 ½ teaspoon salt

 ¼ teaspoon black pepper

 1 teaspoon olive oil

 1 head romaine lettuce

 1 medium-size sweet red pepper, cored, seeded,
 and thinly sliced

Dressing:

 1 clove garlic, mashed

 2 canned anchovy fillets, drained

 2 tablespoons fresh lemon juice
 (about 1 lemon)

 2 tablespoons olive oil

 ⅓ cup reduced-sodium, fat-free chicken broth

 2 teaspoons Dijon mustard

 ½ teaspoon black pepper

 1 teaspoon Worcestershire sauce

 2 tablespoons grated Parmesan cheese

1 Salad: Cook pasta in large, deep pot of lightly
salted boiling water until al dente, firm yet
tender. Drain.

2 Meanwhile, season scallops with salt and
pepper. Heat oil in large nonstick skillet over
medium-high heat. Working in two batches, sauté
scallops just until opaque in center, 6 minutes.

3 Tear romaine into bite-size pieces; place in
large bowl. Add sweet red pepper, pasta, and
scallops.

4 Dressing: Place garlic in small bowl. Add
anchovy fillets; mash until a paste forms. Add
lemon juice; stir to combine. Whisk in oil, then
broth, mustard, black pepper, Worcestershire
sauce, and cheese. Reserve ½ cup dressing for
another use.

5 Drizzle remaining dressing over salad;
toss to coat.

*Nutrient Value Per Serving: 334 calories, 8 g fat
(1 g saturated), 15 g protein, 52 g carbohydrate,
5 g fiber, 795 mg sodium, 12 mg cholesterol.*

Lemon-Tarragon
Shrimp Salad

MAKES: 4 servings
PREP: 15 minutes
COOK: about 5 minutes
REFRIGERATE: 20 minutes

Salad:

 1 pound medium-size shrimp in shells, cleaned
 and halved lengthwise

 ½ pound asparagus, cut into 1-inch pieces

 1 sweet red pepper, cored, seeded, and chopped

 1 rib celery, sliced

 3 scallions, thinly sliced

Dressing:

- **½ cup reduced-fat mayonnaise dressing**
- **1 tablespoon chopped fresh tarragon OR 1 teaspoon dried**
- **2 teaspoons grated lemon rind**
- **2 tablespoons fresh lemon juice**
- **½ teaspoon salt**
- **⅛ teaspoon cayenne**
- **Boston or Bibb lettuce leaves, for serving**

1 Salad: Boil shrimp in medium-size saucepan of boiling water just until firm, about 2 minutes. With slotted spoon, remove. Return water to a boil. In same saucepan, cook asparagus until just tender, about 2 minutes. Drain; rinse asparagus and shrimp with cold water.

2 In large bowl, combine shrimp, asparagus, red pepper, celery, and scallions.

3 Dressing: In small bowl, stir together mayonnaise, tarragon, lemon rind, lemon juice, salt, and cayenne. Add to shrimp mixture; toss to evenly coat shrimp. Cover and refrigerate until well chilled, about 20 minutes. Serve on lettuce leaves.

Nutrient Value Per Serving: 198 calories, 6 g fat (1 g saturated), 25 g protein, 11 g carbohydrate, 2 g fiber, 735 mg sodium, 172 mg cholesterol.

Spicy Shrimp Salad

MAKES: 6 servings
PREP: 20 minutes

- **1¾ pounds medium-size shrimp in shells, cleaned and halved lengthwise**
- **1 cantaloupe (about 2½ pounds), peeled, seeded, and cut into ¾-inch chunks**
- **1 small red onion, thinly sliced**
- **1 jalapeño chile, cored, seeded, and finely chopped**
- **¼ cup cider vinegar**
- **3 tablespoons fresh lime juice**
- **1 teaspoon chili powder**
- **½ teaspoon salt**
- **⅛ teaspoon black pepper**
- **2 dashes liquid hot-pepper sauce**
- **¼ cup vegetable oil**
- **1 medium-size semifirm avocado, peeled, pitted, and cut into chunks**

1 Combine shrimp, cantaloupe, red onion, and jalapeño in large bowl; toss to mix.

2 Whisk together cider vinegar, lime juice, chili powder, salt, black pepper, and hot sauce in small bowl. Gradually whisk in oil until well blended.

3 Add the vinegar dressing to shrimp mixture; toss to mix. Gently stir in avocado, being careful not to mash. Chill salad, if desired. Serve in hollowed-out cantaloupe halves, if desired.

Nutrient Value Per Serving: 248 calories, 15 g fat (2 g saturated), 16 g protein, 13 g carbohydrate, 3 g fiber, 349 mg sodium, 135 mg cholesterol.

Shrimp Taco Salad

MAKES: 8 servings
PREP: 10 minutes
COOK: 9 minutes

1 head green leaf lettuce, torn into bite-size pieces

1 large tomato, cored and diced

1 can (15 ounces) black beans, drained and rinsed

4 cups crumbled baked salsa-flavored tortilla chips

4 ounces reduced-fat cheddar cheese, shredded

1 tablespoon vegetable oil

1 small onion, diced

1 teaspoon chili powder

1½ pounds medium-size shrimp in shells, cleaned

¼ teaspoon salt

¼ teaspoon black pepper

1 tablespoon fresh lime juice

¾ cup reduced-fat Thousand Island dressing

1 Combine lettuce, tomato, black beans, crumbled tortilla chips, and shredded cheddar in large salad bowl.

2 Heat oil in large skillet. Add onion and chili powder; cook 5 minutes. Add shrimp, salt, pepper, and lime juice; cook until shrimp are pink and curled, about 4 minutes. Add to salad bowl along with dressing; toss to coat. Serve warm or chilled.

Nutrient Value Per Serving: 267 calories, 7 g fat (1 g saturated), 20 g protein, 32 g carbohydrate, 5 g fiber, 759 mg sodium, 107 mg cholesterol.

Crab Salad Stir-Fry

MAKES: 4 servings
PREP: 10 minutes
COOK: 2 minutes

¼ cup reduced-sodium soy sauce

2 tablespoons rice-wine vinegar

1 tablespoon sugar

8 cups cleaned Bibb, Boston, or romaine lettuce leaves, torn into bite-size pieces

1 tablespoon vegetable oil

4 scallions, finely chopped

1 tablespoon finely chopped, peeled fresh ginger

3 cloves garlic, finely chopped

2 large sweet red peppers, cored, seeded, and finely chopped

½ pound crabmeat, shell and cartilage removed

1 In small bowl, stir together soy sauce, vinegar, and sugar. Arrange lettuce leaves on serving platter.

2 In large nonstick skillet, heat oil over medium-high heat. Add scallions, ginger, and garlic; stir-fry 30 seconds. Add red peppers; stir-fry 1 minute.

3 Stir soy sauce mixture; add to skillet. Add crab; gently stir-fry until heated through, about 30 seconds. Spoon over lettuce leaves. Serve warm or at room temperature.

Nutrient Value Per Serving: 168 calories, 5 g fat (0 g saturated), 18 g protein, 14 g carbohydrate, 3 g fiber, 1,028 mg sodium, 62 mg cholesterol.

Asian Warm Chicken Slaw

MAKES: 6 servings
PREP: 10 minutes
REFRIGERATE: 30 minutes
COOK: about 20 minutes

½ cup rice vinegar

¼ cup soy sauce

2 tablespoons light brown sugar

2 cloves garlic, minced

1 tablespoon minced peeled fresh ginger

4 boneless, skinless chicken breast halves (about 1 pound total)

1 tablespoon dark Asian sesame oil

½ pound snow peas, halved crosswise

1 sweet red pepper, cored, seeded, and cut into ¼-inch-wide strips

½ cup chicken broth

2 packages (1 pound each) coleslaw mix

2 scallions, sliced

¼ cup sliced almonds, toasted

1 Combine vinegar, soy sauce, brown sugar, garlic, and ginger in large plastic food-storage bag. Add chicken; seal. Refrigerate 30 minutes.

2 Remove chicken from marinade; pat dry; reserve marinade (¾ cup). Heat oil in large, deep, heavy pot over medium-high heat. Add chicken; cook 5 minutes each side or until internal temperature registers 170° on instant-read thermometer. Remove to plate.

3 In same pot, cook snow peas and sweet pepper 2 minutes. Add marinade and broth; simmer 3 minutes. Add coleslaw. Cover; cook until slaw mix is wilted, about 3 minutes.

4 Slice chicken ¼ inch thick. Toss with coleslaw. Top with scallions and almonds.

Nutrient Value Per Serving: 224 calories, 7 g fat (1 g saturated), 20 g protein, 20 g carbohydrate, 6 g fiber, 856 mg sodium, 42 mg cholesterol.

Lean Greens

Invest in prep when you have time on the weekend, and reap the diet dividends throughout the workweek.

- **CLEAN GREENS** Wash and dry a variety of salad greens—such as romaine, Bibb, Boston, mustard, arugula, and escarole—in a salad spinner and store in a see-through container on the bottom shelf of the fridge. Then you know exactly what you have on hand, and you can use the ingredients all week for quick salads, sandwiches, and roll-ups.

- **RECIPE-READY VEGGIES** As soon as you get vegetables home from the market, wash and cut them up and store in the vegetable bin in the refrigerator. Now they're all set for main-dish salads, quick-to-fix stir-fries, toss-together pasta dishes, or just plain snacking.

- **FLAVOR HITS** Keep a supply of good-quality vinegars—balsamic, raspberry, rice-wine, and cranberry are some good choices—for splashing on greens. You may not even need oil, which adds calories.

Warm Chicken and Roast Vegetable Salad

MAKES: 6 servings

PREP: 15 minutes

ROAST: at 425° for 30 minutes

COOK: 10 minutes

¼ cup olive oil

1½ pounds small red potatoes with skins, cut into quarters (eighths if large)

½ pound green beans, halved crosswise

1 sweet red pepper, cored, seeded, and cut into 12 slices

1 teaspoon salt

4 boneless, skinless chicken breast halves (1¼ pounds total)

2 tablespoons fresh lemon juice

¼ teaspoon black pepper

2 tablespoons finely chopped fresh parsley

6 cups chopped romaine or leaf lettuce

1 Into large roasting pan, pour 2 tablespoons olive oil. Place pan in oven while heating to 425°.

2 In hot roasting pan, combine potatoes, green beans, and sweet pepper. Season with ¾ teaspoon salt.

3 Roast vegetables for 30 minutes or until potatoes are tender and vegetables are browned.

4 Meanwhile, in large skillet, bring enough lightly salted water to cover chicken to a simmer. Add chicken; simmer just until cooked through, about 10 minutes (internal temperature should register 170° on instant-read thermometer). Remove chicken to cutting board; let stand 5 minutes. Cut into small pieces.

5 In large bowl, whisk together remaining olive oil, lemon juice, remaining salt, and the pepper. Add vegetables, chicken, and parsley; gently toss.

6 Divide lettuce among 6 bowls or plates. Top with chicken mixture. Serve warm.

Nutrient Value Per Serving: 286 calories, 12 g fat (2 g saturated), 24 g protein, 26 g carbohydrate, 5 g fiber, 440 mg sodium, 52 mg cholesterol.

DELICIOUS DIET DRESSINGS

Whip up one of our easy salad toppers and keep on hand to toss with greens or steamed vegetables. They will be fine up to a week, covered, in the refrigerator.

Creamy Dijon

MAKES: 1½ cups

Combine 1 cup buttermilk, 8-ounce container nonfat sour cream, ⅓ cup grated Parmesan cheese, 1 tablespoon Dijon mustard, 1 teaspoon fresh lemon juice, and ¼ teaspoon black pepper in food processor or blender. Whirl until smooth.

Nutrient Value Per Tablespoon: 17 calories, 1 g fat (0 g saturated), 2 g protein, 2 g carbohydrate, 0 g fiber, 57 mg sodium, 2 mg cholesterol.

Russian

MAKES: 1½ cups

Whisk together ½ cup light mayonnaise, ½ cup low-fat plain yogurt, and 2 tablespoons *each* chili sauce, pickle relish, and chopped sweet red pepper in small bowl until well blended.

Nutrient Value Per Tablespoon: 15 calories, 1 g fat (0 g saturated), 1 g protein, 2 g carbohydrate, 0 g fiber, 75 mg sodium, 2 mg cholesterol.

Honey–Poppy Seed

MAKES: 1 cup

Stir together 8-ounce container low-fat plain yogurt, 1 tablespoon poppy seeds, 1 tablespoon honey, 1 teaspoon orange juice, ½ teaspoon cider vinegar, and ¼ teaspoon grated orange rind in small bowl.

Nutrient Value Per Tablespoon: 16 calories, 0 g fat (0 g saturated), 1 g protein, 2 g carbohydrate, 0 g fiber, 10 mg sodium, 1 mg cholesterol.

Tomato-Basil

MAKES: 1 cup

Combine 1 tomato, peeled, seeded, and chopped, ½ sweet red pepper, chopped, ½ cup packed fresh basil leaves, 1 clove garlic, 2 tablespoons white-wine vinegar, 1 tablespoon tomato paste, ½ teaspoon sugar, ¼ teaspoon salt, ⅛ teaspoon black pepper, and ⅓ cup light mayonnaise in processor or blender. Whirl until blended.

Nutrient Value Per Tablespoon: 18 calories, 1 g fat (0 g saturated), 0 g protein, 2 g carbohydrate, 0 g fiber, 95 mg sodium, 0 mg cholesterol.

Cran-Vinaigrette

MAKES: 1½ cups

Force ¾ cup raspberries with back of spoon through fine sieve over small bowl; discard seeds. Combine raspberries, ½ cup cranberry juice, ½ cup red-wine vinegar, ¼ cup hot water, 1 tablespoon olive oil, ¾ teaspoon salt, and ¼ teaspoon sugar in food processor or blender. Whirl until smooth.

Nutrient Value Per Tablespoon: 11 calories, 1 g fat (0 g saturated), 0 g protein, 2 g carbohydrate, 0 g fiber, 54 mg sodium, 0 mg cholesterol.

Herb Chicken with Warm Vinaigrette

MAKES: 4 servings
PREP: 15 minutes
COOK: 14 minutes

4 boneless, skinless chicken breast halves (about 1 pound total)

4 tablespoons balsamic vinegar

2 teaspoons dried Italian herb seasoning

1 teaspoon salt

½ teaspoon black pepper

3 tablespoons olive oil

1 pound Italian-style plum tomatoes, cored, seeded, and chopped (about 2 cups)

6 cups mixed salad greens

1 Brush chicken with 1 tablespoon vinegar. Sprinkle with Italian seasoning, ¾ teaspoon salt, and ¼ teaspoon pepper.

2 Heat 1 tablespoon olive oil in large nonstick skillet over medium-high heat. Working in batches if necessary to avoid crowding skillet, add chicken to hot oil; sauté about 6 to 7 minutes per side or until browned (internal temperature should register 170° on instant-read thermometer). Remove chicken to platter; keep warm.

3 Add remaining 3 tablespoons vinegar to skillet. Heat over medium heat, stirring with wooden spoon to loosen any browned bits from bottom of skillet. Add remaining 2 tablespoons oil, ¼ teaspoon salt, and ¼ teaspoon pepper to skillet. Stir in tomatoes; heat through. Pour warm vinaigrette over chicken. Serve over mixed greens.

Nutrient Value Per Serving: 261 calories, 14 g fat (2 g saturated), 25 g protein, 11 g carbohydrate, 3 g fiber, 671 mg sodium, 63 mg cholesterol.

Cobb Salad

MAKES: 6 servings
PREP: 15 minutes
COOK: 15 minutes

4 boneless, skinless chicken breast halves (about 1 pound total)

2 tablespoons white-wine vinegar

1 tablespoon Dijon mustard

2 tablespoons finely chopped shallots

¼ teaspoon salt

¼ teaspoon black pepper

¼ cup olive oil

2 tablespoons crumbled blue cheese

6 cups mixed salad greens

2 large tomatoes, cored and cut into chunks

1 avocado, pitted, peeled, and cut into chunks

3 slices turkey bacon, cooked and crumbled

1 Place chicken in large skillet; add just enough water to cover. Simmer, covered, until internal temperature registers 170° on instant-read thermometer, about 15 minutes. Let cool completely. Tear chicken into thin strips.

2 Whisk together vinegar, mustard, shallots, salt, and pepper in a small bowl. Gradually whisk in oil until well blended. Stir in cheese.

3 Arrange greens on platter with chicken, tomatoes, and avocado. Top with bacon. Drizzle with dressing. Serve immediately.

Nutrient Value Per Serving: 266 calories, 19 g fat (3 g saturated), 19 g protein, 8 g carbohydrate, 3 g fiber; 336 mg sodium, 50 mg cholesterol.

Buffalo Chicken Salad

MAKES: 6 servings
PREP: 15 minutes
REFRIGERATE: 30 minutes
BROIL: about 14 minutes

Dressing:

½ cup reduced-fat mayonnaise dressing

¼ cup bottled barbecue sauce

¼ cup crumbled blue cheese

1 teaspoon liquid hot-pepper sauce

2 tablespoons nonfat milk

Salad:

4 boneless, skinless chicken breast halves (about 1 pound total)

½ teaspoon liquid hot-pepper sauce

1 large carrot, peeled and shredded

3 cups bite-size pieces romaine lettuce (about 1 head)

4 cups bite-size pieces iceberg lettuce (about 1 head)

4 ribs celery, from the heart, cut into 1-inch-long matchstick pieces

1 tablespoon crumbled blue cheese

1 Dressing: Stir together mayonnaise, barbecue sauce, blue cheese, hot-pepper sauce, and milk in small bowl.

2 Salad: Place chicken in glass dish. Add ⅓ cup dressing and hot-pepper sauce; turn to coat. Cover; refrigerate 30 minutes.

3 Meanwhile, mix together carrot, romaine, iceberg, and celery in large bowl.

4 Heat broiler. Transfer chicken to broiler-pan rack; discard marinade. Broil 4 inches from heat for 8 minutes; turn over and broil 6 minutes or until internal temperature registers 170° on instant-read thermometer.

5 Add remaining dressing to greens in bowl. Cut chicken into thin slices. Arrange on salad. Sprinkle with cheese.

Nutrient Value Per Serving: 157 calories, 6 g fat (2 g saturated), 18 g protein, 7 g carbohydrate, 2 g fiber, 392 mg sodium, 47 mg cholesterol.

Picnic Pasta

MAKES: 6 servings
PREP: 30 minutes
COOK: 20 minutes

 1 whole chicken breast, on the bone

 1 cup chicken broth

 ½ pound medium-size pasta shells

 ½ bunch broccoli, cut into bite-size pieces

 ¼ cup chopped red onion

 ¾ cup light mayonnaise

 2 tablespoons light sour cream

 2 tablespoons Dijon mustard

 2 teaspoons white-wine vinegar

 2 teaspoons sugar

 ¼ teaspoon dried tarragon

 ½ teaspoon salt

 ¼ teaspoon black pepper

1 Place chicken in deep 10-inch skillet. Add broth and 2 cups water. Bring to boiling. Reduce heat to low; simmer, turning over once, until no longer pink near bone, about 20 minutes (internal temperature should register 170° on instant-read thermometer). Remove from skillet. When cool enough to handle, remove skin and bones. Pull meat into small pieces; place in bowl.

2 Cook pasta in large, deep pot of lightly salted boiling water until al dente, firm yet tender, about 12 minutes. Add broccoli for last 7 minutes.

3 Drain pasta and broccoli; rinse under cold running water. Drain. Add to chicken. Add onion.

4 Stir together mayonnaise, sour cream, mustard, vinegar, sugar, tarragon, salt, and pepper in small bowl. Fold into salad. Cover; refrigerate until serving.

Nutrient Value Per Serving: 312 calories, 13 g fat (3 g saturated), 11 g protein, 38 g carbohydrate, 3 g fiber, 751 mg sodium, 25 mg cholesterol.

Turkey Waldorf Salad

MAKES: 6 servings
PREP: 10 minutes
REFRIGERATE: at least 1 hour

Dressing:

 ½ cup light mayonnaise

 ¼ cup nonfat milk

 2 tablespoons fresh lemon juice

 1 teaspoon sugar

 ½ teaspoon salt

 ½ teaspoon lemon pepper

Salad:

 1½ pounds cooked turkey, cut into ¼-inch cubes

 1 large apple with skin, cored, and cut into ¼-inch cubes

 2 ribs celery, thinly sliced

 1 head Bibb lettuce, separated into leaves and washed

 ¼ cup chopped walnuts, toasted

1 Dressing: In small bowl, whisk together mayonnaise, milk, lemon juice, sugar, salt, and lemon pepper until smooth.

2 Salad: In large bowl, combine turkey, apple, and celery. Stir in mayonnaise mixture. Cover; refrigerate at least 1 hour.

3 Serve salad on top of Bibb lettuce leaves. Garnish with walnuts.

Nutrient Value Per Serving: 232 calories, 12 g fat (2 g saturated), 20 g protein, 12 g carbohydrate, 1 g fiber, 1,662 mg sodium, 52 mg cholesterol.

Zucchini Stuffed with Curried Turkey Salad

MAKES: 6 servings
PREP: 20 minutes
REFRIGERATE: 30 minutes
COOK: 5 minutes

½ cup reduced-fat mayonnaise dressing

1 tablespoon olive oil

1 teaspoon mild curry powder

½ large Red Delicious apple, cored and diced

1 large rib celery, diced

¾ pound cooked turkey breast, diced

6 medium-size zucchini (2 to 2¼ pounds total)

2 tablespoons chopped dry-roasted unsalted cashews, toasted

1 In medium-size bowl, whisk together mayonnaise dressing, oil, and curry powder. Fold in apple, celery, and turkey. Cover; refrigerate 30 minutes.

2 Cut ⅛- to ¼-inch thick lengthwise slice from each zucchini. Cut slices into "sticks" and save for snacking.

3 Using melon baller or small spoon and starting from cut side, scoop out most of flesh from each zucchini, leaving a shell. Reserve flesh for another salad or other uses.

4 In ½ inch of water in a large skillet, simmer zucchini boats, cut side down, until firm-tender, about 5 minutes. Remove zucchini from skillet; let cool.

5 Fill each boat with generous ⅓ cup turkey salad. Sprinkle tops with cashews.

Nutrient Value Per Serving: 210 calories, 11 g fat (3 g saturated), 17 g protein, 11 g carbohydrate, 2 g fiber, 218 mg sodium, 34 mg cholesterol.

Beef-Couscous Salad

MAKES: 8 servings
PREP: 20 minutes

1 can (14.5 ounces) chicken broth

¼ cup water

1 box (10 ounces) couscous

1 teaspoon chopped fresh oregano OR ¼ teaspoon dried

1 teaspoon sugar

½ teaspoon Dijon mustard

1 tablespoon fresh lemon juice

¼ cup red-wine vinegar

⅓ cup olive oil

8 cherry tomatoes, each quartered

1 medium-size cucumber, peeled and sliced (about ¾ cup)

3 ounces feta cheese, crumbled

3 scallions, diagonally sliced

6 ounces sliced roast beef, cut into strips

1 Bring broth and the water in medium-size saucepan to boiling. Remove from heat; stir in couscous. Cover and let stand 5 minutes.

2 Whisk together oregano, sugar, mustard, lemon juice, and vinegar in small bowl. Gradually whisk in oil until well blended.

3 Transfer couscous to large bowl. Add tomatoes, cucumber, feta, scallions, and roast beef. Add dressing; toss to combine. Serve at room temperature or chilled.

Nutrient Value Per Serving: 284 calories, 13 g fat (3 g saturated), 10 g protein, 32 g carbohydrate, 2 g fiber, 510 mg sodium, 18 mg cholesterol.

Steak and Roquefort Salad

MAKES: 6 servings
PREP: 15 minutes
BROIL: 12 minutes

Steak:

1 beef flank steak (1 pound)

¼ teaspoon salt

¼ teaspoon black pepper

Salad:

2 tablespoons red-wine vinegar

¼ cup olive oil

½ teaspoon Dijon mustard

¼ teaspoon salt

⅛ teaspoon black pepper

1 cucumber, peeled and chopped

1 cup cherry tomatoes, each halved

12 cups assorted salad greens

6 tablespoons crumbled Roquefort cheese

1 Steak: Heat broiler. Season steak with salt and pepper. Broil 6 inches from heat 6 minutes per side for medium-rare. Let stand 10 minutes.

2 Salad: Whisk together vinegar, oil, mustard, salt, and pepper in small bowl. Combine cucumber, tomatoes, and greens in large bowl. Thinly slice steak across grain.

3 Arrange greens on 6 plates. Top with steak and cheese. Drizzle with dressing.

Nutrient Value Per Serving: 258 calories, 18 g fat (5 g saturated), 20 g protein, 6 g carbohydrate, 3 g fiber, 402 mg sodium, 45 mg cholesterol.

Sausage and Potato Salad

MAKES: 6 servings
PREP: 15 minutes
COOK: about 20 minutes

> 1½ **pounds red new potatoes**
>
> ½ **cup chicken broth**
>
> ¼ **cup red-wine vinegar**
>
> 2 **teaspoons sugar**
>
> ½ **teaspoon powdered mustard**
>
> ½ **teaspoon salt**
>
> ¼ **teaspoon black pepper**
>
> ¼ **teaspoon fennel seeds, crushed**
>
> 1 **pound hot Italian-style turkey sausage, cut into bite-size pieces**
>
> 1 **sweet red pepper, cored, seeded, and cut into strips**
>
> 1 **sweet yellow pepper, cored, seeded, and cut into strips**
>
> 1 **medium-size onion, halved and sliced crosswise**
>
> 3 **packed cups escarole, cut into bite-size pieces**

1 Cook potatoes in large saucepan of lightly salted boiling water until knife-tender, about 20 minutes.

2 Meanwhile, combine chicken broth, vinegar, sugar, mustard, salt, pepper, and fennel seeds in small saucepan. Heat to simmering; keep warm.

3 Add sausage to large skillet; cook over medium-high heat just until beginning to brown, about 7 minutes. Add sweet peppers and onion. Reduce heat to medium-low; cook until vegetables are tender and sausage is cooked through, about 9 minutes.

4 Drain potatoes; cut in half or in quarters. Place in large bowl; add broth mixture and sausage mixture; toss to coat. Add escarole; toss. Serve slightly warm.

Nutrient Value Per Serving: 219 calories, 5 g fat (1 g saturated), 18 g protein, 25 g carbohydrate, 4 g fiber, 820 mg sodium, 54 mg cholesterol.

Fruited Barley and Ham Salad

MAKES: 6 servings
PREP: 25 minutes
COOK: 15 minutes
REFRIGERATE: 2 hours

> 1 **tablespoon olive oil**
>
> 1 **medium-size red onion, chopped**
>
> 1 **sweet red pepper, cored, seeded, and cut into strips**
>
> 1 **cup quick-cooking barley**
>
> 1½ **cups vegetable broth**
>
> ¾ **teaspoon dried marjoram**
>
> ½ **teaspoon dried thyme**
>
> 1½ **cups frozen baby lima beans**
>
> 2 **cups baby carrots, halved lengthwise**
>
> 2 **cups sliced white mushrooms**
>
> 1 **cup chopped mixed dried fruit**
>
> ½ **teaspoon salt**
>
> ½ **cup apple juice**
>
> 3 **tablespoons red-wine vinegar**
>
> 1 **tablespoon honey**
>
> ¼ **teaspoon liquid hot-pepper sauce**
>
> ½ **pound cooked ham, cut in strips**
>
> **Assorted salad greens, for serving**

1 Heat oil in medium-size saucepan over medium heat. Add onion; cook until softened, about 5 minutes.

2 Add red pepper, barley, broth, marjoram, thyme, lima beans, carrots, and mushrooms. Bring just to a boil over medium heat. Reduce heat to low. Cover saucepan; simmer 10 minutes or until peppers and carrots are crisp-tender.

3 Remove saucepan from heat. Stir in dried fruit and salt. Let stand, covered, 10 minutes. Scrape mixture into large bowl. Refrigerate, covered, 2 hours or until well chilled.

4 Whisk together apple juice, vinegar, honey, and hot-pepper sauce in small bowl. Add to barley mixture; toss to coat. Stir in ham. Serve salad on salad greens.

Nutrient Value Per Serving: 339 calories, 5 g fat (1 g saturated), 17 g protein, 61 g carbohydrate, 11 g fiber, 1,051 mg sodium, 17 mg cholesterol.

Pasta Salad with Ham and Cheese

MAKES: 8 servings
PREP: 15 minutes
COOK: about 12 minutes
REFRIGERATE: 3 hours or overnight

1 pound medium-size pasta shells

1 cup cherry tomatoes, each halved

1 small sweet red pepper, cored, seeded, and cut into strips

1 small sweet green pepper, cored, seeded, and cut into strips

1 cup shredded peeled carrot

¾ cup fat-free mayonnaise

3 tablespoons fresh lemon juice

2 tablespoons Dijon mustard

3 tablespoons water

1 teaspoon sugar

1 teaspoon salt

¼ teaspoon celery seeds

¼ teaspoon black pepper

½ pound smoked ham, cut into strips

¼ pound reduced-fat Jarlsberg cheese, cut into strips

1 Cook pasta shells in large, deep pot of lightly salted boiling water until al dente, firm yet tender. Drain; let cool.

2 Mix pasta, tomatoes, sweet peppers, and carrot in large bowl.

3 Stir together mayonnaise, lemon juice, mustard, water, sugar, salt, celery seeds, and pepper in small bowl.

4 Fold ham, cheese, and all but ⅓ cup mayonnaise into pasta mixture until evenly coated.

5 Refrigerate, covered, at least 3 hours or preferably overnight. Can be prepared up to 2 days ahead. Stir in remaining dressing just before serving.

Nutrient Value Per Serving: 336 calories, 5 g fat (2 g saturated), 18 g protein, 55 g carbohydrate, 4 g fiber, 981 mg sodium, 21 mg cholesterol.

Pear and Pork Tenderloin Salad

MAKES: 8 servings
PREP: 20 minutes
MARINATE: 2 hours or overnight
ROAST: at 350° for 30 minutes
COOK: about 8 minutes

1 teaspoon chopped fresh rosemary

1 clove garlic, finely chopped

½ teaspoon salt

½ teaspoon black pepper

1 tablespoon vegetable oil

2 pork tenderloins (about 2 pounds)

½ cup Madeira wine

2 tablespoons finely chopped shallots

1 tablespoon white-wine vinegar

2 tablespoons finely chopped fresh chives

2 bags (6 ounces each) baby spinach leaves

½ head radicchio, torn

1 head Boston lettuce, torn into bite-size pieces

4 ripe pears

4 ounces goat cheese

1 Combine rosemary, garlic, salt, pepper, and oil in small bowl. Rub over pork tenderloins. Cover with plastic wrap. Refrigerate to marinate for 2 hours or overnight.

2 Heat oven to 350°.

3 Coat ovenproof medium-size skillet with cooking spray. Place over medium-high heat (if skillet is not ovenproof, cover handle with aluminum foil). Add pork; cook, turning, until browned on all sides, 4 to 5 minutes.

4 Transfer skillet to oven. Roast for 20 minutes or until instant-read thermometer inserted in center registers 160°. Transfer pork to platter; let cool to room temperature.

5 Pour Madeira into skillet; simmer over medium-high heat, scraping up any browned bits from bottom of skillet, 2 minutes. Remove from heat. Add shallots, vinegar, and chives.

6 In large bowl, combine spinach, radicchio, and Boston lettuce. Add Madeira mixture; toss to mix.

7 Arrange greens on 8 plates. Cut pork into ¼-inch-thick slices; divide among plates on top of greens. Core pears; cut into thin slices and tuck into greens. Sprinkle with cheese.

Nutrient Value Per Serving: 279 calories, 9 g fat (4 g saturated), 29 g protein, 17 g carbohydrate, 3 g fiber, 282 mg sodium, 74 mg cholesterol.

Gazpacho Salad with Feta

MAKES: 6 servings
PREP: 15 minutes

- ¾ cup reduced-fat balsamic dressing-and-marinade
- 1 pound ripe tomatoes (2 to 3 medium-size), seeded and coarsely chopped (2 to 3 cups)
- ½ pound reduced-fat feta cheese, coarsely crumbled
- 1 medium-size seedless cucumber, peeled and coarsely chopped
- 2 cups arugula, coarsely chopped (about 1 small bunch)
- 1 head Boston lettuce, coarsely chopped
- 1 medium-size red onion, coarsely chopped
- 6 regular-size pita breads

1 Combine marinade, tomatoes, feta, cucumber, arugula, lettuce, and onion in large bowl; toss to coat.

2 Cut pita breads in half; split each half open to form pocket. Evenly divide salad into 6 servings and fill pitas. Serve immediately.

Nutrient Value Per Serving: 299 calories, 5 g fat (3 g saturated), 15 g protein, 49 g carbohydrate, 3 g fiber, 1,292 mg sodium, 14 mg cholesterol.

Mediterranean Bread Salad

MAKES: 6 servings
PREP: 15 minutes
BAKE: at 400°F for 5 minutes

- 3 (6-inch) pita breads
- 2 cups cubed tomatoes
- 2 cups watercress, stemmed
- 1½ cups diced, seeded, unpeeled cucumber
- 1 cup chopped fresh mint
- ¾ cup diced sweet green pepper
- ¾ cup thinly sliced scallions
- ¼ cup olive oil
- ¼ cup fresh lemon juice
- 1 teaspoon salt
- 1 teaspoon black pepper
- 1 teaspoon ground coriander

1 Heat oven to 400°F. Split pitas in half. Cut into bite-size pieces. Place on ungreased baking sheet.

2 Bake until golden, about 5 minutes.

3 Combine tomatoes, watercress, cucumber, mint, green pepper, and scallions in large bowl.

4 Combine oil, lemon juice, salt, pepper, and coriander in small bowl. Add to tomato mixture. Add toasted pita pieces just before serving.

Nutrient Value Per Serving: 202 calories, 10 g fat (1 g saturated), 5 g protein, 25 g carbohydrate, 4 g fiber, 567 mg sodium, 0 mg cholesterol.

4 PERFECT PASTA PRONTO

IT'S QUICK. IT'S DELICIOUS. IT'S DIET-FRIENDLY. Yes, pasta definitely has a place in our *Eat What You Love & Lose* plan. How could we leave it out when everybody adores it so?

The way we slid it in was to come up with scrumptious, yet fat-smart, sauces—everything from tomato to meat to cream. And with toppings this good, you won't need heaps of noodles. A modest serving, about 1 cup cooked, is perfect. Just sit down, and eat it the way the Italians do. Slowly. Lovingly. Pausing between mouthfuls to let the flavors tickle your palate and to experience the al dente bite of the pasta itself.

Trust us: This is pasta like you've never had before.

Take that popular classic, Fra Diavolo (page 61). Ours is as pungent as ever but even better-tasting, enlivened with shrimp and surimi. Pasta with Spicy Red-Pepper Cream Sauce (page 54) may sound like a diet no-no, but light sour cream and sliced almonds give the sauce all the heft it needs. Roasted vegetables and balsamic vinegar add an extra layer of flavor to a rib-sticking penne dish (page 56). But do remember to save yourself for the Rigatoni with Gorgonzola Sauce (page 56). This wonderfully creamy dish was the hands-down favorite of our *FC* crew.

Baked pastas are also on the menu. Broccoli and Cheese Stuffed Shells (page 58) are sure to please, with three different cheeses in the filling. For fun, we've also included two all-vegetable dishes that behave like pasta. Sample our Cauliflower Parmesan (page 69) with mozzarella and marinara and Spaghetti Squash with an olive-y Provençal Sauce (page 69) and we're certain you'll agree.

Three fast fixes for jarred marinara sauces are here too (page 63), for fast-forwarding dinner when there's no time to prep.

Penne with Cherry Tomatoes, Smoked Mozzarella, and Basil (page 52).

Penne with Cherry Tomatoes, Smoked Mozzarella, and Basil

MAKES: 6 servings
PREP: 10 minutes
COOK: 12 minutes

¾ pound penne

1 tablespoon olive oil

2 large cloves garlic, finely chopped

1 pint cherry tomatoes, each tomato halved

½ teaspoon salt

¼ teaspoon black pepper

½ pound smoked mozzarella cheese, diced

1 cup packed fresh basil leaves, finely chopped

1 Cook penne in large, deep pot of lightly salted water until al dente, firm yet tender. Drain.

2 Meanwhile, in large nonstick skillet, heat oil over medium heat. Add garlic; sauté 1 minute. Add tomatoes, salt, and pepper; sauté 2 minutes or until heated through.

3 Toss penne with tomato mixture, cheese, and basil. Serve at once.

Nutrient Value Per Serving: 339 calories, 13 g fat (7 g saturated), 15 g protein, 41 g carbohydrate, 3 g fiber, 443 mg sodium, 27 mg cholesterol.

Linguine with Zucchini Sauce

MAKES: 6 servings
PREP: 15 minutes
COOK: 10 minutes
STAND: 10 minutes

¾ pound linguine

2 pounds zucchini, coarsely shredded (about 6 cups)

¾ teaspoon garlic salt

⅛ teaspoon black pepper

1 cup shredded reduced-fat sharp cheddar cheese

½ cup prepared Alfredo sauce

1 teaspoon fresh lemon juice

¼ teaspoon ground nutmeg

¼ teaspoon liquid hot-pepper sauce

1 Cook linguine in large, deep pot of lightly salted boiling water until al dente, firm yet tender. Drain.

2 Meanwhile, coat large skillet with cooking spray. Place over high heat. Add zucchini, garlic salt, and black pepper; cook, stirring often, until softened, 3 to 4 minutes. Stir in cheese, Alfredo sauce, lemon juice, nutmeg, and pepper sauce; gently heat through.

3 Turn into large bowl. Toss with drained linguine. Cover; let stand 10 minutes. Toss and serve.

Nutrient Value Per Serving: 242 calories, 5 g fat (3 g saturated), 13 g protein, 38 g carbohydrate, 4 g fiber, 589 mg sodium, 12 mg cholesterol.

Orecchiette Arrabbiata

MAKES: 6 servings
PREP: 10 minutes
COOK: 30 minutes

1 medium-size onion, finely chopped

3 large cloves, finely chopped

1 tablespoon water

2 cans (14.5 ounces each) zesty diced tomatoes OR diced tomatoes with green chiles

1 can (8 ounces) tomato sauce

½ teaspoon red-pepper flakes

½ teaspoon dried oregano

Pinch cayenne

¾ pound orecchiette (ear-shaped) pasta OR any tubular shape

1 bag (6 ounces) baby spinach, cleaned

¼ teaspoon salt

¼ teaspoon black pepper

2 tablespoons grated Parmesan cheese

1 Coat medium-size saucepan with cooking spray. Place over medium-high heat. Add onion; cook until softened, about 5 minutes, being careful not to let brown. Add garlic and water; cook 2 minutes.

2 Stir diced tomatoes, tomato sauce, pepper flakes, oregano, and cayenne into saucepan; simmer, uncovered, stirring occasionally, 15 minutes.

3 Meanwhile, cook orecchiette in large, deep pot of lightly salted boiling water until al dente, firm yet tender.

4 Slice spinach. Add to sauce; cook 5 minutes. Add salt and pepper.

5 Drain orecchiette; transfer to large serving bowl.

6 Pour sauce over orecchiette; toss. Sprinkle with Parmesan cheese.

Nutrient Value Per Serving: 253 calories, 2 g fat (1 g saturated), 10 g protein, 50 g carbohydrate, 4 g fiber, 972 mg sodium, 2 mg cholesterol.

Pasta with Spicy Red-Pepper Cream Sauce

MAKES: 6 servings
PREP: 15 minutes
BROIL: 10 to 12 minutes
COOK: 12 minutes

3 large sweet red peppers, halved and seeded

2 large shallots, peeled and halved

2 cloves garlic, peeled

2 tablespoons sliced almonds, toasted

2 tablespoons grated Parmesan cheese

2 teaspoons red-wine vinegar

2 teaspoons honey

½ teaspoon salt

⅛ teaspoon cayenne

⅓ cup light sour cream

¾ pound rotelle

1 Heat broiler. Place peppers, cut side down, on broiler pan. Place shallots and garlic around peppers.

2 Broil vegetables 4 inches from heat for 10 to 12 minutes or until charred and crisp-tender. Let cool. Peel peppers. Dice 2 pepper halves; place in large pasta bowl.

3 Combine remaining sweet pepper, shallots, garlic, almonds, Parmesan, vinegar, honey, salt, and cayenne in food processor or blender. Whirl until smooth. Add sour cream. Whirl just until blended. Transfer to bowl.

4 Meanwhile, cook rotelle in large deep pot of lightly salted boiling water until al dente, firm yet tender. Drain. Add to red pepper mixture in bowl; toss to mix. Serve hot.

Nutrient Value Per Serving: 256 calories, 4 g fat (1 g saturated), 9 g protein, 48 g carbohydrate, 4 g fiber, 251 mg sodium, 6 mg cholesterol.

Chunky Veggie Sauce with Penne

MAKES: 6 servings
PREP: 15 minutes
COOK: 45 minutes

1 tablespoon olive oil

1 large onion, chopped

2 cloves garlic, finely chopped

1 medium-size sweet green pepper, cored, seeded, and chopped

1 medium-size zucchini, chopped

1 cup chopped white mushrooms (about 2 ounces)

3 canned flat anchovies, drained and chopped

2 cans (28 ounces each) chopped tomatoes

1 can (6 ounces) tomato paste

½ teaspoon sugar

¼ cup chopped fresh parsley

1 tablespoon balsamic vinegar

1 teaspoon salt

½ teaspoon black pepper

¾ pound penne

1 Heat olive oil in 4-quart saucepan over medium-high heat. Add onion and garlic; sauté until almost tender, about 4 minutes. Add green pepper, zucchini, mushrooms, and anchovies; sauté 8 to 10 minutes or until vegetables are almost tender.

2 Stir in chopped tomatoes, tomato paste, and sugar. Bring to a boil. Lower heat; simmer, uncovered, 30 minutes or until thickened, stirring occasionally. Stir in parsley, vinegar, salt, and pepper.

3 Meanwhile, cook penne in large deep pot of lightly salted boiling water until al dente, firm yet tender. Drain.

4 Toss penne with sauce.

Nutrient Value Per Serving: 342 calories, 4 g fat (1 g saturated), 13 g protein, 67 g carbohydrate, 9 g fiber, 1,040 mg sodium, 2 mg cholesterol.

Lite Fettuccine Alfredo

MAKES: 6 servings
PREP: 10 minutes
COOK: about 12 minutes

1 pound fettuccine

½ pound green beans, halved crosswise

1 large onion, halved and sliced crosswise

½ pound portabella mushroom caps, sliced

4 ounces ⅓-less-fat cream cheese

1 cup nonfat milk

1 teaspoon salt

1 small clove garlic, finely chopped

½ teaspoon dried basil

¼ teaspoon black pepper

1 jar (7 ounces) roasted red peppers, drained and cut into strips

½ cup grated Parmesan cheese

1 Cook fettuccine in large deep pot of lightly salted boiling water until al dente, firm yet tender. Add beans for last 3 minutes of cooking.

2 Meanwhile, coat skillet with cooking spray. Place over medium-high heat. Add onion and mushrooms; cook, stirring, 8 minutes or until mushrooms release their liquid. Stir in cream cheese until it begins to melt. Stir in milk, salt, garlic, basil, black pepper, and roasted peppers; simmer 2 minutes.

3 Drain fettuccine and beans. Toss with cream sauce and ¼ cup Parmesan in large bowl. Top with remaining cheese.

Nutrient Value Per Serving: 342 calories, 9 g fat (4 g saturated), 16 g protein, 52 g carbohydrate, 4 g fiber, 903 mg sodium, 21 mg cholesterol.

Penne with Roasted Vegetables

MAKES: 6 servings
PREP: 20 minutes
BAKE: at 450° for 35 minutes
COOK: about 12 minutes

1 eggplant (1 pound), cut into 1-inch pieces

1 small butternut squash (1 pound), peeled, seeded, and cut into 1-inch pieces

2 zucchini (about 1 pound), halved lengthwise and cut into 1-inch pieces

2 sweet red peppers, cored, seeded, and cut into 1-inch pieces

1 red onion, cut into ¼-inch-wide wedges

1 teaspoon salt

¼ teaspoon black pepper

¾ pound penne

3 tablespoons balsamic vinegar

3 cloves garlic, minced

1 Heat oven to 450°. Coat 2 shallow roasting pans with cooking spray.

2 Combine eggplant, squash, zucchini, sweet peppers, onion, ½ teaspoon salt, and ⅛ teaspoon pepper in large bowl. Coat vegetables with cooking spray; toss to evenly coat. Divide between 2 pans.

3 Roast for 35 minutes or until nicely browned and tender.

4 Cook penne in large deep pot of lightly salted boiling water until al dente, firm yet tender. Reserve 1 cup liquid; drain.

5 Toss together roasted vegetables, penne, vinegar, garlic, and remaining salt and pepper with enough reserved liquid to moisten.

Nutrient Value Per Serving: 256 calories, 1 g fat (0 g saturated), 9 g protein, 54 g carbohydrate, 7 g fiber, 398 mg sodium, 0 mg cholesterol.

Rigatoni with Gorgonzola Sauce

MAKES: 8 servings
PREP: 10 minutes
COOK: about 15 minutes

1 pound rigatoni

3 sweet peppers (red, yellow, and/or orange), cored, seeded, and cut into ¼-inch-thick slices

1½ cups fat-free half-and-half

⅓ pound Gorgonzola cheese, crumbled

½ cup grated Parmesan cheese

¼ teaspoon salt

¼ teaspoon black pepper

¼ teaspoon ground nutmeg

⅛ teaspoon cayenne

¼ cup fresh basil leaves, torn into small pieces

1 Cook rigatoni in large deep pot of lightly salted boiling water until al dente, firm yet tender.

2 Meanwhile, coat medium-size saucepan with cooking spray. Place over medium heat. Add sweet peppers; cook, stirring occasionally, for 5 to 7 minutes or until peppers are slightly softened. Remove peppers to a plate.

3 In same saucepan, heat half-and-half over medium-high. When it begins to simmer, stir in Gorgonzola and Parmesan cheeses, salt, pepper, nutmeg, and cayenne; heat, stirring, until cheeses have melted and sauce is smooth.

4 Drain rigatoni. In large serving bowl, toss together rigatoni with cheese sauce. Stir in basil. Arrange sweet pepper strips over the top. Garnish with additional fresh basil, if desired. Serve pasta immediately.

Make-Ahead Tip: The sauce can be made ahead. To serve, gently rewarm sauce in medium-size saucepan. Toss with freshly cooked hot pasta.

Nutrient Value Per Serving: 327 calories, 8 g fat (5 g saturated), 15 g protein, 47 g carbohydrate, 3 g fiber, 426 mg sodium, 25 mg cholesterol.

Tricolor Fusilli alla Lasagna

MAKES: 6 servings
PREP: 5 minutes
COOK: 10 minutes

> ¾ pound tricolor fusilli
>
> 1½ cups prepared fat-free spaghetti sauce
>
> 1 bag (6 ounces) baby spinach
>
> ½ cup fat-free ricotta cheese
>
> ¼ cup grated Parmesan cheese
>
> ½ teaspoon salt
>
> ½ teaspoon black pepper
>
> ⅛ teaspoon ground nutmeg

1 Cook fusilli in large deep pot of lightly salted boiling water until al dente, firm yet tender.

2 Meanwhile, heat spaghetti sauce in medium-size saucepan over medium heat until heated through. Stir in spinach; heat until wilted, about 3 minutes.

3 In large serving bowl, whisk together ricotta and Parmesan cheeses, salt, pepper, and nutmeg until well blended.

4 Drain fusilli; add to cheese mixture. Add spinach sauce mixture; toss to combine.

Nutrient Value Per Serving: 261 calories, 2 g fat (1 g saturated), 13 g protein, 47 g carbohydrate, 4 g fiber, 516 mg sodium, 5 mg cholesterol.

Vegetable Pasta Bake

MAKES: 6 servings
PREP: 10 minutes
COOK: about 10 minutes
BAKE: at 375° for 35 minutes

6 ounces bow-tie pasta

4 cups broccoli flowerets (about ¾ pound)

1 cup nonfat sour cream

1 container (10 ounces) refrigerated light Alfredo sauce

1 small onion, finely chopped

½ teaspoon salt

⅛ teaspoon cayenne

⅛ teaspoon ground nutmeg

½ cup frozen peas, thawed

½ cup shredded peeled carrots

½ cup shredded reduced-fat American cheese

1 Heat oven to 375°. Coat shallow 2-quart casserole dish with cooking spray.

2 Cook bow ties in large deep pot of lightly salted boiling water until al dente, firm yet tender. Add broccoli to boiling water for last 2 minutes; drain.

3 Meanwhile, stir together sour cream, Alfredo sauce, onion, salt, cayenne, and nutmeg in large bowl. Add bow ties, broccoli, peas, and carrots; toss to combine. Pour into prepared casserole.

4 Bake for 30 minutes or until bubbly. Sprinkle with cheese. Return to oven for 5 minutes or until cheese is melted.

Nutrient Value Per Serving: 297 calories, 9 g fat (5 g saturated), 14 g protein, 41 g carbohydrate, 3 g fiber, 797 mg sodium, 27 mg cholesterol.

Broccoli and Cheese Stuffed Shells

MAKES: 6 servings
PREP: 30 minutes
COOK: 8 minutes
BAKE: at 375° for 45 minutes

24 jumbo pasta shells (about 7 ounces), from 12-ounce package

1 container (1 pound) low-fat (1%) cottage cheese

1 cup shredded part-skim mozzarella cheese

1 large egg white

1 tablespoon grated Parmesan cheese

½ teaspoon garlic powder

½ teaspoon dried basil

⅛ teaspoon salt

⅛ teaspoon black pepper

2 packages (10 ounces each) frozen chopped broccoli

3 medium-size carrots, shredded (½ cup)

2 cups fat-free marinara pasta sauce

1 Cook shells in large deep pot of lightly salted boiling water until al dente, firm yet tender. Drain; let cool.

2 Heat oven to 375°.

3 In food processor (see Note), pulse together cottage cheese, ½ cup mozzarella, egg white, Parmesan, garlic powder, basil, salt, and pepper until well blended and smooth. Transfer mixture to large bowl. Stir in broccoli and carrots.

4 Coat 2-quart oval or rectangular baking dish (12 x 8 inch) with cooking spray. Spread ½ cup marinara sauce over bottom of dish.

5 Fill each shell with a heaping tablespoon of cheese mixture. Transfer filled shells to prepared dish, packing them slightly to fit. Top with remaining 1½ cups marinara sauce. Sprinkle with remaining ½ cup mozzarella. Cover with nonstick foil (or regular foil coated with cooking spray).

6 Bake for 35 minutes. Carefully uncover dish. Bake 10 minutes. Let cool slightly before serving.

Note: If you do not have a food processor, use hand mixer. Beat for 3 minutes or until smooth.

Nutrient Value Per Serving: 331 calories, 5 g fat (3 g saturated), 26 g protein, 47 g carbohydrate, 7 g fiber, 749 mg sodium, 14 mg cholesterol.

Pasta Power

To come up with a diet-friendly serving of pasta, put your kitchen scale to good use: Weigh out 2 ounces of the dried version per person. No scale? Measure out 1 cup of a tube-type pasta such as rigatoni or ziti, ½ cup of a small pasta like elbow macaroni or orzo. Go with a nickel-size bundle of dry spaghetti. Once cooked, these amounts will make about 1 cup or roughly the size of a fist, with the smaller shapes measuring in at a scant cup and larger like rigatoni coming in at a little over.

Interestingly, there is a small variation in the calorie count for various pasta shapes. In general, you can estimate about 200 calories per serving, ranging from 184 for 2 ounces of dried rotini, cooked, to 222 for the same weight of dried spaghetti, cooked. Go figure.

For perfect pasta every time, follow these steps:

■ In heavy deep pot, bring to a rolling boil 4 quarts of water for each pound of pasta. Add salt, then pasta. (If you are using long pasta shapes, add in batches.)

■ Stir to separate pasta. Cover; return to boil; immediately remove lid. Stir occasionally during cooking.

■ Taste for doneness; *al dente*—the Italian phrase literally means "to the tooth"—pasta should have firmness to the bite but no crunch or raw flavor.

■ Drain immediately into a large colander, but do not rinse unless you plan to serve it cold.

Four-Cheese
Baked Macaroni

MAKES: 10 servings
PREP: 20 minutes
COOK: about 8 minutes
BAKE: at 350° for 45 minutes

1 pound rotelle

2 cups shredded reduced-fat sharp cheddar cheese (8 ounces)

1 cup shredded reduced-fat mozzarella cheese (4 ounces)

½ cup shredded reduced-fat Jarlsberg cheese (2 ounces)

½ cup grated Parmesan cheese

¼ cup all-purpose flour

4 cups milk

1½ teaspoons salt

¼ to ½ teaspoon ground nutmeg

⅛ to ¼ teaspoon cayenne

3 large ripe tomatoes, cored and thinly sliced

1 Heat oven to 350°. Coat 13 x 9 x 2-inch glass baking dish with cooking spray.

2 Cook rotelle in large deep pot of lightly salted boiling water until al dente, firm yet tender. Drain well.

3 Meanwhile, mix together cheddar, mozzarella, Jarlsberg, and Parmesan in large bowl.

4 In small bowl, whisk together flour and 1 cup milk until smooth. Pour into large saucepan. Bring to a simmer over medium heat, stirring, until consistency of mashed potatoes.

5 Gradually mix in remaining milk, 1 cup at a time. Stir in salt, nutmeg, and cayenne; simmer, whisking constantly, until thickened and smooth, about 2 minutes. Remove saucepan from heat. Stir in 2 cups of cheese mixture, whisking until sauce is very smooth. Add rotelle to cheese sauce; stir until well blended.

6 Sprinkle ½ cup of remaining cheese mixture over bottom of prepared baking dish. Spoon half of rotelle mixture into baking dish, spreading evenly. Sprinkle 1 cup of cheese mixture over rotelle. Spoon remaining rotelle mixture over cheese mixture. Sprinkle remaining cheese mixture over top of pasta. Arrange sliced tomatoes to completely cover top of casserole.

7 Bake for 45 minutes or until top is lightly golden. Let stand for at least 10 minutes before serving.

Nutrient Value Per Serving: 330 calories, 9 g fat (5 g saturated), 21 g protein, 40 g carbohydrate, 2 g fiber, 752 mg sodium, 28 mg cholesterol.

Linguine
with Clam Sauce

MAKES: 6 servings
PREP: 10 minutes
COOK: 10 minutes

¾ pound linguine

2 tablespoons olive oil

1 medium-size onion, chopped

4 cloves garlic, chopped

2 cans (6.5 ounces each) chopped clams

1 large tomato, cored, seeded, and chopped

½ teaspoon dried oregano

½ teaspoon dried basil

¼ teaspoon red-pepper flakes

⅛ teaspoon salt

⅛ teaspoon black pepper

2 tablespoons chopped fresh parsley

1 clove garlic, pressed (optional)

1 Cook linguine in large deep pot of lightly salted boiling water until al dente, firm yet tender.

2 Meanwhile, heat oil in medium-size saucepan over medium heat. Add onion and chopped garlic; sauté 5 minutes or until onion is slightly softened.

3 Meanwhile, strain liquid from clams; add liquid to onion in skillet, reserving clams. Add tomato, oregano, basil, pepper flakes, salt, and pepper; simmer 5 minutes.

4 Stir in clams, parsley, and garlic, if using; remove from heat.

5 Drain linguine. Add to sauce; toss to mix. Serve immediately.

Nutrient Value Per Serving: 303 calories, 7 g fat (1 g saturated), 22 g protein, 39 g carbohydrate, 3 g fiber, 223 mg sodium, 41 mg cholesterol.

Pasta Fra Diavolo

MAKES: 8 servings
PREP: 10 minutes
COOK: about 22 minutes

2 teaspoons olive oil

1 large onion, chopped

3 cloves garlic, sliced

1 can (28 ounces) whole tomatoes

1 can (8 ounces) tomato sauce

1 teaspoon dried oregano

1 teaspoon salt

¾ teaspoon red-pepper flakes

¾ pound linguine

1¼ pounds medium-size shrimp in shells, cleaned

½ pound surimi (imitation crab), shredded

¼ cup fresh basil, cut into strips

1 Heat oil in large skillet over medium heat. Add onion and garlic; sauté 8 minutes or until softened, without letting garlic brown.

2 Add tomatoes, tomato sauce, oregano, salt, and pepper flakes. Bring to a simmer, breaking up tomatoes with wooden spoon; simmer over medium heat 10 minutes.

3 While sauce is simmering, cook linguine in large deep pot of lightly salted boiling water until al dente, firm yet tender.

4 Stir shrimp into sauce; cook 3 to 4 minutes or until shrimp is cooked through. Stir in surimi; heat through, about 1 minute.

5 Drain linguine. Toss with shrimp sauce. Garnish with basil.

Nutrient Value Per Serving: 285 calories, 3 g fat (1 g saturated), 19 g protein, 45 g carbohydrate, 4 g fiber, 929 mg sodium, 86 mg cholesterol.

Ravioli with Sausage Sauce

MAKES: 6 servings
PREP: 10 minutes
COOK: 20 minutes

2 large onions, halved and sliced crosswise

3 cloves garlic, sliced

2 tablespoons water

½ pound hot Italian-style turkey sausage links, casings removed

¾ cup chicken broth

2 packages (9 ounces each) refrigerated light cheese ravioli

4 ounces sliced assorted mushrooms

2 medium-size tomatoes, cored and diced

½ teaspoon salt

¼ teaspoon fennel seeds, crushed

¼ teaspoon black pepper

2 small bunches arugula (about ¾ pound total) or spinach, cleaned and cut into large pieces

1 Coat large skillet with cooking spray. Place over medium-high heat. Add onions and garlic; cook 5 minutes, adding the water halfway through to keep onions from burning.

2 Stir in turkey sausage, breaking up clumps with wooden spoon; cook until no longer pink, about 5 minutes, adding ¼ cup of broth halfway through.

3 Meanwhile, cook ravioli in large deep pot of lightly salted boiling water until al dente, firm but tender. Drain.

4 While ravioli are cooking, add mushrooms and another ¼ cup broth to skillet; simmer 3 minutes. Add tomatoes, salt, fennel seeds, and pepper; cook 3 minutes. Add remaining broth and arugula; cook until wilted, about 2 minutes.

5 Gently stir ravioli into skillet. Serve warm.

Nutrient Value Per Serving: 341 calories, 8 g fat (3 g saturated), 21 g protein, 47 g carbohydrate, 5 g fiber, 1,028 mg sodium, 73 mg cholesterol.

SKINNY SAUCES

No time to cook? Start with a fat-free plain tomato-based pasta sauce at 50 calories for a half-cup serving. Then jazz it up with these speedy ideas:

Hearty Vegetable

MAKES: **4 servings**

Spray a medium nonstick skillet with cooking spray; heat over medium heat. Add 1 clove garlic, sliced, and 4 ounces sliced mushrooms. Sauté 4 minutes. Add 2 cups small broccoli flowerets and ¼ cup white wine or water. Cover pan with foil and cook 4 minutes. Uncover, add 2 cups prepared pasta sauce, and heat through.

Nutrient Value Per ⅔ Cup Sauce: 68 calories, 0 g fat (0 g saturated), 4 g protein, 14 g carbohydrate, 3 g fiber, 402 mg sodium, 0 mg cholesterol.

Bacon and Onion

MAKES: **4 servings**

Spray a medium skillet with nonstick spray. Heat over medium heat. Add 4 slices turkey bacon, chopped, and 1 medium onion, diced. Cook 8 minutes or until bacon is cooked and onion is softened. Add 3 tablespoons balsamic vinegar and cook for 1 minute or until most of the liquid has evaporated. Add 2 cups prepared pasta sauce and heat through.

Nutrient Value Per ⅔ Cup Sauce: 105 calories, 3 g fat (1 g saturated), 5 g protein, 16 g carbohydrate, 3 g fiber, 578 mg sodium, 13 mg cholesterol.

Roasted Garlic and Pepper

MAKES: **4 servings**

Place 2 heads garlic in a medium glass bowl or microwave-safe dish. Coat with nonstick cooking spray. Add 2 tablespoons water and cover with plastic. Microwave on high power for 3½ to 4 minutes. Let stand 3 minutes. Meanwhile, coat a medium skillet with nonstick spray. Heat over medium heat. Add 2 red peppers, cored and cut into ¾-inch pieces. Cook 5 minutes, until softened. Add 2 cups prepared pasta sauce. Cut the tops off the garlic, and carefully squeeze softened cloves into skillet. Mash with spoon; stir to distribute. Before serving, stir in 2 tablespoons grated Parmesan cheese.

Nutrient Value Per ⅔ Cup Sauce: 94 calories, 1 g fat (1 g saturated), 4 g protein, 18 g carbohydrate, 3 g fiber, 451 mg sodium, 3 mg cholesterol.

Peanut Noodles
with Chicken

MAKES: 6 servings
PREP: 15 minutes
COOK: about 12 minutes

   4 boneless, skinless chicken breast halves
   (about 1 pound total), cut into ¼-inch-thick
   slices

   3 cloves garlic, minced

   2 medium-size sweet green peppers, cored,
   seeded, and cut into thin strips

   2 medium-size sweet red peppers, cored,
   seeded, and cut into thin strips

   ½ cup reduced-fat creamy peanut butter

   2 cups water

   2 tablespoons balsamic vinegar

   1 tablespoon reduced-sodium soy sauce

   ½ to 1 teaspoon red-pepper flakes

   2 packages (3 ounces each) chicken-flavored
   ramen noodles, reserving 1 seasoning packet

   3 scallions, thinly sliced

1   Coat large skillet with cooking spray. Place
over medium-high heat. Add chicken and garlic;
stir-fry 3 minutes or until chicken is no longer
pink. Remove skillet from heat. Remove chicken
from skillet to bowl.

2   Coat skillet again with cooking spray. Add
sweet peppers; stir-fry 3 minutes or until
softened. Add to chicken in bowl.

3   Spoon peanut butter into skillet. In medium-
size bowl, whisk together water, vinegar, soy
sauce, pepper flakes, and 1 seasoning packet
from noodles. Stir into peanut butter in skillet;
bring to a boil. Add noodles from both packages,
breaking up slightly. Add chicken and sweet
peppers. Lower heat; cover and simmer
5 minutes, stirring occasionally to separate
noodles. Sprinkle with scallions.

*Nutrient Value Per Serving: 325 calories, 10 g fat
(2 g saturated), 27 g protein, 35 g carbohydrate,
4 g fiber, 567 mg sodium, 42 mg cholesterol.*

Creamy Sausage Sauce
with Ziti

MAKES: 6 servings
PREP: 5 minutes
COOK: 25 minutes

   1 teaspoon olive oil

   ½ small onion, chopped

   1 clove garlic, finely chopped

   ½ pound Italian-style turkey sausages,
   casings removed

   1 can (14.5 ounces) recipe-ready diced
   tomatoes

   1 cup fat-free half-and-half

   ¼ teaspoon salt

   ⅛ teaspoon black pepper

   1 teaspoon cornstarch

   1 tablespoon cold water

   1 cup frozen peas, thawed

   ¾ pound ziti

1 Heat oil in large skillet over medium heat. Add onion and garlic; sauté until fragrant, about 1 minute. Crumble turkey sausages into skillet; sauté, breaking up pieces with wooden spoon, until lightly browned, about 7 minutes.

2 Stir in diced tomatoes, half-and-half, salt, and pepper; simmer, uncovered, stirring occasionally, for 15 minutes or until slightly thickened.

3 Dissolve cornstarch in water in small bowl. Gently stir into sausage mixture. Add peas; cook until mixture is heated through.

4 Meanwhile, cook ziti in large deep pot of lightly salted boiling water until al dente, firm yet tender. Drain well.

5 Transfer ziti to large serving bowl; top with sausage sauce.

Nutrient Value Per Serving: 308 calories, 4 g fat (1 g saturated), 17 g protein, 49 g carbohydrate, 4 g fiber, 518 mg sodium, 27 mg cholesterol.

Creamy Pesto Tortellini

MAKES: 6 servings
PREP: 10 minutes
COOK: 13 minutes

1 pound frozen or fresh light cheese tortellini

1 medium-size zucchini, halved lengthwise and cut crosswise into ¼-inch-thick slices

1 small sweet red pepper, cored, seeded, and diced

1 small sweet yellow pepper, cored, seeded, and diced

1 cup fat-free half-and-half

¼ cup prepared pesto

¼ pound ham, cubed

1 Cook tortellini in large deep pot of lightly salted boiling water until al dente, firm yet tender. For the last 2 minutes of cooking, add zucchini and peppers. Drain in colander.

2 Add half-and-half, pesto, and ham to pot. Heat over medium-high heat 3 minutes. Return tortellini and vegetables to sauce in pot; toss to coat. Remove from heat. Let stand 10 minutes to thicken slightly before serving.

Nutrient Value Per Serving: 306 calories, 9 g fat (3 g saturated), 18 g protein, 39 g carbohydrate, 3 g fiber, 688 mg sodium, 13 mg cholesterol.

Rotelle and Mini Meatballs

MAKES: 6 servings
PREP: 20 minutes
COOK: about 25 minutes

3 tablespoons packaged seasoned bread crumbs

2 tablespoons milk

¾ pound ground turkey

½ teaspoon dried Italian herb seasoning

¼ teaspoon liquid hot-pepper sauce

¼ teaspoon salt

1 medium-size red onion, chopped

1 can (14.5 ounces) diced tomatoes with Italian herbs

1 can (8 ounces) tomato sauce

½ cup halved pitted black olives

¾ pound rotelle

Shredded Parmesan cheese (optional)

1 Combine crumbs and milk in medium-size bowl. Add turkey, Italian seasoning, pepper sauce, and salt; mix well. Shape into 24 meatballs, using a slightly rounded tablespoon for each.

2 Coat nonstick 10-inch skillet with cooking spray. Place over medium-high heat. Add onion; cook until softened, about 8 minutes.

3 Add diced tomatoes, tomato sauce, and olives. Bring to a boil. Add meatballs; cover. Lower heat; simmer 15 minutes, turning meatballs over halfway through.

4 Meanwhile, cook rotelle in large deep pot of lightly salted boiling water until al dente, firm yet tender. Drain. Add to meatballs and sauce; toss to combine. Sprinkle with shredded Parmesan cheese, if desired.

Nutrient Value Per Serving: 342 calories, 8 g fat (2 g saturated), 18 g protein, 49 g carbohydrate, 3 g fiber, 850 mg sodium, 46 mg cholesterol.

Tagliatelle Bolognese

MAKES: 6 servings
PREP: 10 minutes
COOK: about 30 minutes

Bolognese Sauce:

2 medium-size carrots, peeled and finely chopped

2 medium-size ribs celery, finely chopped

1 medium-size onion, finely chopped

¾ pound lean ground beef

½ cup dry white wine

¾ cup chicken broth

½ cup tomato sauce

2 tablespoons tomato paste

1 teaspoon salt

½ teaspoon black pepper

1 cup fat-free half-and-half

Pasta:

¾ pound tagliatelle or fettuccine

Grated Parmesan cheese (optional)

1 Sauce: Coat large nonstick saucepan with cooking spray. Place over medium-high heat. Add carrots, celery, and onion; cook 5 minutes or until onion is softened.

2 Add ground beef. Lower heat to medium; cook, stirring occasionally, until no longer pink, about 5 minutes. Add wine, broth, tomato sauce, tomato paste, salt, and pepper; simmer, uncovered, stirring occasionally, until liquid is absorbed, about 15 minutes. Add half-and-half; heat through, about 2 minutes.

3 Pasta: Cook tagliatelle in large deep pot of lightly salted boiling water until al dente, firm yet tender. Drain. Serve with sauce, and Parmesan cheese, if desired.

Nutrient Value Per Serving: 350 calories, 4 g fat (1 g saturated), 21 g protein, 57 g carbohydrate, 5 g fiber, 710 mg sodium, 30 mg cholesterol.

Ham-and-Spinach-Filled Cannelloni

MAKES: 4 servings
PREP: 25 minutes
BAKE: at 400° for 25 minutes

2 cups bottled fat-free pasta sauce

1 package (10 ounces) frozen chopped spinach, thawed and squeezed dry

2 scallions, sliced

1 container (16 ounces) low-fat dry-curd cottage cheese

¼ cup grated Parmesan cheese

2 tablespoons flavored bread crumbs

1 large egg white

2 ounces lean ham, diced

8 no-boil lasagna sheets, about 7 x 7 inches

3 tablespoons grated Parmesan

1 Heat oven to 400°. Coat 13 x 9 x 2-inch baking dish with nonstick cooking spray. Combine 3 tablespoons water and ⅓ cup pasta sauce in baking dish. Set aside.

2 Whirl spinach, scallions, cottage cheese, Parmesan, crumbs, and egg white in food processor to combine. Add ham. Whirl just to blend.

3 Fill another 13 x 9 x 2-inch dish with hot tap water. Add half of lasagne sheets; soak to soften, 5 minutes. Remove to toweling to drain. Repeat with remaining sheets.

4 Place sheet on cutting board. Spoon scant ½ cup filling down center; roll up; place, seam side down, in prepared dish. Repeat with remaining ingredients. Top with remaining sauce; cover with foil.

5 Bake for 25 minutes or until heated through. Sprinkle with Parmesan.

Nutrient Value Per Serving: 349 calories, 5 g fat (2 g saturated), 30 g protein, 49 g carbohydrate, 6 g fiber, 1,268 mg sodium, 19 mg cholesterol.

5 SIMPLY SENSATIONAL SOUPS

AT *FAMILY CIRCLE,* MANY OF US—and not just those in the Food Department—eat lunch at our desks. One of the most popular takeout choices is soup, usually from a local chain that serves up everything from classic tomato to more exotic concoctions. This got us to thinking that soup not only is a palate-pleaser, but cooked up right, it can also be a weight-whittler.

For starters, it's easy to limit calories on soup recipes. Most call for little fat; the flavor comes from the magical simmering of fixings like vegetables, poultry, meat, or seafood along with herbs and spices. For another thing, there's something immensely gratifying about dipping a spoon into the bowl and savoring the combination of tastes. Add some bread or a green salad and you're home free—satisfied and secure in the fact that you haven't overloaded.

Better yet, our recipes go beyond the usual. Minestrone (page 80) has the rich addition of turkey meatballs; gazpacho (page 76) takes on an island aura with shrimp and clam juice; tomatoes and jalapeños jazz up clam chowder (page 77). And if rib-sticking is what you want, we can deliver. Puttanesca Stew (page 83) is a robust medley of chicken, olives, tomatoes, and red wine to serve over noodles. Ground beef and sweet potatoes are the hearty ingredients in a Tex-Mex dish (page 85) that also includes corn, green chiles, and black beans. Spring Gumbo (page 76), a top choice in the office, serves up shrimp, scallops, and rice in zesty Creole style.

There's also a bonus of five 5-ingredient soups on pages 82–83 that you can whip up in no time. So when you say "soup's on," it's ready.

Shrimp-Gazpacho Soup (page 76).

Tortilla Soup

MAKES: 4 servings
PREP: 10 minutes
COOK: 30 minutes
BAKE: at 400° for 10 minutes

1 tablespoon olive oil

1 medium-size onion, finely chopped

1 clove garlic, finely chopped

2 tomatoes, peeled, seeded, and chopped

2 jalapeño chiles, seeded and finely chopped

1 teaspoon black pepper

¾ teaspoon cumin seeds, crushed

4 corn tortillas, cut into ⅛-inch-wide strips

Pinch chili powder

1 large can (2 pints, 14 ounces) chicken broth (5¾ cups)

¼ cup shredded Monterey Jack cheese

2 tablespoons chopped fresh cilantro

1 Heat oven to 400°.

2 Heat oil in large saucepan over medium heat. Add onion and garlic; sauté until softened, about 8 minutes. Add tomatoes, jalapeño, black pepper, and cumin; cook 10 minutes.

3 Meanwhile, sprinkle tortilla strips with chili powder. Place on baking sheet and toast for 10 minutes or until crispy.

4 Add broth to saucepan; simmer 10 minutes. Ladle into 4 soup bowls. Sprinkle with tortilla strips, cheese, and cilantro.

Nutrient Value Per Serving: 194 calories, 12 g fat (3 g saturated), 6 g protein, 17 g carbohydrate, 3 g fiber, 1,513 mg sodium, 14 mg cholesterol.

Black Bean and Corn Soup

MAKES: 6 servings
PREP: 5 minutes
COOK: 15 minutes

1 tablespoon vegetable oil

1 medium-size red onion, chopped

2 cans (15 ounces each) black beans, drained and rinsed

1 can (11 ounces) corn kernels, drained and rinsed

1 can (14.5 ounces) chicken broth

1 cup bottled chunky salsa

1 tablespoon fresh lime juice

½ teaspoon salt

⅛ teaspoon black pepper

Garnish (optional):

Sour cream

Lime wedges

1 Heat oil in medium-size saucepan over medium heat. Add onion; sauté until softened, about 5 minutes.

2 Mash 1 cup beans in small bowl. Stir mashed beans, whole beans, corn, broth, salsa, lime juice, salt, and pepper into saucepan; simmer, uncovered, 10 minutes or until heated through. Serve with dollop of sour cream and lime, if desired.

Nutrient Value Per Serving: 171 calories, 5 g fat (1 g saturated), 8 g protein, 25 g carbohydrate, 7 g fiber, 1,171 mg sodium, 2 mg cholesterol.

Split Pea Soup

MAKES: 6 servings

PREP: 20 minutes

COOK: 2 hours

1 bag (1 pound) dried split green peas, picked over and rinsed

2 large onions, chopped

3 cloves garlic

5 small vegetable bouillon cubes (each cube makes 1 cup bouillon)

1 bay leaf

12 cups water

1 cup chopped baked ham (about 6 ounces)

4 ribs celery, chopped (about 1 cup)

4 medium-size carrots, peeled and chopped (about 1¼ cups)

2 large sprigs fresh thyme OR ½ teaspoon dried

¼ teaspoon black pepper

Dash liquid hot-pepper sauce

1 jar (4 ounces) chopped pimiento

1 Combine split peas, onion, garlic, bouillon cubes, bay leaf, and water in 8-quart pot. Bring to a boil, breaking up cubes with wooden spoon. Reduce heat to medium-low; simmer, uncovered, 1 hour.

2 Stir mixture in pot. Add ham, celery, carrots, and thyme. Simmer, stirring occasionally, 1 hour or until desired smoothness. Add black pepper and hot-pepper sauce.

3 Remove fresh thyme sprigs, if using, bay leaf, and garlic. Adjust seasonings, if necessary. Stir in pimiento. Serve warm.

4 To freeze, let cool slightly. Spoon into freezer containers or heavy-duty freezer bags. Seal; label. Refrigerate until cold, then freeze.

Nutrient Value Per Serving: 306 calories, 4 g fat (1 g saturated), 23 g protein, 49 g carbohydrate, 18 g fiber, 1,093 mg sodium, 14 mg cholesterol.

The Fit Freezer

Having your freezer stocked with ready-to-go diet soups and pasta portions helps keep you on the right track. Cut down on future prep time by doing up double batches of soup and pasta sauces, then freeze half. Follow these tips for best results.

■ Most soups are a safe bet for freezing, except those containing cheese, cream, or other dairy products, since they may separate and curdle when thawed and reheated. The trick is to omit these particular ingredients, then add when gently reheating.

■ Tomato-based pasta sauces are good candidates for the freezer; pack them up in appropriate units— either individual servings or enough for your family.

■ Some vegetable pieces, such as potatoes and green beans, as well as pasta in soups become soft when frozen and reheated. For a better texture, add these ingredients to the soup when you reheat.

■ Freeze soups and complete pasta meals in individual microwave-safe containers for a quick microwavable lunch or snack.

Lentils with Greens Soup

MAKES: 6 servings
PREP: 10 minutes
COOK: about 25 minutes

- ½ cup dried lentils, picked over and rinsed
- 8 cups water
- 1 teaspoon vegetable oil
- ½ pound Italian sausage, casings removed
- ½ medium-size onion, chopped
- 1 pound escarole, stemmed and coarsely chopped OR spinach
- 3 teaspoons chicken broth granules
- ⅛ teaspoon red-pepper flakes
- 4 tablespoons grated Parmesan cheese

1 Combine lentils and 4 cups water in medium-size saucepan; simmer, uncovered, 20 minutes or just until tender. Drain.

2 Meanwhile, heat oil in 4-quart pot over medium-high heat. Add sausage; cook, breaking up any clumps with wooden spoon, until no longer pink, about 3 minutes. Add onion and escarole; cook, stirring occasionally, 3 minutes. Add remaining 4 cups water and broth granules; bring to a boil. Lower heat; simmer, covered, 15 minutes.

3 Add lentils and pepper flakes to pot; simmer 3 minutes.

4 Ladle into 4 bowls. Top each with cheese, dividing equally.

Nutrient Value Per Serving: 163 calories, 7 g fat (3 g saturated), 11 g protein, 14 g carbohydrate, 7 g fiber, 857 mg sodium, 19 mg cholesterol.

Roasted Butternut Squash Soup

MAKES: 8 servings
PREP: 10 minutes
BAKE: at 350° for 1 hour
COOK: 30 minutes

- 3 pounds butternut squash (1 large or 2 small), seeded, peeled, and cut into 8 wedges
- 2 tablespoons vegetable oil
- 4 cloves garlic, crushed
- 1 onion, coarsely chopped
- 1 Granny Smith apple, peeled, cored, and coarsely chopped
- 5 cups chicken broth
- 1 cup apple cider
- 1 teaspoon salt
- ⅛ teaspoon black pepper
- ⅛ teaspoon ground nutmeg
- ½ cup light sour cream
- ⅛ teaspoon ground cinnamon

1 Heat oven to 350°. In roasting pan, mix squash and 1 tablespoon oil. Arrange squash, curved side up; place garlic in curved part of squash.

2 Roast for 1 hour or until tender. Turn halfway through cooking.

3 In large pot, heat remaining tablespoon oil. Add onion; sauté 5 minutes or until softened. Add squash, garlic, apple, broth, cider, salt, black pepper, and nutmeg. Bring to a boil over high heat. Cover; lower heat to medium. Simmer 25 minutes or until apple and squash are very soft.

4 Working in batches, puree soup in food processor. Return to pot; gently heat through. Garnish with sour cream and cinnamon.

Nutrient Value Per Serving: 146 calories, 7 g fat (2 g saturated), 2 g protein, 21 g carbohydrate, 4 g fiber, 936 mg sodium, 8 mg cholesterol.

Creamy Mushroom-Barley Soup

MAKES: 6 servings
PREP: 10 minutes
COOK: 25 minutes

1 medium-size onion, chopped

1 pound assorted mushrooms, sliced

1 large carrot, peeled and chopped

½ cup quick-cooking barley

1 can (14.5 ounces) reduced-sodium, fat-free chicken broth

¼ cup water

1 cup milk

2 cups fat-free half-and-half

1 tablespoon all-purpose flour

1 teaspoon salt

¼ teaspoon black pepper

1 Coat large saucepan with cooking spray; place over medium-high heat. Add onion, mushrooms, and carrots; cook until onion is softened, about 6 minutes. Add barley, broth, and water; bring to a boil. Lower heat; simmer, covered, 15 minutes or until barley is tender.

2 Meanwhile, stir together milk, half-and-half, flour, salt, and pepper in small bowl. Stir into saucepan.

3 Cook, stirring constantly, until mixture comes to a boil. Boil, stirring, for 1 minute or until thickened.

4 Puree 2 cups of soup in food processor. Stir back into soup in saucepan; gently heat through.

Nutrient Value Per Serving: 160 calories, 2 g fat (1 g saturated), 10 g protein, 25 g carbohydrate, 3 g fiber, 555 mg sodium, 6 mg cholesterol.

Salsa Fish Soup

MAKES: 4 servings
PREP: 5 minutes
COOK: 10 minutes

1 can (13.75 ounces) chicken broth

⅔ cup instant white rice

1 package (10 ounces) frozen corn kernels

1½ cups bottled chunky salsa

1 pound skinned, mild-flavored fish fillets, such as haddock, cod, or halibut, cut into 2-inch pieces

Fresh lime wedges, for garnish

1 Combine broth with enough water to equal 6 cups. Combine with rice in large saucepan; simmer, covered, 5 minutes. Add corn and salsa.

2 Add fish to saucepan; simmer, covered, 5 minutes or until fish is opaque and flakes when touched lightly with a fork. Serve with lime wedges.

Nutrient Value Per Serving: 275 calories, 3 g fat (1 g saturated), 29 g protein, 34 g carbohydrate, 4 g fiber, 919 mg sodium, 74 mg cholesterol.

Spring Gumbo

MAKES: 6 servings

PREP: 10 minutes

COOK: 35 minutes

2 tablespoons olive oil

1 medium-size onion, thinly sliced

2 cloves garlic, finely chopped

1 sweet green pepper, cored, seeded, and chopped

3 ribs celery, thinly sliced

1 jalapeño chile, seeded and diced

2 chicken bouillon cubes, dissolved in 9 cups hot water

2 cans (14.5 ounces each) stewed tomatoes

1 teaspoon paprika

⅛ teaspoon cayenne pepper

3 to 5 drops liquid hot-pepper sauce

1 cup uncooked white rice

¼ cup all-purpose flour

1¼ pounds shrimp, cleaned and sliced in half

½ pound scallops

½ teaspoon salt

1 In a large heavy deep pot, heat oil. Add onion, garlic, green pepper, celery, and jalapeño; cook until celery is softened, 10 to 12 minutes. Reserve 1 cup bouillon liquid. Add remaining bouillon liquid, tomatoes, paprika, cayenne, pepper sauce, and rice to pot; simmer, covered, 20 minutes.

2 Stir together reserved bouillon liquid and flour in small bowl. Stir into pot. Add shrimp, scallops, and salt; simmer until seafood is opaque, about 3 minutes. Spoon into bowls.

Nutrient Value Per Serving: 290 calories, 7 g fat (1 g saturated), 25 g protein, 33 g carbohydrate, 3 g fiber, 1,070 mg sodium, 136 mg cholesterol.

Shrimp-Gazpacho Soup

MAKES: 4 servings

PREP: 20 minutes

REFRIGERATE: several hours or overnight

1 cucumber, peeled, seeded, and diced

1 small red onion, minced

2 cloves garlic, minced

3 large ripe tomatoes, cored, peeled, seeded, and diced

1 small sweet green pepper, cored, seeded, and diced

2 cups thick tomato juice

1 cup reduced-sodium chicken broth

1 bottle (8 ounces) clam juice

¼ cup red-wine vinegar

1 tablespoon minced fresh oregano OR 1 teaspoon dried

1 tablespoon minced fresh basil OR 1 teaspoon dried

¼ teaspoon liquid hot-pepper sauce

½ teaspoon salt

¼ teaspoon black pepper

1 pound fully-cooked peeled shrimp, chopped

1 In large bowl, combine cucumber, onion, garlic, tomatoes, and green pepper. In medium-size bowl, stir together tomato juice, chicken broth, clam juice, vinegar, oregano, basil, pepper sauce, salt, and black pepper. Pour over vegetables. Refrigerate, covered, several hours or overnight.

2 Divide soup among 4 bowls. Top with chopped shrimp. Serve chilled.

Nutrient Value Per Serving: 194 calories, 2 g fat (1 g saturated), 27 g protein, 16 g carbohydrate, 3 g fiber, 1,298 mg sodium, 222 mg cholesterol.

Spicy Clam Chowder

MAKES: 6 servings
PREP: 10 minutes
COOK: 25 minutes

- ¼ pound turkey bacon, chopped
- 1 teaspoon vegetable oil
- ½ small onion, chopped
- 2 small ribs celery, chopped
- ½ teaspoon dried thyme
- 1 pound russet potatoes, peeled and cut into ½-inch pieces
- 2 cans (14.5 ounces each) chopped tomatoes with jalapeño chiles
- 2 bottles (8 ounces each) clam juice
- ½ teaspoon black pepper
- 2 cans (10 ounces each) chopped clams with juice
- 1 can (7 ounces) corn kernels, drained and rinsed

1 Brown bacon in 5-quart saucepan over medium-high heat, 2 minutes. Remove bacon to paper toweling. Heat oil in saucepan. Add onion, celery, thyme, and potatoes; sauté 5 minutes. Add tomatoes, clam juice, and pepper; simmer, covered, 15 minutes or until potatoes are just tender.

2 Stir in clams with juice and corn kernels; heat through. Top with bacon.

Nutrient Value Per Serving: 172 calories, 5 g fat (1 g saturated), 7 g protein, 27 g carbohydrate, 3 g fiber, 1,483 mg sodium, 20 mg cholesterol.

Country Captain Soup

MAKES: 6 servings
PREP: 10 minutes
COOK: about 20 minutes

- 2 teaspoons olive oil
- 1 medium-size onion, chopped
- 1 sweet green pepper, cored, seeded, and chopped
- 1 Granny Smith apple, peeled, cored, and chopped
- 2 cloves garlic, minced
- 1 tablespoon curry powder
- 1 teaspoon grated peeled fresh ginger
- 1¼ pounds boneless, skinless chicken thighs, cut into 1-inch pieces
- 2 cans (14.5 ounces each) chicken broth
- 1 can (14.5 ounces) chopped tomatoes with jalapeño chiles

1 Heat oil in large saucepan over medium-high heat. Add onion, green pepper, apple, and garlic; sauté until onion is softened, about 5 minutes. Add curry powder and ginger; sauté 1 minute.

2 Add chicken pieces, broth, and tomatoes to saucepan; simmer, covered, 15 minutes or until chicken is cooked through.

Nutrient Value Per Serving: 199 calories, 8 g fat (2 g saturated), 20 g protein, 11 g carbohydrate, 2 g fiber, 937 mg sodium, 81 mg cholesterol.

Hot and Sour Chicken and Noodles

MAKES: 6 servings
PREP: 20 minutes
COOK: 15 minutes

2 quarts reduced-sodium, fat-free chicken broth

¼ to ⅓ cup rice vinegar

1 tablespoon dark Asian sesame oil

2 to 3 teaspoons liquid hot-pepper sauce

¼ cup cornstarch

2 tablespoons miso paste (see Note)

1 pound boneless, skinless chicken breast halves, cut into 1 x ½-inch strips

8 white mushrooms, sliced

1 cup coarsely shredded peeled carrots (1 to 2 medium-size)

4 scallions, thinly sliced

1 package (5 ounces) curly dried noodles, cooked following package directions and drained

1 Heat broth in large saucepan to simmering.

2 Stir together vinegar, oil, and hot-pepper sauce in small bowl. Stir in cornstarch until smooth and well blended.

3 Stir miso paste into hot broth to dissolve. Add chicken, mushrooms, and carrots; return to simmering. Re-whisk cornstarch mixture; stir into soup along with scallions. Simmer until slightly thickened, about 1 minute.

4 Divide noodles among serving bowls; ladle in soup.

Note: Made from fermented soybeans and with a peanut-butter-like texture, miso paste is used in Japanese cooking to season and thicken soups. Look for it in Japanese markets or well-stocked supermarkets.

Nutrient Value Per Serving: 260 calories, 5 g fat (1 g saturated), 22 g protein, 30 g carbohydrate, 1 g fiber, 944 mg sodium, 42 mg cholesterol.

Beef-and-Pineapple Soup

MAKES: 6 servings
PREP: 20 minutes
MARINATE: 15 minutes
COOK: about 15 minutes

½ pound beef chuck or bottom round

2 teaspoons plus 3 tablespoons Vietnamese
or Thai fish sauce

¼ teaspoon plus 1 tablespoon sugar

2 cloves garlic, finely chopped

2 shallots, finely sliced

⅛ teaspoon black pepper

½ onion, cut into thin slivers

1 large ripe tomato, cored, seeded, and cut
into wedges

½ fresh ripe pineapple, cored, peeled, and cut
into ¼-inch-thick slices, then into small pieces
(about 2½ cups)

5 cups water

2 ounces dried rice noodles

2 scallions, thinly sliced

2 tablespoons chopped fresh cilantro

1 Slice beef against grain into ⅛-inch-thick strips. Combine with 2 teaspoons fish sauce, ¼ teaspoon sugar, garlic, shallots, and pepper in medium-size bowl. Marinate at room temperature for 15 minutes.

2 Coat bottom of 3-quart saucepan with cooking spray. Place over medium-high heat. Add beef; cook 1 minute. Transfer to clean medium-size bowl.

3 Add onion to saucepan; cook until lightly browned, about 2 minutes. Add tomato, pineapple, and 1 tablespoon sugar; cook over medium heat, 2 minutes. Add water and 3 tablespoons fish sauce. Bring to a boil. Add rice noodles. Reduce heat; simmer, covered, 5 minutes. Stir beef into soup. Remove from heat. Stir in scallions and cilantro.

Nutrient Value Per Serving: 212 calories, 7 g fat (3 g saturated), 9 g protein, 30 g carbohydrate, 2 g fiber, 621 mg sodium, 26 mg cholesterol.

Meatball Minestrone

MAKES: 8 servings
PREP: 20 minutes
COOK: about 25 minutes

1 medium-size onion, chopped

2 medium-size carrots, peeled and chopped

2 cloves garlic, finely chopped

1 medium-size zucchini, unpeeled and diced

4 cubes vegetable bouillon

8 cups hot water

¼ teaspoon dried Italian herb seasoning

1 can (14.5 ounces) diced tomatoes

1 cup tubetti pasta

1 can (15 ounces) small white beans, drained and rinsed

1 can (15.25 ounces) dark red kidney beans, drained and rinsed

1 head escarole, trimmed and chopped (about 3 packed cups)

1 package (12 ounces) refrigerated, fully-cooked turkey meatballs, each quartered

Grated Parmesan cheese (optional)

1 Coat bottom of large deep pot with cooking spray. Place over medium heat. Add onion; cook 3 minutes. Add carrots and garlic; cook 3 minutes. Add zucchini; cook 5 minutes.

2 Dissolve vegetable bouillon in hot water in medium-size saucepan. Add to pot, along with Italian seasoning and tomatoes. Bring to a boil. Add pasta; boil until pasta is tender, about 10 minutes. Stir in drained beans and escarole; cook until escarole is wilted, 2 to 3 minutes. (Can be made ahead and reheated.)

3 Stir meatballs into soup. Cook over medium-high until heated through, about 5 minutes. Spoon soup into individual bowls. Top with grated Parmesan if desired.

Nutrient Value Per Serving: 177 calories, 4 g fat (1 g saturated), 13 g protein, 26 g carbohydrate, 7 g fiber, 317 mg sodium, 23 mg cholesterol.

Stuffed-Cabbage Soup

MAKES: 8 servings
PREP: 15 minutes
COOK: 55 minutes

1 pound beef chuck for stew, cut into 1-inch chunks

1 package (1 pound) classic coleslaw mix

1 large onion, chopped

1 can (28 ounces) crushed tomatoes in puree

2 cans (14.5 ounces each) beef broth

1 cup water

½ cup packed light-brown sugar

1 tablespoon fresh lemon juice

¾ teaspoon salt

⅓ cup uncooked long-grain white rice

1 Coat 6-quart pot with cooking spray. Place over medium heat. Add beef; cook until browned, about 6 minutes. Add coleslaw mix and onion; cook, covered, 4 minutes, stirring after 2 minutes.

2 Add tomatoes, beef broth, water, brown sugar, lemon juice, and salt. Bring to a boil. Add rice. Lower heat to medium-low; simmer, covered, 45 minutes or until beef and rice are tender.

3 Spoon into soup bowls.

Nutrient Value Per Serving: 230 calories, 4 g fat (2 g saturated), 16 g protein, 32 g carbohydrate, 3 g fiber, 944 g sodium, 35 mg cholesterol.

FIVE-INGREDIENT FLAIR

A mere five items—plus the salt, pepper, and oil you always have on hand—is all it takes to turn out filling, yet slimming, soups. We have five to get you going, from a hearty and rich onion soup, ideal for cool winter evenings, to a fresh and light tomato and crab spoonable meal to serve on sultry summer nights.

Hearty Onion Soup

MAKES: 6 servings

Cook 6 large Spanish onions, sliced, in 1 tablespoon olive oil in large pot (not nonstick) over medium-high heat until softened and caramelized or dark brown, stirring frequently to avoid burning, 30 to 35 minutes. Stir in 3 tablespoons all-purpose flour; cook 1 minute. Stir in three 14.75-ounce cans beef broth; cover and simmer over medium-low heat 20 minutes. Spoon soup into 6 ovenproof bowls. Top each with 1-ounce slice of crusty bread and 1-ounce slice reduced-fat Swiss cheese. Broil until cheese is melted and lightly browned, about 1 minute.

Nutrient Value Per Serving: 258 calories, 6 g fat (2 g saturated), 14 g protein, 39 g carbohydrate, 3 g fiber, 1,153 mg sodium, 7 mg cholesterol.

Escarole Meatball Soup

MAKES: 6 servings

Cook 2 large onions, sliced, in 1 tablespoon olive oil in large nonstick pot over medium-high heat until softened, about 6 minutes. Add four 14.75-ounce cans reduced-sodium chicken broth. Bring to a boil. Add 12-ounce package refrigerated fully-cooked Italian seasoned turkey meatballs, each halved. Stir

in ¼ teaspoon salt, ¼ teaspoon black pepper, and 2 bunches escarole, rinsed and cut into ½-inch-wide strips. Bring to a boil. Lower heat; cover and simmer 8 minutes. Ladle into soup bowls. Sprinkle 1 teaspoon grated Parmesan cheese over each serving.

Nutrient Value Per Serving: 209 calories, 12 g fat (3 g saturated), 13 g protein, 15 g carbohydrate, 7 g fiber, 600 mg sodium, 37 mg cholesterol.

Springtime Soup

MAKES: 6 servings

Cook 2 leeks, white and 1 inch green parts sliced, in 1 tablespoon olive oil in large nonstick pot, stirring occasionally, until softened, about 15 minutes. Add three 14.5-ounce cans vegetable broth and one 10-ounce box frozen green peas. Bring to a boil. Lower heat; simmer, uncovered, 8 minutes. Stir in two 10-ounce bags romaine salad blend, ½ teaspoon salt, and ¼ teaspoon black pepper. Bring to a boil. Remove from heat. Let cool slightly. Blend in batches in blender or food processor until smooth. Stir in ½ cup light sour cream. Serve immediately.

Nutrient Value Per Serving: 127 calories, 5 g fat (1 g saturated), 6 g protein, 19 g carbohydrate, 4 g fiber, 1,157 mg sodium, 7 mg cholesterol.

Cream of Tomato–Crab Soup

MAKES: 6 servings

Heat 2 teaspoons vegetable oil in large nonstick saucepan over medium heat. Add 1 medium-size sweet onion, finely chopped; sauté 5 minutes or until softened. Add two 28-ounce cans chopped tomatoes and their juice, ½ teaspoon dried thyme, ¼ teaspoon salt, and ¼ teaspoon black pepper; simmer, covered, 20 minutes. Working in batches, in blender or food processor, puree tomato mixture until smooth. Return to saucepan. Stir in ½ pound imitation crabmeat, coarsely chopped, and one 12-ounce can evaporated milk; simmer 5 minutes or just until heated through.

Nutrient Value Per Serving: 223 calories, 7 g fat (3 g saturated), 13 g protein, 31 g carbohydrate, 6 g fiber, 825 mg sodium, 24 mg cholesterol.

Hearty Sausage-Spinach Soup

MAKES: 6 servings

In 5- or 6-quart saucepan, combine 8 ounces turkey kielbasa, halved lengthwise and cut crosswise into ¼-inch-thick slices, 3 cups frozen cubed potato, onion, and pepper mixture (O' Brien), thawed, one 10-ounce package frozen leaf spinach, thawed and coarsely chopped, 2 medium-size carrots, peeled and thinly sliced, two 14.5-ounce cans reduced-sodium, fat-free chicken broth, 2 cups water, and ⅛ teaspoon black pepper. Cover; bring to a boil. Lower heat; simmer 15 minutes or until vegetables are tender.

Nutrient Value Per Serving: 138 calories, 3 g fat (1 g saturated), 10 g protein, 17 g carbohydrate, 4 g fiber, 661 mg sodium, 25 mg cholesterol.

Puttanesca Stew

MAKES: 6 servings
PREP: 15 minutes
COOK: 30 minutes

1 medium-size red onion, finely chopped

1½ pounds boneless, skinless chicken thighs, cut into 1-inch pieces

1 can (28 ounces) chopped tomatoes

1 can (8 ounces) tomato sauce

¼ cup dry red wine

2 tablespoons tomato paste

½ cup pitted green olives, halved

3 tablespoons drained capers

½ teaspoon dried Italian herb seasoning

¼ teaspoon salt

¼ teaspoon black pepper

Dash liquid hot-pepper sauce

¼ teaspoon red-pepper flakes

½ pound egg noodles, cooked following package directions

1 Coat large saucepan with cooking spray. Place over medium-high heat. Add onion and chicken; cook until onion is softened, about 5 minutes.

2 Add chopped tomatoes, tomato sauce, wine, tomato paste, olives, capers, Italian seasoning, salt, black pepper, pepper sauce, and red pepper flakes. Bring to a boil. Lower heat; simmer, covered, 25 minutes or until chicken is tender.

3 Serve over cooked noodles.

Nutrient Value Per Serving: 327 calories, 7 g fat (2 g saturated), 29 g protein, 35 g carbohydrate, 5 g fiber, 1,163 mg sodium, 125 mg cholesterol.

Black-Bean Chili

MAKES: 6 servings
PREP: 20 minutes
COOK: 45 minutes

2 tablespoons dried oregano

1 tablespoon cumin seeds

2 large yellow onions, finely chopped

½ sweet green pepper, cored, seeded, and finely chopped

1 sweet red pepper, cored, seeded, and finely chopped

1 can (4.5 ounces) chopped green chiles

2 cloves garlic, finely chopped

1 teaspoon salt

½ teaspoon paprika

1 teaspoon cayenne

1 can (28 ounces) crushed tomatoes

3 cans (15 ounces each) black beans, drained and rinsed

1 tablespoon red-wine vinegar

Garnish (optional):

Nonfat sour cream

Chopped scallions

1 Toast oregano and cumin in small skillet over medium heat, shaking often, 3 minutes. Don't burn.

2 Coat large saucepan with cooking spray. Place over medium-high heat. Add onions, peppers, chiles, garlic, salt, paprika, cayenne, and oregano-cumin mixture; cook until onion is softened, about 10 minutes. Add tomatoes; simmer, covered, 10 minutes. Add beans, 1 cup water, and vinegar; cover and simmer 20 minutes.

3 Ladle into bowls. Top with sour cream and scallions, if desired.

Nutrient Value Per Serving: 238 calories, 1 g fat (0 g saturated), 14 g protein, 51 g carbohydrate, 16 g fiber, 1,109 mg sodium, 0 mg cholesterol.

Turkey Chili

MAKES: 8 servings
PREP: 10 minutes
COOK: 40 minutes

2 tablespoons vegetable oil

1 medium-size onion, diced

3 cloves garlic, chopped

1 sweet green pepper, cored, seeded, and diced

¼ cup chili powder

1½ pounds ground turkey

1 can (28 ounces) diced tomatoes

1 can (8 ounces) tomato sauce

¼ cup ketchup

¼ to ½ teaspoon cayenne

1 packet (.19 ounce) instant beef-flavored broth granules

½ teaspoon salt

1 can (19 ounces) red kidney beans, drained and rinsed

Accompaniments (optional):

Cooked white rice

Nonfat sour cream

Chopped scallions

1 Heat oil in 5- to 6-quart pot over medium heat. Add onion, garlic, green pepper, and chili powder; sauté until onion and green pepper are softened, 10 minutes.

2 Add turkey; cook, breaking up clumps with wooden spoon, until no longer pink, about 6 minutes.

3 Add diced tomatoes, tomato sauce, ketchup, cayenne, instant broth granules, and salt; simmer, uncovered, stirring occasionally, for 20 minutes. Add kidney beans; cook until heated through, about 4 minutes.

4 Serve with accompaniments, if desired.

Note: Chili is always better with the extra punch of a tasty garnish, from scallions to sour cream. Try this easy-on-you guacamole.

Guacamole: Mash flesh from 3 ripe avocados in medium-size bowl. Stir in 3 tablespoons finely chopped red onion, 3 tablespoons fresh lime juice, 2 tablespoons chopped fresh cilantro, 1 jalapeño chile, seeded and finely chopped, ¼ teaspoon salt, and ¼ teaspoon liquid hot-pepper sauce. Refrigerate. Spoon a dollop on each chili serving.

Nutrient Value Per Serving (without guacamole): 234 calories, 10 g fat (2 g saturated), 17 g protein, 20 g carbohydrate, 7 g fiber, 853 mg sodium, 56 mg cholesterol.

Tex-Mex Stew

MAKES: 8 servings
PREP: 10 minutes
COOK: about 20 minutes

1½ pounds lean ground beef (90%)

1 sweet green pepper, cored, seeded, and chopped

1 tablespoon ground cumin

½ teaspoon salt

½ teaspoon dried oregano

¼ teaspoon cayenne

1¾ pounds sweet potatoes, peeled and cut into ½-inch cubes

1 can (15.5 ounces) black beans, drained and rinsed

1 can (11 ounces) corn kernels, drained and rinsed

1 can (4.5 ounces) chopped green chiles

1 packet onion soup mix

3¼ cups water

2 tablespoons all-purpose flour

1 lime, cut into 8 wedges

1 Brown beef and pepper in 5- to 6-quart large deep pot over medium-high heat, breaking up clumps of meat with wooden spoon but leaving some large pieces, until no longer pink, about 5 minutes. Stir in cumin, salt, oregano, and cayenne; cook 1 minute. Add sweet potatoes, beans, corn, chiles, soup mix, and 3 cups water. Bring to a boil. Lower heat; simmer, covered, 10 minutes or just until potatoes are tender.

2 Stir together remaining ¼ cup water and flour in small cup until smooth. Stir into stew. Bring to a boil; cook until thickened, about 1 minute.

3 Ladle into bowls. Serve with lime wedges.

Nutrient Value Per Serving: 350 calories, 9 g fat (3 g saturated), 25 g protein, 44 g carbohydrate, 8 g fiber, 968 mg sodium, 31 mg cholesterol.

6 FAST & FIT FISH AND SEAFOOD

DIET GURUS ARE ALWAYS PUSHING FISH: It's good for you, they say, stocked with nutrients, and is an excellent weight-loss enhancer because it's both low-fat and low-cal. But many of us suffer from fish phobia. Can you really cook up tasty seafood in your own kitchen? Are there enough variations to have fish more than once in a blue moon? Absolutely, we say. Seafood takes beautifully to all kinds of preparations, from tropical to Indian to south-of-the-border. We've come up with recipes that work for an ocean's worth, and most come in at under 300 calories. (What's more, many cook up quick—think 6, 8, 10 minutes.)

Picture Maui Tuna (page 88), a tempting steak, marinated in piña colada mix laced with lime juice and ginger. Broil for 6 minutes and dine without guilt, because it's only 226 calories. Our international variations include a pungent Tandoori Salmon (page 92), alive with cayenne, curry, and cinnamon and served with cucumber sauce and rice pilaf. Crispy Fish 'n' Chips (page 94) tweaks the English classic with a cornflakes-based crumb topping and dashes of chili powder and Old Bay seasoning for zest.

Shellfish lovers will be tempted by scallops simmered in orange juice with three kinds of peppers (page 107), and a fresh, sprightly Pesto Shrimp (page 106). Our crab cakes (page 108), kept trim with a mix of egg whites and reduced-fat mayonnaise dressing, are out of this world, topped with a tangy corn relish. And last, but not at all least, there's Classic Lobster Rolls (page 107). Marvelously creamy, just savory enough, and still under 300 calories.

Speaking of shellfish, turn to page 101 for three terrific Slim Shrimp Dippers—exactly the thing to bring out when company's coming.

Blackened Swordfish with Green Goddess Sauce and Potato Salad (page 94).

Maui Tuna

MAKES: 4 servings
PREP: 10 minutes
REFRIGERATE: 4 hours
BROIL: about 6 minutes

- ½ cup frozen piña colada mix, thawed
- ½ cup water
- 1 teaspoon grated lime rind
- 1 tablespoon fresh lime juice
- 1 teaspoon grated peeled fresh ginger
- ¼ teaspoon red-pepper flakes
- ¼ teaspoon salt
- ⅛ teaspoon black pepper
- 4 tuna steaks (1 pound total)
- 1 scallion, sliced

1 To make marinade, combine piña colada mix, ½ cup water, lime rind and juice, ginger, pepper flakes, salt, and pepper in small bowl.

2 Pour half of marinade into 11 x 7 x 2-inch baking dish. Place tuna in dish; pour remaining marinade over tuna. Cover. Refrigerate 4 hours, turning once.

3 Heat broiler.

4 Place tuna on broiler-pan rack. Discard marinade.

5 Broil tuna 3 inches from heat for 3 minutes. Turn tuna over. Sprinkle with scallion. Broil 3 to 4 minutes or until desired doneness.

Nutrient Value Per Serving: 226 calories, 3 g fat (2 g saturated), 30 g protein, 18 g carbohydrate, 0 g fiber, 203 mg sodium, 58 mg cholesterol.

Tuna Steaks in Spicy Tomato Sauce with Mashed Potatoes

MAKES: 6 servings
PREP: 15 minutes
COOK: potatoes 15 minutes, tuna 18 minutes

Potatoes:

- 4 medium-size all-purpose potatoes (1½ pounds total), with skins, cut into ½-inch cubes
- ¾ cup fat-free half-and-half
- ½ teaspoon salt
- ⅛ teaspoon black pepper
- ⅛ teaspoon ground nutmeg
- ⅛ teaspoon garlic powder

Fish:

- 1 pint (about 12 ounces) grape tomatoes, each cut in half (about 2 cups)
- 3 cloves garlic, sliced
- 1 can (8 ounces) tomato sauce
- ½ teaspoon salt
- ½ teaspoon dried Italian herb seasoning
- ¼ teaspoon onion powder
- ¼ teaspoon red-pepper flakes
- ⅓ cup small pimiento-stuffed green olives, each cut in half
- 6 tuna steaks, 1-inch thick (about 1½ pounds total)
- Lemon wedges, for garnish

1 **Potatoes:** In large pot, add water to potatoes to cover by 1 inch. Cover; boil until tender, 12 to 15 minutes. Drain. Return potatoes to pot; mash. Heat half-and-half, salt, pepper, nutmeg, and garlic powder in saucepan over medium-low until steaming; stir into potatoes until well blended. Cover with foil.

2 **Fish:** Meanwhile, coat large nonstick skillet with cooking spray. Place over medium-high heat. Add tomatoes and garlic; cook 3 minutes. Add tomato sauce, salt, Italian seasoning, onion powder, and pepper flakes; cook 5 minutes. Stir in olives. Add tuna; turn to coat. Spoon sauce over tuna. Simmer, covered, over medium heat 10 minutes or until fish flakes when tested with a fork, turning over halfway through; baste occasionally. Serve with mashed potatoes and lemon.

Nutrient Value Per Serving: 311 calories, 7 g fat (2 g saturated), 30 g protein, 32 g carbohydrate, 4 g fiber, 1,125 mg sodium, 42 cholesterol.

Tuna Puttanesca Baked Potatoes

MAKES: 4 servings
PREP: 20 minutes
BAKE: at 400° for 45 minutes
COOK: 4 minutes

4 large baking potatoes, pierced

2 teaspoons olive oil

2 cloves garlic, finely chopped

3 scallions, chopped

¾ teaspoon dried basil

¼ teaspoon dried oregano

1 can (14.5 ounces) pasta-ready tomatoes

1½ tablespoons slivered, pitted, oil-cured black olives

1 tablespoon drained capers

¼ teaspoon liquid hot-pepper sauce

1 can (6 ounces) light tuna packed in water, drained and flaked

1 Bake potatoes in 400° oven for 45 minutes, or microwave at full power for 20 minutes, or until fork-tender.

2 Heat oil in large skillet. Add garlic, scallion, basil, and oregano; sauté 1 minute. Add tomatoes, olives, capers, and pepper sauce; cook until reduced slightly, about 3 minutes. Add tuna; remove from heat.

3 Score top of potatoes in cross pattern; push ends to open potato. Spoon tuna mixture over potatoes and serve.

Nutrient Value Per Serving: 350 calories, 6 g fat (1 g saturated), 17 g protein, 58 g carbohydrate, 6 g fiber, 890 mg sodium, 13 mg cholesterol.

Roasted Salmon

MAKES: 4 servings
PREP: 10 minutes
REFRIGERATE: 30 minutes
ROAST: at 425° for 10 to 12 minutes

> 1 tablespoon sugar
>
> 1 tablespoon grated lemon rind
>
> 1 teaspoon salt
>
> ¼ teaspoon black pepper
>
> 1 salmon fillet (1⅓ pounds), about 1 inch thick

1 Combine sugar, lemon rind, salt, and pepper in small bowl. Rub over salmon. Cover and refrigerate at least 30 minutes.

2 Heat oven to 425°. Coat shallow baking dish with cooking spray. Cut salmon into 4 pieces. Place salmon, skin side down, in baking dish.

3 Roast for 10 to 12 minutes or until fish is easily flaked with a fork.

Nutrient Value Per Serving: 177 calories, 5 g fat (1 g saturated), 28 g protein, 3 g carbohydrate, 0 g fiber, 676 mg sodium, 74 mg cholesterol.

Moroccan-Style Salmon: Add 1 teaspoon ground cumin, 1 teaspoon ground coriander, and ½ teaspoon ground cinnamon to rub in step 1 above. Roast as above.

Latin-Style Salmon: Omit salt from rub in recipe above. Add 1 tablespoon jarred bitter-orange-flavored adobo seasoning* to rub. Roast as above.

*Note: Look for adobo seasoning in the spice section or Spanish food section of your supermarket.

Smoked Lemon Salmon

MAKES: 8 servings
PREP: 5 minutes
SOAK: wood chips at least 1 hour
GRILL: 30 minutes

> 2 cups mesquite wood chips

Green Mayonnaise:

> ½ cup light mayonnaise
>
> 1 tablespoon fresh lemon juice
>
> 2 tablespoons chopped fresh dill
>
> 1 tablespoon snipped fresh chives
>
> ⅛ teaspoon salt

Salmon:

> 1 tablespoon grated lemon rind
>
> 1 tablespoon chopped fresh dill
>
> ½ teaspoon salt
>
> ¼ teaspoon black pepper
>
> 2 pounds salmon fillet (about 1¼ inches thick), with skin left on and bones removed
>
> 1 tablespoon vegetable oil

1 Soak wood chips following package directions, at least 1 hour.

2 Green Mayonnaise: In food processor, pulse together mayonnaise, lemon juice, dill, chives, and salt until blended. Scrape into bowl; cover and refrigerate.

3 Drain soaked wood chips; place in small foil pan. Prepare outdoor grill with hot coals arranged for indirect grilling. Place foil pan with chips in corner of grill and over direct heat. Or heat gas grill for indirect grilling with foil pan. (See oven method below.) Grill is ready when chips begin to smoke, about 5 minutes.

4 Salmon: In small bowl, combine lemon rind, dill, salt, and pepper. Brush salmon with oil; rub lemon-dill mixture over salmon. Oil grill or place salmon in fish basket.

5 Grill salmon over indirect heat, covered, 30 minutes. Serve with Green Mayonnaise.

Oven Method: Heat oven to 375°. Place salmon fillet on oiled rack in broiler pan. Bake salmon about 20 minutes or until fish flakes easily when tested with a fork. (Do not try smoking fish with wood chips in oven.)

Nutrient Value Per Serving: 230 calories, 14 g fat (2 g saturated), 23 g protein, 2 g carbohydrate, 0 g fiber, 352 mg sodium, 69 mg cholesterol.

Basque-Style Fish Bake

MAKES: 6 servings

PREP: 15 minutes

BAKE: at 375° for 70 minutes

2 onions, halved and cut crosswise into ½-inch-thick slices

2 sweet green peppers, cored, seeded, and cut into ½-inch-thick slices

2 sweet red peppers, cored, seeded, and cut into ½-inch-thick slices

1 pound red potatoes, with skins and cut into ⅛-inch-thick slices

3 tablespoons olive oil

1 teaspoon salt

½ teaspoon black pepper

4 cloves garlic, smashed

2 tablespoons fresh lemon juice

2 cans (14.5 ounces each) diced tomatoes

½ teaspoon liquid hot-pepper sauce

6 cod fillets (1½ pounds total)

⅓ cup fresh parsley leaves

1 Heat oven to 375°. Toss together onions, sweet peppers, potatoes, oil, and half the salt and pepper in large bowl. Spread in 13 x 9 x 2-inch baking dish.

2 Bake, uncovered, for 40 minutes. Stir halfway through cooking.

3 After 40 minutes, add garlic, lemon juice, 1 can of tomatoes, and hot sauce to baking dish; stir to combine.

4 Season fish with remaining salt and pepper. Arrange over top of potato mixture. Spoon remaining can of tomatoes over fish and vegetables. Cover baking dish.

5 Bake 30 minutes. Let covered baking dish stand 10 minutes before serving. Garnish with parsley.

Nutrient Value Per Serving: 240 calories, 8 g fat (1 g saturated), 17 g protein, 27 g carbohydrate, 6 g fiber, 612 mg sodium, 30 mg cholesterol.

Tandoori Salmon with Raita and Rice Pilaf

MAKES: 6 servings
PREP: 25 minutes
REFRIGERATE: 30 minutes
COOK: 20 minutes
BAKE: at 450° for 12 to 15 minutes

Salmon:

2 cloves garlic, chopped

1 piece (1 inch) fresh ginger, peeled and chopped

1 teaspoon curry powder

1 teaspoon fresh lemon juice

½ teaspoon paprika

½ teaspoon salt

⅛ teaspoon ground cinnamon

⅛ teaspoon cayenne

1½ pounds salmon fillet, 1 inch thick

Raita:

½ cup low-fat plain yogurt

½ large cucumber, peeled, seeded, and thinly sliced

1 teaspoon fresh lemon juice

⅛ teaspoon salt

Pilaf:

1 can (14.5 ounces) reduced-sodium, fat-free chicken broth

¼ teaspoon salt

⅛ teaspoon black pepper

1 cup basmati rice

2 cloves garlic, chopped

2 large scallions, chopped

1½ cups frozen peas, thawed

¼ cup flat-leaf parsley, chopped

1 **Salmon:** In small bowl, combine garlic, ginger, curry powder, lemon juice, paprika, salt, cinnamon, and cayenne. Place salmon in glass baking dish. Spread spice mixture over salmon. Cover; refrigerate 30 minutes.

2 **Raita:** In small bowl, stir together yogurt, cucumber, lemon juice, and salt. Cover; refrigerate for at least 30 minutes.

3 Heat oven to 450°.

4 **Pilaf:** In medium-size saucepan, combine chicken broth, salt, pepper, and rice. Bring to a boil. Lower heat; cover and gently simmer 10 minutes. Stir in garlic and scallions; cook, covered, 5 minutes. Gently stir in thawed peas; cook, covered, until peas are heated through and all liquid is absorbed, 3 to 5 minutes. Stir in parsley.

5 While rice is cooking, bake salmon until cooked through, 12 to 15 minutes. Serve salmon with raita and rice pilaf.

Nutrient Value Per Serving: 344 calories, 8 g fat (1 g saturated), 31 g protein, 35 g carbohydrate, 4 g fiber, 491 mg sodium, 65 mg cholesterol.

Crispy Fish 'n' Chips

MAKES: 6 servings
PREP: 20 minutes
BAKE: at 450°F for 20 minutes

2 tablespoons olive oil

2 tablespoons all-purpose flour

1 teaspoon Old Bay crab boil seasoning

1½ teaspoons salt

⅛ teaspoon cayenne

2 large egg whites

1 cup cornflake crumbs

1 teaspoon chili powder

1½ teaspoons dried oregano

6 cod, scrod, or other thick white fish fillets (about 2¼ pounds total)

1½ pounds new red potatoes, with skins and thinly sliced

6 cloves garlic, sliced

¼ teaspoon black pepper

1 Heat oven to 450°F. Pour oil into roasting pan. Place pan on lowest oven rack while heating.

2 Meanwhile, line jelly-roll pan with foil. Lightly coat with cooking spray. On sheet of waxed paper, combine flour, crab boil seasoning, ½ teaspoon salt, and the cayenne. In small bowl, beat egg whites until stiff, glossy peaks form. On second sheet of waxed paper, combine crumbs, chili powder, and 1 teaspoon oregano.

3 Dip fillets in flour mixture to coat both sides, shaking off excess. Spread beaten whites on one side of floured fillets. Cover egg white sides with crumbs. Repeat coating other sides of fillets. Place fish on foil-lined pan.

4 When oven is heated, add potatoes, garlic, remaining ½ teaspoon oregano, remaining 1 teaspoon salt, and the black pepper to hot roasting pan; toss to coat potatoes. Return to oven. Place fish on pan on middle rack in oven.

5 Bake until fish is crisp and cooked through, 15 minutes; remove from oven and keep warm. Bake potatoes another 5 minutes or until tender.

Nutrient Value Per Serving: 277 calories, 5 g fat (1 g saturated), 25 g protein, 36 g carbohydrate, 3 g fiber, 884 mg sodium, 45 mg cholesterol.

Blackened Swordfish with Green Goddess Sauce and Potato Salad

MAKES: 6 servings
PREP: 20 minutes
COOK: 8 minutes
REFRIGERATE: 1 hour
GRILL: 7 minutes

Green Goddess Sauce:

⅓ cup reduced-fat mayonnaise dressing

⅓ cup light sour cream

2 tablespoons red-wine vinegar

1 tablespoon fresh lemon juice

½ teaspoon salt

⅛ teaspoon black pepper

2 tablespoons finely chopped fresh flat-leaf parsley leaves

2 scallions, finely chopped (¼ cup)

2 tablespoons snipped fresh chives

Swordfish and Potato Salad:

1½ pounds all-purpose potatoes, peeled and cut into 1-inch cubes

2 tablespoons lemon-pepper dry marinade

6 swordfish steaks, ¾- to 1-inch thick (about 2 pounds total)

1 Sauce: In medium-size bowl, whisk together mayonnaise, sour cream, vinegar, lemon juice, salt, and pepper. Stir in parsley, scallions, and chives. Cover and refrigerate until ready to use.

2 Swordfish and Potato Salad: Place potatoes in medium-size saucepan; cover with cold water. Bring to a boil over high heat. Reduce heat to medium-high; simmer until fork-tender, about 8 minutes. Drain potatoes. Place in medium-size bowl; let cool slightly. Reserve ½ cup of sauce to serve with fish. Add remaining sauce to potatoes; gently stir to coat potatoes. Cover and refrigerate for at least 1 hour.

3 Prepare outdoor grill with hot coals or heat gas grill. Lightly brush grill grid with vegetable oil. (Or cook using oven method, below.)

4 Sprinkle ½ teaspoon lemon pepper on each side of swordfish. Grill 4 minutes on one side. Turn over; grill 3 minutes or until cooked through. Serve swordfish with potato salad and reserved sauce on the side.

Oven Method: Heat broiler. Coat broiler-pan rack with cooking spray. Place seasoned swordfish steaks on rack in broiler pan. Broil 4 to 6 inches from heat 4 minutes on one side. Turn fish over; broil 3 minutes.

Nutrient Value Per Serving: 273 calories, 10 g fat (3 g saturated), 23 g protein, 24 g carbohydrate, 2 g fiber, 871 mg sodium, 49 mg cholesterol.

The Fish Swap

If your recipe calls for:	You can also use:	Characteristics:
Sole	Flounder, tilapia, rainbow trout, catfish, fluke	Thin, tender, lean, mild- to medium-flavored fillets
Red snapper	Rockfish, weakfish (sea trout), sea bass, grouper, orange roughy	Thin, firm, lean, mild- to medium-flavored fillets
Bluefish	Lake trout, mackerel, shad, sturgeon	Thick, firm, dark-fleshed, oily, strongly flavored fillets
Cod	Tilefish, haddock, halibut	Thick, firm, lean, mild-flavored steaks and fillets
Tuna	Swordfish, mahi-mahi, mako shark, salmon	Thick, firm, slightly oily, full-flavored steaks and fillets

Baked Catfish with Vegetables

MAKES: 4 servings
PREP: 15 minutes
BAKE: at 350° for 35 minutes

1 tablespoon butter, cut into pieces

4 catfish fillets (1½ pounds total)

¼ teaspoon salt

⅛ teaspoon black pepper

1⅓ cups broccoli slaw mix (from 12-ounce bag)

2 large scallions, sliced

⅓ cup small pimiento-stuffed green Spanish olives, sliced

¼ cup dry white wine

8 sprigs fresh thyme

⅓ cup fresh basil leaves, sliced

1 Heat oven to 350°.

2 Cut four 12 x 12-inch pieces of foil; divide butter among foil. Season both sides of fish with salt and pepper. Place fish on top of butter. Top with broccoli slaw, scallions, and olives. Fold edges of foil up. Sprinkle each with 1 tablespoon wine. Top each with 2 sprigs of thyme. Evenly distribute basil on top. Crimp edges of foil together to form tight seal. Place on baking sheet.

3 Bake 35 minutes or until fish is opaque; carefully open one packet to test. Let each diner open his or her own packet.

Nutrient Value Per Serving: 300 calories, 20 g fat (5 g saturated), 30 g protein, 3 g carbohydrate, 2 g fiber, 645 mg sodium, 92 mg cholesterol.

Catfish with Poblano Sauce

MAKES: 6 servings
PREP: 15 minutes
BROIL: 5 to 10 minutes
COOK: 25 minutes
BAKE: at 375° for 20 minutes

Sauce:

1 fresh poblano chile

1 sweet red pepper

2 cups fat-free half-and-half

1 medium-size onion, diced

2 cloves garlic, chopped

½ teaspoon dried oregano

¾ teaspoon salt

Fish:

¼ cup dry white wine

6 small catfish fillets (1½ pounds total)

¼ teaspoon salt

⅛ teaspoon black pepper

1 Heat broiler.

2 Sauce: Broil poblano chile and sweet pepper until blackened, turning several times, 5 to 10 minutes. Place in plastic bag 10 minutes. Peel, seed, and chop chile and red pepper.

3 Combine half-and-half, poblano, red pepper, onion, garlic, and oregano in medium-size saucepan. Bring to a boil. Lower heat; simmer 25 minutes. Pour into blender; add salt. Puree; return to pot. Keep warm. (Sauce improves if prepared up to a day ahead; cover, refrigerate, and gently reheat before serving.)

4 Heat oven to 375°.

5 Fish: Coat baking pan large enough to hold fish fillets in single layer generously with cooking spray. Add wine. Place fish in pan. Sprinkle with salt and pepper. Cover with aluminum foil.

6 Bake for 20 minutes or until fish easily flakes when tested with a fork. Spoon sauce over top.

Nutrient Value Per Serving: 240 calories, 10 g fat (2 g saturated), 23 g protein, 11 g carbohydrate, 1 g fiber, 531 mg sodium, 61 mg cholesterol.

Swordfish Brochettes

MAKES: 4 servings
PREP: 10 minutes
REFRIGERATE: 30 minutes
BROIL: 8 minutes

2 tablespoons fresh lemon juice

1½ tablespoons olive oil

2 cloves garlic, finely chopped

1 tablespoon finely chopped fresh rosemary OR ¼ teaspoon dried

¼ teaspoon salt

⅛ teaspoon black pepper

1 yellow summer squash, cut into ½-inch-thick slices

1 sweet green pepper, cored, seeded, and cut into 1-inch pieces

8 cherry tomatoes

1 pound swordfish steaks, cut into 1-inch cubes

4 cups leafy greens, such as Boston or Bibb

1 Stir together lemon juice, olive oil, garlic, rosemary, salt, and black pepper in medium-size bowl. Add squash, green pepper, cherry tomatoes, and fish to bowl; gently stir to evenly coat swordfish cubes. Refrigerate, covered, for 30 minutes.

2 Heat broiler.

3 Thread squash, green pepper, cherry tomatoes, and fish, alternating pieces, on four 10-inch metal skewers.

4 Broil skewers 6 inches from heat, turning once, for 8 minutes or until swordfish is just opaque in center and vegetables are crisp-tender. Serve on a bed of leafy greens.

Nutrient Value Per Serving: 179 calories, 9 g fat (2 g saturated), 17 g protein, 9 g carbohydrate, 3 g fiber, 222 mg sodium, 30 mg cholesterol.

Gingered Flounder in Parchment

MAKES: 4 servings
PREP: 15 minutes
MARINATE: 10 minutes
BAKE: at 375° for 15 to 20 minutes

   3 tablespoons reduced-sodium soy sauce

   2 tablespoons olive oil

   1 clove garlic, finely chopped

   1 tablespoon grated peeled fresh ginger

   4 flounder fillets (1¼ pounds total)

   3 ounces snow peas

   1 small sweet red pepper, cored, seeded, and cut into thin strips

   1 medium-size carrot, peeled and cut into thin strips

   3 scallions, chopped

1 Combine soy sauce, oil, garlic, and ginger in large bowl. Add fish; turn gently to coat. Cover and marinate at room temperature for 10 minutes.

2 Heat oven to 375°.

3 Cut four 20-inch lengths of parchment paper or aluminum foil; fold each in half. Starting at folded side, cut out half a heart shape in each, using folded side as center of heart. Open hearts on flat surface. Spread one-quarter of snow peas, sweet pepper, carrot, and scallions on one side of each heart. Place a fish fillet on top of each. Spoon any remaining marinade over fillets. Fold paper over; seal tightly by double pleating edges all around. Place packets on large baking sheet.

4 Bake for 15 to 20 minutes or until fish is just opaque in the center; carefully open one packet to test. If using foil packets, check fish after 12 minutes. Let each diner open his or her own packet.

Nutrient Value Per Serving: 213 calories, 8 g fat (1 g saturated), 26 g protein, 7 g carbohydrate, 2 g fiber, 571 mg sodium, 67 mg cholesterol.

Cajun Fish with Creamy Sauce

MAKES: 4 servings
PREP: 10 minutes
COOK: 7 minutes
BAKE: at 400° for 15 minutes

   1 teaspoon olive oil

   1 medium-size onion, finely chopped

   1 sweet red pepper, cored, seeded, and finely chopped

   1 clove garlic, finely chopped

   1 teaspoon dried thyme

   ⅔ cup canned black beans, drained and rinsed

   ⅔ cup packaged corn bread stuffing

   4 flounder fillets (1¼ pounds total)

   ½ teaspoon paprika

   1 cup vegetable broth

   2 teaspoons cornstarch

   ¼ teaspoon liquid hot-pepper sauce

   ⅛ teaspoon salt

   2 tablespoons nonfat sour cream

   1 teaspoon fresh lemon juice

1 Heat oven to 400°. Coat medium-size baking dish, just large enough to hold folded-over fish fillets in single layer, with cooking spray.

2 Heat oil in medium-size nonstick skillet over medium heat. Add onion, sweet pepper, garlic, and thyme; sauté until softened, about 5 minutes. Remove half the mixture to medium-size bowl. Set aside skillet with remaining red pepper mixture. Stir beans and cornbread stuffing into onion mixture in bowl.

3 Place fillets flat on work surface. Spoon bean and corn bread stuffing mixture from bowl in center of each fillet, dividing equally. Fold fillets in half over stuffing mixture. Place fillets, seam side down, in prepared baking dish. Sprinkle with paprika.

4 Bake fish for 15 minutes or until fillets are just opaque all the way through.

5 Meanwhile, prepare sauce: Whisk together vegetable broth, cornstarch, hot pepper sauce, and salt in small bowl. Stir into red pepper mixture in skillet. Heat over medium heat, stirring, until thickened, about 2 minutes. Remove skillet from heat. Stir in sour cream and lemon juice. Serve sauce with fish.

Nutrient Value Per Serving: 229 calories, 4 g fat (1 g saturated), 28 g protein, 21 g carbohydrate, 4 g fiber, 692 mg sodium, 67 mg cholesterol.

Tropical Snapper

MAKES: 8 servings
PREP: 15 minutes
BROIL: 8 to 10 minutes

1 can (20 ounces) pineapple tidbits in juice
½ cup chopped cucumber
½ cup chopped sweet red pepper
¼ cup chopped red onion
¼ cup fresh lime juice
2 tablespoons honey
½ teaspoon chili powder
¼ teaspoon cayenne
¼ teaspoon salt
8 small red snapper fillets (about 2½ pounds total)

1 Heat broiler. Coat broiler-pan rack with cooking spray.

2 Drain pineapple, reserving ¼ cup juice. Combine pineapple, cucumber, sweet pepper, and onion in medium-size bowl. In small bowl, whisk together reserved pineapple juice, lime juice, honey, chili powder, cayenne, and salt. Reserve ¼ cup sauce. Pour remaining sauce over pineapple-cucumber mixture; toss to mix. Set salsa aside.

3 Place fillets, skin side down, on broiler-pan rack. Brush fillets with reserved sauce.

4 Broil about 4 inches from heat 8 to 10 minutes or until fish flakes when tested with a fork. Serve with pineapple salsa.

Nutrient Value Per Serving: 151 calories, 1 g fat (0 g saturated), 20 g protein, 16 g carbohydrate, 1 g fiber, 124 mg sodium, 35 mg cholesterol.

Lemon-Herb Grilled Fish

MAKES: 4 servings
PREP: 10 minutes
GRILL: about 25 minutes

2 whole cleaned red snappers, small bluefish, or striped bass (2½ to 3 pounds total)

¼ teaspoon salt

¼ teaspoon black pepper

1 lemon, cut into 8 slices

2 sprigs fresh thyme

4 cloves garlic, peeled

Remoulade:

½ cup light mayonnaise

1 tablespoon sweet pickle relish

2 teaspoons fresh lemon juice

Liquid hot-pepper sauce, to taste

1 Prepare outdoor grill with medium-low to medium coals, or heat gas grill to medium-low to medium (see broiler method, below).

2 Rinse fish; pat dry. Cut 3 slashes on each side. Season with salt and pepper.

3 Stuff 3 lemon slices in cavity of each fish. Add thyme and 2 cloves garlic to each cavity.

4 Remoulade: Meanwhile, stir together mayonnaise, relish, lemon juice, and hot-pepper sauce to taste. Cover and refrigerate until serving.

5 Grill fish 6 inches from heat, covered, 10 to 12 minutes or just until fish begins to char. Flip over carefully. Cover each eye with one of remaining lemon slices. Grill 12 to 15 minutes more or until flesh is white throughout.

6 Transfer fish to platter. For each, pry up top fillet in one piece, flipping over, skin side down. Beginning at tail, carefully pull up end of spine of fish, and lift up, removing whole backbone. Remove any small bones from fish. Serve with Remoulade.

Broiler Method: Broil 6 inches from heat 10 to 12 minutes; then flip over and broil 12 to 15 minutes.

Nutrient Value Per Serving with Remoulade:
258 calories, 12 g fat (2 g saturated), 31 g protein,
4 g carbohydrate, 0 g fiber, 486 mg sodium,
66 mg cholesterol.

SLIM SHRIMP DIPPERS

Cold cooked shrimp are a dieter's dream: You get 10 large shrimp (about 2 ounces) for a mere 55 calories. The point, of course, is to keep the sauce under control. These fast-fix options are delicious and top out at 28 calories per tablespoon.

PREPARING SHRIMP
Clean 1½ pounds of shrimp: Pull shell backward, starting from center of legs; leave the tail attached. Using a sharp knife, cut in about ¼ of an inch along outer edge. With tip of knife, scrape out exposed inner vein. You will have about 1¼ pounds after cleaning.

COOKING SHRIMP
Bring 3 quarts of water to a boil. Add shrimp, 1½ teaspoons salt, 1 bay leaf, and 8 whole black peppercorns. Boil 1 to 2 minutes or until pink and cooked through. Drain in colander; run under cold water to stop cooking.

Horseradish Dipping Sauce

MAKES: 1½ cups

Stir together ¾ cup reduced-fat mayonnaise dressing, ⅓ cup ketchup, 1 tablespoon bottled horseradish, 1 tablespoon fresh lemon juice, ¼ teaspoon liquid hot-pepper sauce, ¼ teaspoon salt, 2 scallions, chopped, and 1 tablespoon chopped fresh parsley in small bowl. Cover; refrigerate at least 1 hour or up to 2 days.

Nutrient Value Per Tablespoon: 18 calories, 1 g fat (0 g saturated), 0 g protein, 3 g carbohydrate, 0 g fiber, 135 mg sodium, 0 mg cholesterol.

Caesar Dipping Sauce

MAKES: 1¼ cups

In food processor, puree ½ pound creamy reduced-fat (2%) cottage cheese, ¼ cup grated Parmesan cheese, 1½ tablespoons fresh lemon juice, 1½ teaspoons Worcestershire sauce, ¾ teaspoon garlic salt, ¼ teaspoon salt, pinch black pepper, ¼ teaspoon liquid hot-pepper sauce, and ¼ teaspoon anchovy paste until smooth, about 2 minutes. Through tube with machine running, gradually add 2 tablespoons olive oil and process 1 minute. Refrigerate, covered, up to 1 day.

Nutrient Value Per Tablespoon: 28 calories, 2 g fat (1 g saturated), 2 g protein, 1 g carbohydrate, 0 g fiber, 170 mg sodium, 3 mg cholesterol.

Mustard Dipping Sauce

MAKES: 1⅓ cups

Whisk together 1 cup reduced-fat (2%) milk, 3 tablespoons grainy mustard, 2 tablespoons all-purpose flour, ⅛ teaspoon dried thyme, and ⅛ teaspoon salt in small saucepan. Heat over medium-high heat, stirring, until thickened and slightly bubbly, 5 minutes. Remove pan from heat. Whisk in 1½ tablespoons white-wine vinegar and 2 tablespoons butter until melted and smooth. Serve warm.

Nutrient Value Per Tablespoon: 20 calories, 1 g fat (1 g saturated), 1 g protein, 1 g carbohydrate, 0 g fiber, 71 mg sodium, 4 mg cholesterol.

Fish Burgers
with Caper Mayonnaise

MAKES: 4 burgers
PREP: 15 minutes
COOK: 6 minutes

Caper Mayonnaise:

½ cup reduced-fat mayonnaise dressing

½ cup nonfat plain yogurt

¼ cup drained capers, crushed

2 teaspoons fresh lemon juice

¼ teaspoon salt

⅛ teaspoon black pepper

Burgers:

1 scallion, cut into 2-inch pieces

¾ pound cod fillets, bones removed and fish cut into 2-inch pieces

½ sweet red pepper, cored, seeded, and finely chopped

2 large ribs celery, peeled and coarsely chopped

½ teaspoon coarse (kosher) salt

¼ teaspoon coarsely ground black pepper

¼ cup packaged unseasoned bread crumbs

1 tablespoon vegetable oil

4 "light" hamburger buns

1 Mayonnaise: Stir together mayonnaise dressing, yogurt, capers, lemon juice, salt, and pepper in a small bowl. Refrigerate, covered, until needed.

2 Burgers: Chop scallion in food processor. Add fish. Whirl until coarsely ground. Scrape into bowl. Add sweet pepper, celery, salt, and black pepper. Shape into 4 equal burgers about 3 inches thick. Coat with bread crumbs.

3 Heat oil in large nonstick skillet over medium-high heat. Add burgers; cover and cook until golden brown, about 3 minutes per side. Remove from skillet. Serve on buns with mayonnaise.

Nutrient Value Per Burger: 240 calories, 5 g fat (0 g saturated), 16 g protein, 37 g carbohydrate, 4 g fiber, 1,233 mg sodium, 37 mg cholesterol.

Honey Scallops
with Couscous

MAKES: 4 servings
PREP: 10 minutes
REFRIGERATE: 20 minutes
BROIL: about 8 minutes

1 lemon

¼ cup honey

¼ cup Dijon mustard

1 pound sea scallops (about 20)

1 package (5.7 ounces) herb-flavored couscous

1 cup packed baby spinach leaves, sliced

1 Grate rind from lemon to make 1 teaspoon; reserve. Halve lemon; squeeze lemon to make 1 tablespoon lemon juice. Stir together lemon juice, honey, and mustard in medium-size bowl. Add scallops; toss to coat. Cover and refrigerate for 20 minutes.

2 Heat broiler.

3 Prepare couscous following package directions, but omitting oil; when you add couscous to boiling water, add spinach and lemon rind.

4 Thread scallops onto four 10-inch metal skewers, dividing equally. Pour remaining marinade into small saucepan; boil marinade 3 minutes on high heat.

5 Coat broiler-pan rack with cooking spray. Place skewers on rack.

6 Broil skewers about 3 inches from heat for 4 minutes a side or until cooked through, basting with marinade.

7 Equally divide couscous among 4 dinner plates; top each with scallops.

Nutrient Value Per Serving: 317 calories, 5 g fat (1 g saturated), 26 g protein, 44 g carbohydrate, 2 g fiber, 742 mg sodium, 40 mg cholesterol.

Stir-Fried Scallops and Snow Peas with Ginger-Citrus Sauce

MAKES: 6 servings
PREP: 15 minutes
COOK: 5 minutes

½ cup chicken broth

¼ cup orange juice

2 tablespoons fresh lemon juice

2 tablespoons soy sauce

1 teaspoon dark Asian sesame oil

1 tablespoon sugar

1 tablespoon cornstarch

½ teaspoon salt

1 tablespoon vegetable oil

2 large cloves garlic, finely chopped

2 tablespoons finely chopped fresh ginger

1½ pounds sea scallops, halved, muscle removed

1 pound snow peas, trimmed

Grated orange rind (optional)

1 In small bowl, combine broth, orange juice, lemon juice, soy sauce, sesame oil, sugar, cornstarch, and salt.

2 In very large (12-inch) nonstick skillet or wok, heat oil over medium-high heat. Add garlic and ginger; stir-fry 1 minute. Increase heat to high. Add scallops. Stir-fry until opaque, about 2 minutes. With slotted spoon, transfer scallops to clean bowl.

3 Add snow peas to skillet. Stir-fry 2 minutes. Stir reserved broth mixture and add to skillet. Simmer 1 minute. Add scallops back to skillet. Simmer 1 minute. Serve hot. Sprinkle with orange rind, if desired.

Nutrient Value Per Serving: 248 calories, 5 g fat (0 g saturated), 33 g protein, 13 g carbohydrate, 2 g fiber, 938 mg sodium, 75 mg cholesterol.

Caribbean Shrimp

MAKES: 6 servings
PREP: 5 minutes
REFRIGERATE: 10 minutes
BROIL: 3 to 4 minutes

1 tablespoon light brown sugar

1 teaspoon ground allspice

1 teaspoon black pepper

1 teaspoon onion powder

1 teaspoon garlic powder

1 teaspoon dried thyme

½ teaspoon salt

¼ teaspoon cayenne

1 tablespoon vegetable oil

1 tablespoon molasses

2 tablespoons fresh lime juice

2 pounds jumbo shrimp in shells, cleaned

1 lime cut into wedges, for garnish

1 Heat broiler. Coat large broiler-pan rack with cooking spray.

2 Mix brown sugar, allspice, black pepper, onion powder, garlic powder, thyme, salt, and cayenne in medium-size bowl. Whisk in oil, molasses, and lime juice until smooth. Add shrimp; toss to coat. Cover and refrigerate for 10 minutes, stirring after 5 minutes.

3 Arrange shrimp in single layer on broiler-pan rack.

4 Broil about 4 inches from heat for 2 minutes. Turn shrimp over. Broil 1 to 2 minutes or until shrimp are cooked through. Serve immediately with white rice, if desired. Garnish with lime wedges. Pour drippings from broiler pan over shrimp, if desired.

Nutrient Value Per Serving: 140 calories, 3 g fat (1 g saturated), 20 g protein, 6 g carbohydrate, 0 g fiber, 413 mg sodium, 188 mg cholesterol.

Corn-Shrimp Tostadas

MAKES: 6 servings
PREP: 20 minutes
BAKE: at 425° for about 14 minutes

12 (6-inch) corn tortillas (9-ounce package)

Nonstick cooking spray

¾ teaspoon salt

1 can (11 ounces) corn kernels, drained and rinsed (about 1½ cups)

1 can (15 ounces) black beans, drained and rinsed

¾ pound cooked, shelled shrimp, chopped

2 small jalapeño chiles, cored, seeded, and chopped

½ small red onion, finely chopped

1 teaspoon grated lime rind

3 tablespoons fresh lime juice

1 tablespoon chopped fresh cilantro

1 teaspoon sugar

½ cup reduced-fat mayonnaise dressing

1 tablespoon water

⅛ teaspoon liquid hot-pepper sauce

1 Heat oven to 425°. Place tortillas in single layer on 2 baking sheets. Coat with cooking spray. Flip tortillas over; coat with spray.

2 Bake for 13 to 15 minutes or until lightly browned, flipping tortillas over once. Transfer to wire rack. Sprinkle each with pinch of salt, ¼ teaspoon total. Let cool completely.

3 Mix corn kernels, beans, chopped shrimp, jalapeño, and onion in large bowl.

4 Whisk together rind, juice, cilantro, sugar, remaining ½ teaspoon salt, mayonnaise, water, and pepper sauce in small bowl. Spoon over corn mixture; stir gently to combine.

5 Divide corn mixture among baked tortillas, about ⅓ cup each. Serve immediately.

Nutrient Value Per Serving: 259 calories, 3 g fat (0 g saturated), 15 g protein, 46 g carbohydrate, 7 g fiber, 913 mg sodium, 74 mg cholesterol.

Pesto Shrimp

MAKES: 6 servings
PREP: 10 minutes
COOK: 20 minutes

3⅓ cups water

½ teaspoon garlic salt

¼ teaspoon black pepper

1½ cups uncooked basmati rice

1 sweet red pepper, cored, seeded,
and thinly sliced

3 tablespoons prepared reduced-fat pesto

3 cloves garlic, coarsely chopped

1½ pounds medium-size shrimp in shells,
cleaned

¼ teaspoon salt

1 In medium-size saucepan, bring water, garlic, salt, and ⅛ teaspoon black pepper to a boil. Add rice. Lower heat; cover and simmer 15 minutes. Sprinkle sweet red pepper over rice. Cover; cook 5 minutes or until rice is tender and liquid is absorbed. Stir 2 tablespoons pesto into rice; keep warm.

2 Meanwhile, coat large nonstick skillet with cooking spray. Place over medium heat. Add garlic; cook 3 minutes. In medium-size bowl, toss together shrimp, salt, remaining 1 teaspoon pepper, and remaining 1 tablespoon pesto. Increase heat to medium-high. Add shrimp to skillet; cook until curled and pink, 4 to 6 minutes.

3 Transfer rice to platter. Top with shrimp and liquid from skillet. Serve immediately.

*Nutrient Value Per Serving: 288 calories, 4 g fat
(1 g saturated), 19 g protein, 44 g carbohydrate,
1 g fiber, 473 mg sodium, 136 mg cholesterol.*

Quick Shrimp Paella

MAKES: 6 servings
PREP: 5 minutes
COOK: 30 minutes

1¼ pounds medium-size shrimp in shells, cleaned

¼ teaspoon garlic salt

⅛ teaspoon black pepper

1 medium-size onion, chopped (1 cup)

2 links seasoned cooked chicken sausage (5 to
6 ounces total), cut into ¼-inch-thick slices

1 box (6.8 ounces) Spanish seasoned rice-and-
vermicelli mix

1 can (14.5 ounces) stewed tomatoes

1 cup frozen peas

¼ teaspoon red-pepper flakes

1 can (14 ounces) artichoke hearts in water,
drained and quartered

⅛ teaspoon salt

1 Combine shrimp, garlic salt, and pepper in medium-size bowl.

2 Coat large skillet with cooking spray. Place over medium-high heat. Add shrimp; cook 3 minutes or just until pink and curled. Transfer shrimp to clean bowl; cover to keep warm.

3 In same skillet, cook onion and sausage, 3 minutes, coating skillet with more spray if needed to prevent sticking. Add rice mix without seasoning packet; cook, stirring occasionally, 2 minutes. Add 2 cups water, tomatoes, peas, seasoning packet, and pepper flakes.

2 tablespoons fresh lime juice

¼ teaspoon salt

Pinch black pepper

Dash liquid hot-pepper sauce, or to taste

1 Crab Cakes: In food processor, combine crabmeat, sweet pepper, scallions, and carrots. Pulse until finely chopped. Add egg whites, mayonnaise, salt, pepper, and tarragon. Pulse until blended and ingredients are evenly moistened. Transfer mixture to medium-size bowl.

2 Heat oven to 425°.

3 Stir ¾ cup bread crumbs into crab mixture; place remaining crumbs in shallow dish. Shape crab mixture into twelve 2½-inch patties or cakes, using about ⅓ cup mixture for each. Coat cakes with remaining crumbs.

4 Coat baking sheet with cooking spray. Transfer crab cakes to prepared sheet. Lightly coat tops with additional spray.

5 Bake crab cakes for 8 minutes. Turn over. Coat with additional spray. Bake 8 minutes. If desired, place cakes under broiler for 1 to 2 minutes per side to crisp coating.

6 Corn Relish: In small bowl, stir together corn kernels, scallions, sweet pepper, cherry tomatoes, lime juice, salt, and black pepper. Season with hot-pepper sauce. Serve relish with crab cakes.

Nutrient Value Per Serving: 243 calories, 3 g fat (0 g saturated), 24 g protein, 28 g carbohydrate, 2 g fiber, 881 mg sodium, 81 mg cholesterol.

Seafood Nachos

MAKES: 6 servings
PREP: 5 minutes
BAKE: at 350° for 16 minutes

½ pound shredded imitation crab (surimi)

½ pound cooked cleaned shrimp, coarsely chopped

1 can (4.5 ounces) chopped green chiles

1 teaspoon hot chili powder

½ teaspoon ground cumin

¼ teaspoon salt

1 bag (8.5 ounces) baked corn tortilla chips

1 cup prepared salsa

4 ounces reduced-fat Monterey Jack cheese, shredded (1 cup)

¼ cup chopped black olives

2 scallions, sliced

1 Heat oven to 350°.

2 In large bowl, mix together surimi, shrimp, chiles, hot chili powder, cumin, and salt. Line bottom and sides of 13 x 9 x 2-inch baking dish with tortilla chips. Spoon surimi mixture evenly over corn chips. Cover surimi mixture with salsa, cheese, olives, and scallions.

3 Bake 16 minutes or until heated through and cheese is melted.

Nutrient Value Per Serving: 320 calories, 7 g fat (0 g saturated), 22 g protein, 43 g carbohydrate, 4 g fiber, 1,359 mg sodium, 91 mg cholesterol.

7 GREAT CHICKEN IN A HURRY

WHETHER WE'RE WATCHING OUR DIETS OR NOT (is there anyone in America in that category?), chicken always seems to be on our preferred list. We love eating it in all its guises and it's a cinch to cook, adapting beautifully to different techniques and different ingredients. Because chicken is naturally low-fat, many of our dishes include tasty go-withs like rice, pasta, and polenta, and the total calorie count is still diet-smart. One winner, served over noodles, is a gutsy marriage of chicken thighs and portabella mushrooms in a creamy white wine sauce (page 125). Not what you'd think of as a weight-loss dinner, but it is! Ditto for our Orange-Glazed Chicken (page 126), cooked in a tangy orange juice and hot mustard sauce and served with squash, sweet red pepper, and couscous.

Since chicken dishes are so popular, we revisited favorites and gave them a trimdown. Enchilada Casserole (page 126) offers everything you'd expect—salsa, black beans, olives, onions, and cheese—for only 293 calories a serving. Chunky Chicken Potpie (page 128) is comfort food, diet-style, courtesy of a hit of Parmesan and (surprise) puff pastry. In our "Fried" Chicken (page 112) the crunch comes from corn bread stuffing; the moist, rich taste from low-fat yogurt and mustard. Because the calories were still at a safe level, we threw in something extra: herbed potato slices, baked to cut down on fat.

When you're tired of chicken, you can usually substitute turkey. But to spur your imagination, we've included some imaginative turkey dishes too, like a Country-Style Turkey Meat Loaf (page 133) and Teriyaki Turkey Burgers (page 134).

In the mood for grilled chicken? We offer three tasty toppings (page 121) to up your satisfaction quotient.

"Fried" Chicken and Potatoes (page 112).

Chicken Breasts with Mustard-Caper Sauce

MAKES: 6 servings
PREP: 5 minutes
COOK: about 17 minutes

6 boneless, skinless chicken breast halves (about 2 pounds total)

¼ teaspoon salt

⅛ teaspoon black pepper

1 can (14.5 ounces) chicken broth

¼ cup drained capers

½ teaspoon dried rosemary

¼ teaspoon dried thyme

2 tablespoons Dijon mustard

1 tablespoon honey

4½ cups cooked hot couscous

1 Coat large skillet with cooking spray. Place over medium-high heat. Season chicken on both sides with salt and pepper. Add chicken to skillet; cook about 5 to 6 minutes on each side or until cooked through. Remove to platter and keep warm.

2 Add broth, capers, rosemary, and thyme to skillet; cook over medium-high heat, scraping up any browned bits from bottom of skillet, for 5 minutes. Remove skillet from heat; stir in mustard and honey. Serve couscous with chicken. Pour sauce over chicken and couscous.

Nutrient Value Per Serving: 325 calories, 5 g fat (1 g saturated), 36 g protein, 31 g carbohydrate, 2 g fiber, 762 mg sodium, 85 mg cholesterol.

"Fried" Chicken and Potatoes

MAKES: 6 servings
PREP: 15 minutes
BAKE: at 425° for 30 minutes

Potatoes:

1 large egg white

½ teaspoon dried thyme

¼ teaspoon salt

⅛ teaspoon black pepper

2 large all-purpose potatoes with skins, scrubbed and cut lengthwise into thin wedges

2 large sweet potatoes with skins, scrubbed and cut lengthwise into thin wedges

½ cup packaged corn bread stuffing, crushed

Chicken:

½ cup low-fat plain yogurt

1 tablespoon spicy brown or Dijon mustard

1 tablespoon fresh lemon juice

½ teaspoon salt

¼ teaspoon black pepper

4 boneless, skinless chicken breast halves (1½ pounds total), each cut into quarters

1¼ cups packaged corn bread stuffing, crushed

1 teaspoon dried thyme

Nonstick cooking spray

1 Heat oven to 425°. Coat 2 large baking sheets with cooking spray.

2 Potatoes: Beat egg white slightly in large bowl. Stir in thyme, salt, and pepper. Add potatoes and sweet potatoes; toss to coat; sprinkle with stuffing crumbs; toss to coat. Place in single layer on prepared baking sheet.

3 Bake for 10 minutes on bottom rack.

4 **Chicken:** Meanwhile, stir together yogurt, mustard, lemon juice, salt, and pepper in large bowl. Add chicken; turn to coat.

5 Combine stuffing crumbs and thyme in pie plate. Add chicken, one piece at a time; roll in crumbs to stick. Transfer to prepared baking sheet. Lightly coat chicken with cooking spray.

6 After potatoes have cooked 10 minutes, place chicken on upper rack. Bake both potatoes and chicken 20 minutes or until chicken is golden brown and potatoes are crispy.

7 To crisp chicken, if desired, increase oven temperature to broil. Broil chicken 3 minutes.

Nutrient Value Per Serving: 344 calories, 8 g fat (2 g saturated), 29 g protein, 38 g carbohydrate, 4 g fiber, 706 mg sodium, 64 mg cholesterol.

Honey-Mustard Chicken and Veggies

MAKES: 6 servings
PREP: 15 minutes
BAKE: at 400° for 25 minutes; 450° for 20 minutes
COOK: 3 minutes

4 small carrots, peeled, halved lengthwise, and cut crosswise into 1-inch-thick half-moons

3 medium-size parsnips, peeled, halved lengthwise, and cut crosswise into 1-inch-thick half-moons

2 heads Belgian endive, trimmed and cut into 1-inch pieces

2 large onions, each cut into 8 wedges

2 tablespoons vegetable oil

1 teaspoon salt

½ cup honey-mustard

2 tablespoons fresh lemon juice

½ teaspoon dried thyme

3 large skinless chicken breast halves on the bone (2½ pounds total), each cut in half and trimmed of visible fat

4 medium-size zucchini (about 2 pounds), cut into 1½-inch pieces

2 cups chopped broccoli rabe (½ bunch)

1 Heat oven to 400°. Place carrots, parsnips, endive, and onions in very large bowl. Add oil; toss. Transfer to large roasting pan. Season with ½ teaspoon salt.

2 In small cup, stir together honey-mustard, lemon juice, and thyme. Place chicken in pan on top of vegetables. Sprinkle chicken evenly with remaining ½ teaspoon salt. Brush evenly with 3 tablespoons of the honey-mustard mixture.

3 Roast for 25 minutes. Remove pan from oven. Add zucchini, moving chicken if necessary. Increase heat to 450°. Roast 10 minutes. Remove chicken to platter; cover with foil to keep warm.

4 Stir remaining honey-mustard mixture into vegetables in roasting pan. Roast 10 minutes. Divide vegetable mixture among plates. Top each with a piece of chicken.

5 While vegetables are roasting, steam broccoli rabe until tender, 2 to 3 minutes. Serve on side with chicken and vegetables.

Nutrient Value Per Serving: 348 calories, 12 g fat (2 g saturated), 32 g protein, 31 g carbohydrate, 4 g fiber, 531 mg sodium, 75 mg cholesterol.

Lemon Chicken

MAKES: 6 servings
PREP: 10 minutes
MARINATE: 20 minutes
COOK: 14 minutes

¼ **cup fresh lemon juice (1 lemon)**

1 **tablespoon finely chopped, peeled fresh ginger**

1 **tablespoon soy sauce**

1 **tablespoon sugar**

1 **tablespoon cornstarch**

6 **boneless, skinless chicken breast halves (about 1½ pounds total), cut into 1-inch chunks**

6 **ounces linguine**

2 **tablespoons olive oil**

2 **cloves garlic, sliced**

⅛ **teaspoon red-pepper flakes**

¾ **pound cherry tomatoes**

¼ **teaspoon salt**

6 **cups shredded romaine lettuce**

Garnish:

2 **scallions, finely chopped**

¼ **cup finely chopped fresh cilantro**

6 **cups green beans, steamed**

1 In steam-proof dish or glass pie plate, stir together lemon juice, ginger, soy sauce, sugar, and cornstarch. Add chicken; stir to coat. Let stand at room temperature 20 minutes.

2 Place dish with chicken and marinade on rack over 1 inch of water in wok or very large skillet with deep lid.

3 Heat water to a simmer over medium heat. Cover tightly; steam 5 minutes. Uncover. With tongs, turn chicken over. Cover and steam over medium heat until chicken is opaque, 5 minutes.

4 Meanwhile, cook linguine in large deep pot of lightly salted boiling water until al dente, firm yet tender. Drain.

5 In large skillet, heat oil over medium heat. Add garlic; sauté 1 minute. Add pepper flakes and tomatoes; cook until tomatoes just start to break up, about 3 minutes. Toss in linguine and salt.

6 Place romaine on plates. Spoon chicken and sauce over top. Divide linguine among plates. Garnish with scallions, cilantro, and green beans.

Nutrient Value Per Serving: 326 calories, 9 g fat (2 g saturated), 30 g protein, 36 g carbohydrate, 7 g fiber, 373 mg sodium, 63 mg cholesterol.

Asian Warm
Chicken Slaw

1

THIS PAGE: Pasta Fra Diavolo

OPPOSITE: Penne with Roasted Vegetables

THIS PAGE: Roasted Butternut Squash Soup
OPPOSITE: Classic Lobster Roll

4

THIS PAGE: Blue-Cheese Dip
OPPOSITE: Very Berry Tart

Trio of cheesecakes
(top to bottom):
Pineapple Cheesecake,
Lemon Cheesecake
with Apricot Glaze,
Marble Cheesecake

Summertime Chicken

MAKES: 8 servings
PREP: 15 minutes
REFRIGERATE: 20 minutes
COOK: 15 minutes
BROIL: 8 minutes

Chicken:

- 1 container (8 ounces) low-fat plain yogurt
- 3 tablespoons balsamic vinegar
- 8 thin-cut boneless, skinless chicken breast halves (about 1½ pounds total)

Tomato-Mozzarella Topping:

- 1 tablespoon olive oil
- 1 medium-size onion, cut into 16 wedges
- ¼ cup balsamic vinegar
- 2 tablespoons water
- 1 pound plum tomatoes, cored, seeded, and chopped (about 4 cups)
- 1 teaspoon salt
- ½ teaspoon black pepper
- 1 piece (8 ounces) fresh mozzarella cheese, cut into ½-inch dice
- 1 cup loosely packed basil leaves, chopped

1 Chicken: In small bowl, whisk together yogurt and vinegar. In plastic food-storage bag, combine chicken and yogurt mixture; seal and turn to coat. Refrigerate 20 minutes to marinate.

2 Meanwhile, heat broiler, or prepare outdoor grill with medium-hot coals, or heat gas grill to medium-hot.

3 Tomato-Mozzarella Topping: In large skillet, heat oil over medium heat. Add onion; sauté for 5 minutes or until slightly softened (the wedges will fall apart into pieces). Add vinegar and water. Bring to a simmer. Reduce heat to medium-low; cook until liquid has reduced to a sauce and onion is tender, about 7 minutes.

4 Increase heat to medium-high. Add tomatoes, salt, and pepper; cook 2 minutes. Remove skillet from heat; let cool 2 to 3 minutes. Stir in mozzarella and chopped basil.

5 Remove chicken from bag; discard marinade.

6 Broil or grill chicken about 4 inches from heat 3 to 4 minutes per side or until cooked through. Place chicken on large platter. Scoop ¼ cup topping on each chicken piece. Serve immediatcly or let cool to room temperature.

Nutrient Value Per Serving: 224 calories, 11 g fat (6 g saturated), 24 g protein, 6 g carbohydrate, 1 g fiber, 527 mg sodium, 68 mg cholesterol.

Chicken Marsala

MAKES: 6 servings
PREP: 10 minutes
COOK: 25 to 30 minutes

3 tablespoons butter

6 boneless, skinless chicken breast halves
(about 1½ pounds total)

3 tablespoons all-purpose flour

1 pound sliced white or small mushrooms

1 medium-size onion, sliced

½ cup marsala wine

1 cup beef broth

¾ teaspoon salt

3 cups water

1 cup instant polenta

1 tablespoon fresh lemon juice

2 tablespoons chopped flat-leaf Italian parsley

6 cups steamed broccoli flowerets

1 Melt butter in large skillet over medium-high
heat.

2 Meanwhile, coat chicken in flour; shake off
excess. Working in batches if necessary to avoid
crowding skillet, add chicken to skillet; sauté
over medium-high heat 4 to 6 minutes or until
golden brown, turning once. Remove chicken
from skillet. Reduce heat to medium.

3 Add mushrooms and onion to skillet; sauté
4 minutes or until browned. Add wine, broth,
and ¼ teaspoon salt; simmer 2 minutes,
scraping up any browned bits from bottom
of skillet with wooden spoon.

4 Return chicken to skillet. Bring to a boil over
high heat. Cover. Lower heat; simmer 15 minutes
or until cooked through, basting occasionally.

5 Meanwhile, bring water to a boil in medium-
size saucepan. Add remaining salt. Slowly
add instant polenta, stirring constantly; cook,
stirring occasionally, 3 to 5 minutes or until
desired consistency. Set aside and keep warm
until serving.

6 Remove chicken to serving platter. Stir lemon
juice into sauce in skillet. To serve, pour sauce
over chicken. Sprinkle with parsley. Serve with
polenta and broccoli.

*Nutrient Value Per Serving: 337 calories, 9 g fat
(4 g saturated), 29 g protein, 34 g carbohydrate,
5 g fiber, 535 mg sodium, 78 mg cholesterol.*

Caribbean Chicken Curry

MAKES: 8 servings
PREP: 15 minutes
COOK: 40 minutes

6 boneless, skinless chicken breast halves
(1½ pounds total), cut into 1-inch pieces

½ teaspoon salt

¼ teaspoon black pepper

1 large onion, sliced

2 cloves garlic, chopped

1 tablespoon curry powder

¼ teaspoon cayenne

2⅔ cups nonfat milk

2 cans (10.75 ounces each) 98% fat-free condensed cream of chicken soup

1 large tomato, seeded and chopped

1 large mango, seeded, peeled, and chopped

¼ cup dark seedless raisins

3 cups hot cooked white rice

1 Coat bottom of 8-quart pot with cooking spray. Place over medium-high heat. Season chicken with salt and pepper. Add to pot; cook for 5 minutes or until lightly brown and cooked through. Remove chicken from pot.

2 Add onion and garlic to pot; cook for 3 minutes or until softened. Stir in curry and cayenne; cook 1 minute.

3 Whisk milk into soup in small bowl. Add to onion mixture. Add chicken, tomato, mango, and raisins. Partially cover; simmer 30 minutes.

4 Serve with white rice.

Nutrient Value Per Serving: 260 calories, 3 g fat (1 g saturated), 29 g protein, 26 g carbohydrate, 2 g fiber, 215 mg sodium, 72 mg cholesterol.

Mahogany Sesame Chicken

MAKES: 4 servings
PREP: 20 minutes
COOK: about 15 minutes

4 boneless, skinless chicken breast halves (about 1 pound total), cut into 1-inch cubes

¼ cup sesame seeds, toasted (see Note) and cooled

5 teaspoons vegetable oil

½ sweet green pepper, cored, seeded, and chopped

½ sweet red pepper, cored, seeded, and chopped

⅓ cup teriyaki sauce

2 teaspoons finely chopped peeled fresh ginger

1 clove garlic, chopped

1 tablespoon fresh lemon juice

2 scallions, thinly sliced

2 cups hot cooked rice

1 Shake together chicken and sesame seeds in plastic food-storage bag to coat chicken.

2 Heat 2 teaspoons oil in large nonstick skillet over medium heat. Add peppers; sauté 3 to 5 minutes or until slightly softened. Remove to bowl and keep warm.

3 Heat remaining 3 teaspoons oil in skillet over medium-high heat. Add chicken; sauté until browned and cooked through, 4 to 5 minutes per side. Add to peppers in bowl.

4 Reduce heat to low. Add teriyaki sauce, ginger, and garlic to skillet. Bring to a boil just to thicken sauce slightly. Return chicken and peppers to skillet; toss to coat with glaze.

5 Sprinkle with lemon juice and scallions. Serve over rice.

Note: Toast sesame seeds in dry skillet over medium-low heat, shaking skillet, until lightly golden, 2 to 3 minutes.

Nutrient Value Per Serving: 347 calories, 12 g fat (2 g saturated), 28 g protein, 30 g carbohydrate, 2 g fiber, 973 mg sodium, 63 mg cholesterol.

Chicken with Spicy Rub

MAKES: 4 servings
PREP: 10 minutes
REFRIGERATE: 1 hour
COOK: 12 minutes
BROIL: 4 minutes

Dip:

1 cup low-fat plain yogurt

1 tablespoon chopped fresh mint

¼ teaspoon salt

⅛ teaspoon black pepper

2 teaspoons fresh lemon juice

Spice Rub:

1 tablespoon light-brown sugar

1 tablespoon paprika

¾ teaspoon salt

½ teaspoon ground cumin

½ teaspoon cayenne

½ teaspoon ground allspice

Chicken and Orzo:

4 thin-sliced boneless, skinless chicken breast cutlets (about ¾ pound total)

1 can (14.5 ounces) chicken broth

¼ teaspoon garlic salt

½ cup orzo

1 cup frozen peas, thawed

½ cup grape tomatoes, each halved

1 Dip: Stir together yogurt, mint, salt, pepper, and lemon juice in small bowl. Refrigerate, covered, at least 1 hour.

2 Heat broiler. Lightly coat broiler-pan rack with cooking spray.

3 Spice Rub: Mix sugar, paprika, salt, cumin, cayenne, and allspice in small bowl.

4 Chicken and Orzo: Rub spice mixture over chicken.

5 In medium-size saucepan, bring chicken broth seasoned with garlic salt to a boil. Add orzo; simmer, stirring occasionally, until almost tender, 8 to 10 minutes. Stir in peas and tomatoes; cook until heated through, 2 minutes. Remove from heat; let stand, covered, 10 minutes.

6 Broil chicken, turning once, about 2 minutes per side or until cooked through. Serve with dip on the side and orzo mixture.

Nutrient Value Per Serving: 308 calories, 6 g fat (2 g saturated), 27 g protein, 37 g carbohydrate, 4 g fiber, 932 mg sodium, 53 mg cholesterol.

Chicken-Asparagus Stir-Fry

MAKES: 4 servings
PREP: 10 minutes
COOK: 13 minutes

2 tablespoons oil

3 boneless, skinless chicken breasts (about ¾ pound), cut into 1 x ½-inch strips

2 bunches (1¾ pounds total) asparagus, trimmed and cut into 1-inch pieces

1 sweet red pepper, cored, seeded, and cut into ¼-inch-wide strips

6 scallions, cut into 1-inch pieces

2 teaspoons chopped peeled fresh ginger

2 large cloves garlic, finely chopped

½ teaspoon dark Asian sesame oil

¼ teaspoon red-pepper flakes

1½ cups chicken broth

1 teaspoon soy sauce

2 tablespoons hoisin sauce

2 teaspoons cornstarch

2 teaspoons water

2 cups hot cooked rice

1　Heat 1 tablespoon oil in large nonstick skillet over high heat. Add chicken; cook 1 minute. Stir and cook 1 minute more or until chicken is almost cooked through. Remove chicken to plate.

2　Add remaining oil to skillet. Add asparagus, sweet pepper, scallions, ginger, garlic, sesame oil, and pepper flakes; stir-fry 5 minutes. Add broth, soy sauce, and hoisin sauce; stir-fry until vegetables are crisp-tender, about 4 minutes. Add chicken.

3　Stir together cornstarch and water in small dish. Add to skillet; cook until heated through and thickened, about 2 minutes.

4　Serve with cooked rice.

Nutrient Value Per Serving: 337 calories, 12 g fat (2 g saturated), 23 g protein, 35 g carbohydrate, 4 g fiber, 640 mg sodium, 49 mg cholesterol.

One-Pot Festive Chicken

MAKES: 6 servings
PREP: 10 minutes
COOK: 28 minutes

　1 package (6 ounces) white-and-wild rice mix

　2⅓ cups reduced-sodium chicken broth

　1 thick slice cooked ham (2 ounces), cut in ¼-inch chunks

　6 boneless, skinless chicken breast halves (1¾ pounds total)

　5 scallions, thinly sliced

　2 sweet red peppers, cored, seeded, and sliced

1　Combine rice and broth in large saucepan. Bring to a boil. Cover tightly. Lower heat; simmer 8 minutes.

2　Stir ham into rice. Place chicken breasts on top of rice. Cover; simmer 8 minutes. Remove lid; turn chicken over. Re-cover; cook 7 minutes or until cooked through. Remove chicken to a platter; keep warm.

3　Stir scallions and red pepper into rice. Cover saucepan; cook rice until liquid is absorbed and rice is tender, 13 minutes. Add a little more water to rice if it becomes dry. Serve rice with chicken.

Nutrient Value Per Serving: 349 calories, 6 g fat (2 g saturated), 47 g protein, 26 g carbohydrate, 2 g fiber, 617 mg sodium, 117 mg cholesterol.

Chicken Kabobs over Fruited Couscous

MAKES: 8 servings

PREP: 20 minutes

REFRIGERATE: 2 hours

COOK COUSCOUS: 6 minutes

STAND: 10 minutes

GRILL OR BROIL: 8 to 12 minutes

Marinade:

1 tablespoon dark Asian sesame oil

⅓ cup rice wine OR dry sherry

⅓ cup reduced-sodium soy sauce

3 tablespoons apricot preserves

1 teaspoon liquid hot-pepper sauce

2 cloves garlic, chopped

1 tablespoon minced peeled fresh ginger

2 scallions, finely chopped

1 tablespoon sesame seeds, toasted
(see Note on page 117)

½ teaspoon Chinese five-spice powder
(optional)

Chicken:

6 boneless, skinless chicken breast halves
(about 1½ pounds total), cut into 1-inch
squares

1 sweet red pepper, cored, seeded, and cut into
1-inch squares

1 sweet yellow or green pepper, cored, seeded,
and cut into 1-inch squares

Fruited Couscous:

1 medium-size onion, chopped

2 cloves garlic, minced

1 rib celery, finely chopped

6 dried apricots, cut in ¼-inch dice

⅓ cup dried cherries OR dark seedless raisins

1 package (10 ounces) couscous

1 can (14.5 ounces) reduced-sodium, fat-free
chicken broth

¼ cup water

½ teaspoon salt

¼ teaspoon black pepper

1 Marinade: Whisk together oil, rice wine, soy, preserves, hot sauce, garlic, ginger, scallions, ½ tablespoon of the sesame seeds, and, if using, five-spice powder, in medium-size bowl.

2 Chicken: Add chicken and sweet peppers to marinade. Cover; refrigerate 2 hours or overnight.

3 Prepare outdoor grill with hot coals, or heat gas grill to hot, or heat oven broiler.

4 Fruited Couscous: Coat large nonstick skillet with cooking spray. Place over medium-high heat. Add onion, garlic, and celery; cook, stirring occasionally, until softened, about 4 minutes. Add apricots and cherries; cook 1 minute or until vegetables are light-golden. Stir in couscous; cook 1 minute. Add broth, ¼ cup water, salt, and pepper. Bring to a boil. Immediately remove skillet from heat. Cover and let stand 10 minutes.

5 Thread chicken on 6 metal skewers, alternating with peppers.

6 Grill kabobs, turning once, until chicken is cooked through, about 8 minutes.

7 Arrange couscous and kabobs on plates. Sprinkle top with remaining sesame seeds.

Nutrient Value Per Serving: 305 calories, 3 g fat (1 g saturated), 24 g protein, 41 g carbohydrate, 4 g fiber, 387 mg sodium, 47 mg cholesterol.

FAT-FREE GRILLING ADD-ONS

There's no question about it: Chicken breast is ultra-trim. Serve 3 ounces of roasted skinless chicken breast for only 140 calories and 3 grams of fat, according to the USDA. The skin adds about 30 calories and 4 grams of fat, but you can cook the chicken with the skin for added moistness, and then ditch it—and all of the fat, too!

We're fond of grilling, since it's speedy with easy clean-up. Just take care not to overcook; according to the USDA, chicken breasts are done at 170° measured on an instant-read thermometer (and legs and thighs at 180°). Lightly coat the breasts with cooking spray and grill over a medium-high heat about 5 minutes per side. Then try one of these great sauces for zippy flavor.

Orange BBQ Sauce

MAKES: 2 cups sauce

In medium-size saucepan, stir together 1 cup ketchup, ½ cup sugar-free orange marmalade, ½ cup cider vinegar, 1 small onion, finely chopped, 2 cloves garlic, chopped, and 1 tablespoon Worcestershire sauce. Bring to a boil. Lower heat; simmer, uncovered, 10 minutes. Use to brush on chicken for last 2 minutes of cooking. (Sauce can be refrigerated for up to 2 days.)

Nutrient Value Per Tablespoon: 15 calories, 0 g fat (0 g saturated), 0 g protein, 4 g carbohydrate, 0 g fiber, 96 mg sodium, 0 mg cholesterol.

Spicy Yogurt Sauce

MAKES: 2 cups sauce

Coat 8-inch nonstick skillet with cooking spray. Place over medium-high heat. Add 1 small onion, finely chopped, 3 cloves garlic, chopped, and 1 tablespoon finely chopped, peeled fresh ginger; cook 3 minutes or until onion is softened. Stir in 1 teaspoon ground cumin, 1 teaspoon salt, ½ teaspoon ground turmeric, ¼ teaspoon each ground cinnamon, cloves, nutmeg, and cayenne; cook 2 minutes. Remove from heat. In medium-size bowl, stir together onion-spice mixture, 8-ounce container low-fat plain yogurt, and 1 cup nonfat sour cream. Serve alongside grilled chicken or use as a marinade.

Nutrient Value Per Tablespoon: 11 calories, 0 g fat (0 g saturated), 1 g protein, 2 g carbohydrate, 0 g fiber, 88 mg sodium, 0 mg cholesterol.

Mango-Chipotle Salsa

MAKES: 6 cups salsa

In large bowl, combine 2 large mangos, peeled and diced, 1 medium-size sweet red pepper, diced, 1 small red onion, finely chopped, 2 tablespoons chopped fresh cilantro, 2 tablespoons fresh lime juice, 1 teaspoon mashed canned chipotle chile in adobo sauce, and 2 teaspoons adobo sauce from can of chipotle chiles. For best flavor, refrigerate, covered, a few hours or overnight. Serve alongside grilled chicken.

Nutrient Value Per ¼ cup: 23 calories, 0 g fat (0 g saturated), 1 g protein, 4 g carbohydrate, 0 g fiber, 23 mg sodium, 0 mg cholesterol.

Barbecue Chicken Tacos

MAKES: 6 servings (2 tacos per serving)
PREP: 15 minutes
BROIL: 8 to 10 minutes

6 boneless, skinless chicken breast halves (about 1½ pounds total)

¾ cup bottled barbecue sauce

1 box (10 ounces) frozen corn kernels, cooked following package directions

¼ teaspoon salt

12 (6-inch) corn tortillas

1 small head lettuce, shredded

1 cup shredded reduced-fat Monterey Jack cheese (4 ounces)

2 scallions, thinly sliced

1 Heat broiler. Brush chicken with ½ cup barbecue sauce.

2 Broil for 4 to 5 minutes on each side or until cooked through.

3 Slice breasts into long ½-inch-thick slices. Mix with remaining barbecue sauce, corn, and salt in medium-size bowl; keep warm.

4 Gently warm tortillas following package directions.

5 To serve, place lettuce on tortillas. Top with chicken. Garnish with cheese and scallions. Roll up.

Nutrient Value Per Serving: 348 calories, 6 g fat (2 g saturated), 30 g protein, 44 g carbohydrate, 6 g fiber, 634 mg sodium, 70 mg cholesterol.

Chicken Parmesan Pita Pizzas

MAKES: 6 servings (2 pizzas each)
PREP: 5 minutes
BROIL: about 8 minutes

2 cloves garlic, finely chopped

2 teaspoons olive oil

¼ teaspoon salt

1 pound uncooked chicken tenders

6 (6-inch) pita breads, split

¾ cup prepared tomato sauce OR pizza sauce

6 tablespoons grated Parmesan cheese

1 cup shredded reduced-fat (50% less fat) mozzarella cheese (4 ounces)

1 Heat broiler.

2 In pie plate, combine garlic, oil, and salt. Add chicken; turn to evenly coat. Arrange chicken in single layer on broiler-pan rack.

3 Broil 4 inches from heat for 3 minutes. Turn chicken over. Broil until cooked through, about 2 minutes. When cool enough to handle, thinly slice. Set aside.

4 Arrange the 12 pita rounds, rough side up, on baking sheets. Toast under broiler until barely golden around edges, 30 to 45 seconds.

5 Spread generous 1 tablespoon tomato sauce on each pita. Divide sliced chicken, adding Parmesan and mozzarella evenly on top. Broil pizzas until cheese is melted, about 1 minute.

Nutrient Value Per Serving: 345 calories, 8 g fat (3 g saturated), 29 g protein, 38 g carbohydrate, 2 g fiber, 897 mg sodium, 53 mg cholesterol.

Skillet Smarts

Boneless, skinless chicken breasts—as well as any lean meat cutlet or fish fillet—take well to quick skillet sautéing. And if you use a nonstick pan, that means less oil and fewer calories. Here are the tricks to maximize your results.

- **TEMPERATURE** All nonstick coatings begin to deteriorate at 500°. Also, the hotter the pan gets, the softer the coating becomes and the easier it scratches. Never leave an empty pot on even medium-high heat for more than a couple of minutes.

- **PREHEATING** You can preheat nonsticks at medium-high heat for browning and searing for short periods; just turn the heat down to low or medium immediately after browning is complete.

- **OVEN COOKING** Nonsticks can go into an oven preheated to 350°. Always check the care label; some can tolerate slightly higher temperatures. But never use under a broiler.

- **UTENSILS** Be cautious with metal utensils, even if their use is approved by the manufacturer. Don't cut meat in the pan with a sharp knife or poke at vegetables with a sharp-pronged fork.

- **CLEANING** Wash interiors with soapy water and a sponge. Look for products that clearly state "safe for nonstick surfaces."

- **ALUMINUM NONSTICK** Check manufacturer's directions to see if the product is dishwasher safe.

- **OIL WIPE** To improve nonstick release performance, periodically rub cooking oil all over any nonstick coating; wipe off excess with paper toweling.

- **STORAGE** If you stack skillets or saucepans, place a clean dishcloth or paper toweling between pans—you'll minimize scratching the nonstick finish.

Ranch-Style Chicken Thighs

MAKES: 6 servings
PREP: 15 minutes
MARINATE: 15 minutes
BROIL: 20 minutes
COOK: 8 minutes

1 package (1 ounce) ranch dressing mix

1 container (8 ounces) low-fat plain yogurt

6 boneless, skinless chicken thighs (about 1½ pounds total)

6 small zucchini (about 2½ pounds), halved lengthwise and cut crosswise into ¼-inch-thick slices

1 medium-size onion, sliced

1 cup grape tomatoes, large tomatoes halved

3 cups hot cooked couscous

1 Reserve 1 tablespoon ranch dressing mix. Stir together remaining dressing mix and yogurt in large bowl. Add chicken; stir to coat. Cover; marinate at room temperature for 15 minutes or refrigerate for an hour or two.

2 Heat broiler. Place chicken on broiler-pan rack.

3 Broil 4 inches from heat 10 minutes on each side or until cooked through.

4 Meanwhile, coat large skillet with cooking spray. Place over medium-high heat. Add zucchini and onion; cook 5 minutes. Add reserved ranch dressing mix and tomatoes; cook 2 to 3 minutes or until tomatoes start to wilt.

5 Serve chicken and zucchini mixture with couscous.

Nutrient Value Per Serving: 313 calories, 10 g fat (3 g saturated), 23 g protein, 32 g carbohydrate, 4 g fiber, 463 mg sodium, 58 mg cholesterol.

Chicken with Portabella Mushrooms and Wine

MAKES: 4 servings
PREP: 10 minutes
COOK: 30 minutes

1 tablespoon olive oil

4 boneless, skinless chicken thighs (about 1 pound total)

½ teaspoon salt

¼ teaspoon black pepper

1 package (6 ounces) sliced portabella mushrooms

¼ cup plus 2 tablespoons chicken broth

¼ cup dry white wine

1 teaspoon dried rosemary

2 teaspoons all-purpose flour

¼ cup reduced-fat sour cream

2 cups hot cooked egg noodles

1 Heat oil in large skillet. Season chicken with salt and pepper. Add to skillet; sauté 6 minutes or until golden, turning over halfway through cooking. Remove to platter. Drain off all but 1 tablespoon drippings.

2 Place skillet over medium heat. Add mushrooms; sauté for 5 minutes, turning over halfway through the cooking.

3 Return chicken to skillet along with the ¼ cup broth, the wine, and rosemary. Cover; simmer 15 minutes or until the chicken is tender and cooked through. Remove chicken to platter and keep warm.

4 Whisk together flour and remaining 2 tablespoons broth in small bowl until smooth and well blended. Whisk into skillet; cook, stirring occasionally, for 3 to 5 minutes or until sauce is thickened and bubbly. Stir in sour cream; gently heat mixture through (do not let boil or sauce may separate). Pour over chicken and serve with noodles.

Nutrient Value Per Serving: 321 calories, 11 g fat (3 g saturated), 28 g protein, 24 g carbohydrate, 2 g fiber, 499 mg sodium, 129 mg cholesterol.

Orange-Glazed Chicken and Squash

MAKES: 4 servings
PREP: 15 minutes
COOK: about 18 minutes

½ cup orange juice

½ cup chicken broth

3 tablespoons soy sauce

1 tablespoon cornstarch

2 teaspoons sugar

1 teaspoon Chinese-style prepared hot mustard or other hot mustard

½ teaspoon red-pepper flakes

1 tablespoon vegetable oil

4 boneless, skinless chicken thighs (about 1 pound total), each cut into ½-inch-thick strips

3 ribs celery, peeled and cut into 2-inch-long matchsticks (about 1¼ cups)

1 medium-size yellow squash, quartered lengthwise, then cut crosswise into ½-inch pieces

2 medium-size zucchini, quartered lengthwise, then cut crosswise into ½-inch pieces

1 sweet red pepper, cored, seeded, and cut into thin strips

2 cups hot cooked couscous

1 Whisk together orange juice, chicken broth, soy sauce, cornstarch, sugar, hot mustard, and pepper flakes in small bowl.

2 Heat oil in large skillet over high heat. Add chicken strips; cook 4 minutes or until no longer pink. Remove with slotted spoon to plate.

3 Reduce heat to medium-high. Add celery to skillet; cook 1 minute. Add squash, zucchini, and 2 tablespoons water; cook, stirring, until vegetables are softened, about 6 minutes.

4 Add chicken strips and sweet red pepper to skillet; cook 2 minutes. Add orange sauce from bowl, stirring to combine; cook until sauce is slightly thickened, about 2 minutes.

5 Serve with hot cooked couscous.

Nutrient Value Per Serving: 349 calories, 14 g fat (3 g saturated), 21 g protein, 36 g carbohydrate, 4 g fiber, 997 mg sodium, 57 mg cholesterol.

Chicken Enchilada Casserole

MAKES: 8 servings
PREP: 20 minutes
BAKE: at 350° for 25 minutes

1 package (10 ounces) frozen corn kernels, thawed slightly

12 (6-inch) corn tortillas

1 cup bottled hot salsa

1 can (14 to 16 ounces) stewed tomatoes

1 container (8 ounces) low-fat plain yogurt

½ cup low-fat (1%) milk

¾ teaspoon salt

24 pitted black olives, sliced

1 can (16 ounces) black beans, rinsed and drained

½ pound cooked chicken, torn into shreds (about 2 x ½ inch)

½ cup sliced scallions OR chopped onion

¼ cup chopped fresh cilantro

¼ teaspoon black pepper

1 teaspoon ground cumin

1 teaspoon dried oregano

1 cup shredded sharp cheddar cheese

1 Heat oven to 350°. Lightly coat 13 x 9 x 2-inch baking dish with cooking spray.

2 Sprinkle ½ cup corn kernels in prepared dish. Tear each of 6 corn tortillas into 4 or 5 pieces; arrange, overlapping, to cover bottom of dish.

3 Mix salsa and tomatoes in medium-size bowl. In another bowl, stir together yogurt, milk, and ¼ teaspoon salt.

4 Spoon 1 cup salsa mixture over tortillas in dish. Drizzle with ½ cup yogurt mixture; sprinkle with olives. Reserve ¼ cup each corn and beans; sprinkle remaining corn and beans over casserole. Top with chicken, scallions, and cilantro. Sprinkle with remaining ½ teaspoon salt, pepper, cumin, and oregano. Sprinkle with half the cheddar; spoon ½ cup salsa mixture over top.

5 Tear remaining tortillas into pieces. Overlap on top to cover. Sprinkle with reserved corn and beans. Spoon on remaining salsa mixture. Drizzle remaining yogurt mixture over top; sprinkle with remaining cheddar.

6 Bake, covered, 15 minutes. Uncover; bake 10 minutes or until hot and lightly browned. Serve with sour cream and radish slices if desired.

Nutrient Value Per Serving: 293 calories, 10 g fat (4 g saturated), 20 g protein, 35 g carbohydrate, 6 g fiber, 930 mg sodium, 43 mg cholesterol.

Chicken Sausage and Apples

MAKES: 4 servings
PREP: 5 minutes
COOK: 30 minutes

1 package (4 to 5 links, 10 to 12 ounces) precooked chicken sausage with apple, cut into ½-inch-thick slices

1 teaspoon unsalted butter

1 large red onion, sliced

1 large Golden Delicious apple, peeled, cored, and sliced

½ cup apple cider OR chicken broth

½ cup bottled mango chutney, chopped

2 cups prepared hot mashed potatoes

1 Sauté sausage in large nonstick skillet over medium-high heat until golden brown, about 5 minutes. Remove to plate; keep warm.

2 Melt butter in skillet over medium heat. Add onion; sauté until slightly softened, 8 minutes. Add apple; cook 5 minutes or until slightly softened.

3 Stir in cider, chutney, and sausage; cook, stirring occasionally, 10 minutes or until onion is softened and sauce is slightly thickened. If too thick, add a little more cider if desired. Serve with mashed potatoes.

Nutrient Value Per Serving: 327 calories, 11 g fat (5 g saturated), 17 g protein, 45 g carbohydrate, 4 g fiber, 730 mg sodium, 106 mg cholesterol.

Chicken Sausage Stir-Fry

MAKES: 6 servings
PREP: 10 minutes
MARINATE: 10 minutes
COOK: about 25 minutes

Marinade:

¼ cup hoisin sauce

2 tablespoons reduced-sodium soy sauce

2 tablespoons rice vinegar

1 clove garlic, finely chopped

1 tablespoon grated peeled fresh ginger

⅛ teaspoon cayenne

Stir-Fry:

½ pound green beans, halved crosswise

1 can (15 ounces) baby corn, drained

1 large sweet red pepper, cored, seeded, and cut into ¼-inch-wide strips

1 teaspoon vegetable oil

1 package (10 to 12 ounces) precooked jalapeño-flavored chicken sausage, sliced diagonally into ½-inch-thick pieces

⅓ cup chicken broth mixed with ½ teaspoon cornstarch

3 cups hot cooked rice

Chopped scallions, for garnish (optional)

1 Marinade: Stir together hoisin, soy sauce, vinegar, garlic, ginger, and cayenne in small bowl.

2 Stir-Fry: Cook green beans in saucepan of boiling water until tender, about 12 minutes. Drain.

3 Place corn, red pepper, and green beans in medium-size bowl. Add ¼ cup marinade; let stand 10 minutes.

4 Meanwhile, heat oil in large nonstick skillet over high heat. Add sausage; sauté until golden brown, 5 minutes. Remove to plate; keep warm.

5 Add green beans, corn, red pepper, and remaining marinade to skillet; sauté over medium-high heat for 4 minutes. Add cornstarch mixture; cook until vegetables are crisp-tender and sauce is thickened, 2 to 3 minutes. Add sausage; heat through.

6 Serve over hot cooked rice. Garnish with chopped scallions, if desired.

Nutrient Value Per Serving: 247 calories, 5 g fat (1 g saturated), 13 g protein, 38 g carbohydrate, 6 g fiber, 889 mg sodium, 51 mg cholesterol.

Chunky Chicken Potpie

MAKES: 6 servings
PREP: 15 minutes
BAKE: at 400° for 30 minutes

3 cups diced cooked chicken (about 1 pound)

1 can (10.75 ounces) condensed cream of chicken soup

1 can (19 ounces) kidney beans, drained and rinsed

1 jar (4.5 ounces) sliced mushrooms, drained

1 can (4.5 ounces) chopped green chiles, drained

¼ cup water

½ teaspoon dried sage

½ teaspoon dried thyme

¼ teaspoon salt

⅛ teaspoon black pepper

1 sheet frozen puff pastry, thawed following package directions

1 large egg mixed with 1 tablespoon water

1 tablespoon grated Parmesan cheese

1 Heat oven to 400°.

2 Stir together chicken, soup, kidney beans, mushrooms, chiles, water, sage, thyme, salt, and pepper in large bowl. Scrape into 8 x 8 x 2-inch square glass baking dish.

3 Place pastry on top of filling; crimp edges along rim of baking dish. Brush egg mixture over pastry. Sprinkle top evenly with Parmesan cheese. Cut about ten 1-inch steam vents in pastry.

5 Bake until filling is bubbly and top is golden brown, about 30 minutes. If top browns too quickly, cover with foil. Let stand 10 minutes before serving.

Nutrient Value Per Serving: 312 calories, 9 g fat (2 g saturated), 32 g protein, 26 g carbohydrate, 7 g fiber, 688 mg sodium, 100 mg cholesterol.

Zesty Chicken Burger

MAKES: 6 burgers
PREP: 5 minutes
COOK: 10 minutes
GRILL OR BROIL: 10 minutes

1 teaspoon vegetable oil

1 small onion, chopped

7 soft hamburger buns

1 pound lean ground chicken

1 large egg, slightly beaten

3 tablespoons bottled barbecue sauce

½ teaspoon salt

¼ teaspoon black pepper

1 cup fresh corn kernels or frozen kernels, thawed

Sliced red onion and barbecue sauce, for garnish

1 Prepare outdoor grill with medium-hot coals, or heat gas grill to medium-hot, or heat oven broiler. Lightly coat grill rack or broiler-pan rack with cooking spray.

2 Heat oil in small nonstick skillet over medium-low heat. Add onion; sauté until softened, about 10 minutes; do not let brown. Remove from heat.

3 Tear 1 hamburger bun into pieces and place in food processor. Whirl until fine crumbs form.

4 Mix together ground chicken, egg, barbecue sauce, salt, pepper, crumbs, and sautéed onion in medium-size bowl. Stir in corn kernels. Shape into 6 equal patties.

5 Grill or broil patties about 4 inches from heat, turning once, for 10 minutes or until instant-read thermometer inserted in centers registers 165°. Serve on soft roll with sliced red onion and extra barbecue sauce.

Nutrient Value Per Burger: 287 calories, 6 g fat (1 g saturated), 22 g protein, 35 g carbohydrate, 2 g fiber, 583 mg sodium, 77 mg cholesterol.

Chicken and Vegetable Burritos

MAKES: 10 burritos
PREP: 20 minutes
COOK: 15 minutes
BAKE: at 375° for 10 minutes

1 medium-size onion, chopped

1 medium-size carrot, peeled, cut in half lengthwise, then crosswise into thin half-moons

1 pound lean ground chicken

2 cloves garlic, finely chopped

1 can (14.5 ounces) stewed tomatoes

1 medium-size zucchini, cut in half lengthwise, then crosswise into thin half-moons

½ cup reduced-sodium, fat-free chicken broth

1 package (1.5 ounces) taco seasoning mix

½ teaspoon salt

½ cup instant white rice

10 burrito-size flour tortillas (99% fat-free)

1 cup shredded taco-flavored cheese

1 Coat large skillet with cooking spray. Place over medium-high heat. Add onion and carrot; cook until softened, 6 minutes. Add chicken and garlic; cook, breaking up chicken into small pieces, until chicken is no longer pink, 5 minutes. Stir in tomatoes, zucchini, broth, taco seasoning, and salt; cook, covered, 4 minutes, just until zucchini is tender. Remove from heat; stir in rice. Cover; let stand 5 minutes.

2 Heat oven to 375°. Divide filling evenly among the 10 tortillas, about ½ cup per tortilla. Fold up each side as if wrapping a package, then roll up.

3 Place, seam side down, in 13 x 9 x 2-inch baking dish. Sprinkle with taco cheese.

4 Bake 10 minutes or until heated through.

Nutrient Value Per Burrito: 335 calories, 12 g fat (6 g saturated), 14 g protein, 47 g carbohydrate, 1 g fiber, 1,160 mg sodium, 75 mg cholesterol.

Turkey-Veggie Stir-Fry

MAKES: 6 servings
PREP: 15 minutes
REFRIGERATE: 1 hour
COOK: about 20 minutes

Sauce:

¼ cup reduced-sodium soy sauce

2 tablespoons ketchup

2 tablespoons rice vinegar

2 tablespoons sugar

¾ cup chicken broth

2 tablespoons cornstarch

½ teaspoon chili paste

Stir-Fry:

4 turkey cutlets, cut into thin strips (1 pound)

4 teaspoons vegetable oil

1 small red onion, sliced

1 medium-size sweet potato, peeled, cut in half lengthwise, halves into quarters lengthwise, then crosswise in ¼-inch-thick slices

2 cups broccoli flowerets

2 small sweet red peppers, cored, seeded, and cut into 1-inch pieces

½ cup water

1 Sauce: Stir together soy sauce, ketchup, vinegar, sugar, broth, cornstarch, and chili paste in small bowl.

2 Stir-fry: Combine 3 tablespoons sauce and the turkey in a bowl. Let marinate, covered, in the refrigerator, for up to 1 hour.

3 Heat 2 teaspoons oil in large nonstick skillet or nonstick wok over medium-high heat. Add turkey; stir-fry 4 minutes; remove to plate. Add remaining oil and onion; stir-fry 2 minutes. Add potato, broccoli, and sweet pepper; stir-fry 3 minutes. Add ½ cup water. Cover; cook 6 to 8 minutes or until sweet potato is tender.

4 Stir remaining sauce. Add with turkey to skillet; cook, stirring, until thickened, 3 minutes.

Nutrient Value Per Serving: 211 calories, 8 fat (2 g saturated), 18 g protein, 17 g carbohydrate, 2 g fiber, 643 mg sodium, 41 mg cholesterol.

Turkey Fajitas

MAKES: 8 servings (2 fajitas each)
PREP: 15 minutes
REFRIGERATE: 1 hour
BROIL: 6 minutes
COOK: 8 minutes

  2 teaspoons grated lime rind

  2 tablespoons fresh lime juice

  4 cloves garlic, finely chopped

  2 tablespoons chopped fresh cilantro

  2 teaspoons olive oil

  ¾ teaspoon salt

  ¾ teaspoon ground cumin

  4 turkey cutlets (about 1 pound)

  2 onions, halved and sliced crosswise

  1 sweet red pepper, cored, seeded, and sliced

  1 sweet green pepper, cored, seeded, and sliced

  ½ teaspoon chili powder

  ½ teaspoon dried oregano

  ⅛ teaspoon black pepper

  16 small (6-inch) fat-free flour tortillas, heated following package directions

Garnish:

  ½ cup salsa

  ½ cup fat-free sour cream

  ¼ cup chopped fresh cilantro

1 Combine lime rind, juice, half the garlic, the cilantro, 1 teaspoon olive oil, ½ teaspoon salt, and ½ teaspoon cumin in gallon-size plastic food-storage bag. Add turkey; seal. Refrigerate to marinate at least 1 hour.

2 Heat broiler. Remove turkey from marinade and place on baking sheet. Discard remaining marinade.

3 Broil turkey until no longer pink in center, about 3 minutes per side. Let cool slightly.

4 Heat remaining 1 teaspoon oil in nonstick skillet. Add onions, remaining garlic, and the sweet peppers. Sprinkle with remaining salt, cumin, the chili powder, oregano, and black pepper; sauté until vegetables are tender, about 8 minutes. Do not let garlic burn.

5 Slice turkey into thin strips. Add to vegetables in skillet; stir to reheat. Divide mixture, about ⅓ cup each, and garnishes among 16 tortillas.

Nutrient Value Per Serving: 347 calories, 7 g fat (1 g saturated), 20 g protein, 53 g carbohydrate, 848 mg sodium, 32 mg cholesterol.

Turkey and Asparagus Roll-Ups

MAKES: 6 servings
PREP: 10 minutes
COOK: 24 minutes

½ teaspoon salt

¼ teaspoon black pepper

1 teaspoon dried poultry seasoning

6 thin-cut turkey cutlets, ¼ inch thick
(1¼ pounds total)

12 large asparagus spears, peeled and
blanched OR 1 package (10 ounces) frozen
asparagus spears, thawed

1 tablespoon vegetable oil

1 small onion, thinly sliced

1 can (10.75 ounces) 98% fat-free condensed
cream of mushroom soup

1 cup nonfat milk

¼ cup light sour cream

1½ teaspoons dried parsley OR 1 tablespoon
chopped fresh parsley

3 cups small new potatoes, steamed

1 Combine salt, pepper, and ½ teaspoon poultry
seasoning in small bowl. Sprinkle one side of
each cutlet with seasoning.

2 Place 2 asparagus spears at narrow end of
each cutlet (or divide thawed frozen spears
evenly among cutlets). Roll up each turkey
cutlet; secure with toothpick to hold in place.

3 Heat oil in large nonstick skillet. Add turkey
rolls; sauté until lightly golden, about 2 minutes
on each side. Remove turkey from skillet.

4 Add onion to skillet; sauté 3 minutes. Whisk
together soup, milk, and remaining ½ teaspoon
poultry seasoning in small bowl; add to onion
in skillet along with turkey rolls. Simmer over
medium-low heat for 8 minutes. Turn turkey
rolls over; simmer 8 minutes or until turkey is
tender. Remove turkey to serving plate; cover
with foil to keep warm.

5 Remove skillet from heat. Stir in sour cream.
Sprinkle parsley over turkey. Serve sauce on side
along with potatoes.

*Nutrient Value Per Serving: 278 calories, 11 g fat
(2 g saturated), 25 g protein, 19 g carbohydrate,
3 g fiber, 603 mg sodium, 53 mg cholesterol.*

Skillet Turkey Parmesan

MAKES: 4 servings
PREP: 5 minutes
COOK: 7 minutes

4 turkey cutlets (1 pound), flattened

⅛ teaspoon salt

⅛ teaspoon black pepper

1½ cups fat-free marinara sauce

½ cup shredded part-skim mozzarella cheese

2 tablespoons grated Parmesan cheese

2 cups hot cooked rotini or other shaped pasta

1 Coat large nonstick skillet with cooking spray. Place over medium heat. Add cutlets; cook until golden brown on bottom, 2 minutes. Turn cutlets over; sprinkle with salt and pepper. Cook until cooked through, about 3 minutes.

2 Reduce heat to low. Add marinara sauce. Sprinkle cheeses over cutlets; simmer, covered, until cheeses are melted, about 2 minutes.

3 Serve with pasta.

Nutrient Value Per Serving: 345 calories, 10 g fat (4 g saturated), 34 g protein, 29 g carbohydrate, 2 g fiber, 550 mg sodium, 71 mg cholesterol.

Country-Style Turkey Meat Loaf

MAKES: 8 servings
COOK: 3 minutes
BAKE: at 350° for 30 to 40 minutes

1 medium-size onion, chopped

2 tablespoons reduced-sodium, fat-free chicken broth

1½ pounds lean ground turkey breast

½ cup sourdough bread crumbs

½ cup plus 2 tablespoons fat-free, reduced-sodium barbecue sauce

2 tablespoons Worcestershire sauce

½ teaspoon Dijon mustard

2 cloves garlic, minced

½ teaspoon dried thyme

1 Heat oven to 350°.

2 Cook onion in broth in small nonstick skillet until lightly browned, about 3 minutes. Let cool slightly.

3 Combine onion, turkey, crumbs, the ½ cup barbecue sauce, Worcestershire, mustard, garlic, and thyme in medium-size bowl. Form mixture into loaf; place in ungreased loaf pan. Brush top with remaining barbecue sauce.

4 Bake 30 to 40 minutes or until cooked through. Carefully drain off fat. Let cool 20 minutes before slicing.

Nutrient Value Per Serving: 171 calories, 8 g fat (2 g saturated), 16 g protein, 8 g carbohydrate, 1 g fiber, 288 mg sodium, 67 mg cholesterol.

Teriyaki Turkey Burgers

MAKES: 6 servings
PREP: 10 minutes
BROIL: 10 minutes
COOK: 8 minutes

1½ pounds lean ground turkey

4 ounces shiitake or cremini mushrooms, stems removed and caps finely chopped

3 scallions, finely chopped

3 tablespoons soy sauce

2 teaspoons finely chopped peeled fresh ginger

3 cups angel hair pasta

2 teaspoons dark Asian sesame oil

2 teaspoons soy sauce

Garnish:

3 cups steamed snow peas

3 cups mandarin orange slices

1 Heat broiler.

2 In large bowl, combine turkey, mushrooms, scallions, soy sauce, and ginger. Shape into 6 equal patties.

3 Broil burgers 4 inches from heat for 5 minutes. Turn burgers over. Broil until internal temperature registers 165° on instant-read thermometer, 5 minutes.

4 Meanwhile, cook pasta in large deep pot of lightly salted boiling water until al dente, firm yet tender. Drain; return to pot. Toss with sesame oil and soy sauce. Serve with pasta, snow peas, and mandarin orange slices.

Nutrient Value Per Serving: 346 calories, 10 g fat (3 g saturated), 25 g protein, 39 g carbohydrate, 6 g fiber, 661 mg sodium, 75 mg cholesterol.

Spinach and Turkey Sausage Casserole

MAKES: 6 servings
PREP: 5 minutes
COOK: 30 minutes

1 medium-size onion, chopped

1 clove garlic, finely chopped

6 hot Italian-style turkey sausage links (about 1¼ pounds), casings removed

1 can (13.5 ounces) reduced-sodium, fat-free chicken broth

2 tablespoons water

¾ cup quick-cooking barley

1 cup shredded peeled carrots

2 packages (10 ounces each) frozen leaf spinach, thawed and squeezed dry

1 Coat large nonstick skillet with cooking spray. Place over medium-high heat. Add onion and garlic; cook until lightly colored, about 3 minutes. Crumble sausage into skillet; cook, breaking up clumps with wooden spoon until no longer pink, about 7 minutes.

2 Add broth, water, barley, and carrots to skillet. Cover; bring to a boil. Lower heat; simmer, covered, 10 minutes.

3 Remove cover. Add spinach. Replace cover; simmer 8 to 10 minutes or until barley is tender.

Nutrient Value Per Serving: 259 calories, 7 g fat (2 g saturated), 24 g protein, 27 g carbohydrate, 7 g fiber, 758 mg sodium, 68 mg cholesterol.

8 MARVELOUS MEAT IN MINUTES

IF YOU'RE LIKE US, sometimes there just isn't anything that will satisfy like a great sirloin steak. Or a gutsy slab of meat loaf. Or some homestyle pork chops. Indeed, it's nice to know that when the mood for meat hits, you can give in. The trick is to choose the right cuts.

When it comes to beef, that means boneless sirloin, beef tenderloin, top round, lean ground, and filet mignon. Stick to these and you can dine on robust delights like Bacon-Wrapped Filet with Bacon-Cheddar Mashed Potatoes (page 138)—(no kidding!)—or Onion-Pepper Braciole (page 146) in a mushroom and tomato sauce. And yes, you can have that sirloin. Our wine-marinated version (page 141) is everything you could wish for, topped with a chili-horseradish glaze.

Pork? You're ahead of the game here, because these days pork is so naturally lean. We have two versions of chops: pan-barbecued with zucchini and frying peppers (page 154) and, for down-home taste, baked with mustard and dill and served on top of pumpernickel stuffing (page 153). Apple-Marinated Pork Tenderloin (page 157) is another keeper. Made with maple syrup and Worcestershire sauce, it's sweet and tangy at the same time and comes accompanied with roasted apple and sweet potato chunks.

On the lamb plan, (pages 160–63), we have chops in a lovely lemon marinade, a spicy broiled leg laced with cumin and mint, and a wholesome and hearty potato and lamb casserole, sprinkled with tiny peas and baby carrots.

Other meat sensations spotlight a Spicy Sausage Pizza (page 159) with both Monterey Jack and Parmesan cheeses and a Garden Meat Loaf (page 148) strewn with coleslaw for only 176 calories a serving.

For menu help: check out our suggestions in Side Dish Savvy (page 140).

Beef and Broccoli Stir-Fry (page 142).

Bacon-Wrapped Filet with Bacon-Cheddar Mashed Potatoes

MAKES: 6 servings
PREP: 15 minutes
COOK: 15 minutes
BROIL: 8 to 10 minutes

Potatoes:

> **2¼ pounds Yukon Gold potatoes, peeled and cut into 1-inch pieces**
>
> **¾ cup fat-free half-and-half**
>
> **½ cup shredded reduced-fat cheddar cheese**
>
> **2 slices reduced-fat turkey bacon, cooked and crumbled**
>
> **½ teaspoon salt**
>
> **2 scallions, sliced**

Filets:

> **6 small filet mignon steaks (about 4 ounces each, about 1 inch thick)**
>
> **¼ teaspoon salt**
>
> **⅛ teaspoon black pepper**
>
> **2 teaspoons dried Italian herb seasoning**
>
> **3 slices reduced-fat turkey bacon**

1 Potatoes: Boil potatoes in water to cover in medium-size saucepan until fork-tender, about 15 minutes.

2 Coat broiler-pan rack with cooking spray. Heat broiler.

3 Filets: Season steaks with salt, pepper, and Italian seasoning. Cut bacon in half lengthwise; wrap a half around edge of each filet; secure with toothpick.

4 Broil 6 inches from heat 8 to 10 minutes, turning once, for medium-rare or longer for desired doneness. Remove to serving platter. Let stand 5 minutes.

5 Meanwhile, drain potatoes. Transfer to medium-size serving bowl. Add half-and-half; mash to desired consistency. Stir in cheddar, bacon, salt, and scallions. Serve with steaks.

Nutrient Value Per Serving: 308 calories, 8 g fat (3 g saturated), 32 g protein, 26 g carbohydrate, 3 g fiber, 596 mg sodium, 75 mg cholesterol.

Beef Tenderloin with Roasted Wild Mushroom Sauce

MAKES: 16 servings
PREP: 15 minutes
ROAST: at 425° for 45 minutes
COOK: 15 minutes

> **1 whole beef tenderloin (about 4 pounds), trimmed and tied for roasting**
>
> **1 teaspoon olive oil**
>
> **¾ teaspoon salt**
>
> **½ teaspoon black pepper**
>
> **2 cloves garlic, finely chopped**

Mushroom Sauce:

> **¾ pound assorted mushrooms, such as cremini, shiitake, and oyster, tough stems removed and caps sliced**
>
> **1 large shallot, finely chopped**
>
> **1 clove garlic, finely chopped**
>
> **2 tablespoons dry sherry**
>
> **2 tablespoons all-purpose flour**

1 can (14.75 ounces) beef broth

⅓ cup fat-free half-and-half

½ teaspoon chopped fresh tarragon
OR ¼ teaspoon dried

⅛ teaspoon salt

⅛ teaspoon black pepper

8 cups hot cooked egg noodles

1 Heat oven to 425°.

2 Rub meat with olive oil. Season on all sides with salt and pepper. Press chopped garlic onto all sides of meat. Place roast on rack in large roasting pan.

3 Roast about 45 minutes for medium-rare or longer for desired doneness. Remove roast from pan; let rest for 10 minutes in warm place, tented with foil.

4 Sauce: Meanwhile, heat large nonstick skillet over medium heat. Add mushrooms and shallot; cook, stirring frequently, until mushrooms release most of their liquid, about 10 minutes. Add garlic and sherry; cook 1 minute. Sprinkle flour over mushroom mixture; cook, stirring, 1 minute.

5 Gradually stir beef broth into mushroom mixture, scraping bottom of skillet. Bring to a boil; cook until sauce is thickened, about 1 minute. Stir in half-and-half, tarragon, salt, and pepper. Heat through. Remove from heat.

6 Remove string from tenderloin. Slice tenderloin. Pour mushroom sauce into gravy boat and serve with sliced tenderloin and ½ cup cooked egg noodles per serving.

Nutrient Value Per Serving: 347 calories, 12 g fat (4 g saturated), 36 g protein, 22 g carbohydrate, 1 g fiber, 324 mg sodium, 116 mg cholesterol.

Pepper Steak with Teriyaki Sauce

MAKES: 6 servings
PREP: 10 minutes
BROIL: 12 to 15 minutes
COOK: 10 minutes

1 boneless sirloin steak (1½ pounds)

1 to 2 teaspoons coarse black pepper

2 teaspoons olive oil

1 onion, chopped

1 sweet red pepper, cored, seeded, and cut into 1-inch-long slivers

½ pound white mushrooms, thinly sliced

½ cup bottled teriyaki basting sauce-and-glaze

1 tablespoon fresh lemon juice

2 to 3 tablespoons steak drippings and/or water

1 Heat broiler. Season steak with black pepper, pressing pepper into meat.

2 Broil steak 5 inches from heat for 12 to 15 minutes, turning over halfway through cooking, for medium or longer for desired doneness. Let stand 10 minutes. Reserve pan drippings.

3 Meanwhile, heat oil in nonstick skillet over medium heat. Add onion and red pepper; cook 3 minutes, stirring. Increase heat to high. Add mushrooms; cook until mushrooms release their liquid, about 6 minutes. Stir in teriyaki sauce, lemon juice, and pan drippings or water. Bring to a simmer. Remove from heat. Slice steak. Serve with sauce.

Nutrient Value Per Serving: 233 calories, 8 g fat (3 g saturated), 29 g protein, 11 g carbohydrate, 2 g fiber, 982 mg sodium, 75 mg cholesterol.

SIDE DISH SAVVY

With our range of lean entrées, all you need are a few side dishes to round out your menus. Here are five of our slim selections.

Moroccan Snap Peas and Carrots

MAKES: 6 servings

Bring 1 inch water to boiling in large skillet. Cut ½ pound peeled and trimmed carrots in half lengthwise; then cut diagonally crosswise. Add carrots to boiling water; cook 6 minutes. Stir in ½ pound sugar snap peas; cook 3 minutes or just until tender. Drain, leaving vegetables in skillet. Add 2 tablespoons salted butter, ¾ teaspoon ground ginger, 1 teaspoon ground cumin, ½ teaspoon curry powder, ½ teaspoon salt, and ¼ teaspoon black pepper to vegetables. Cook over medium heat, stirring, 3 minutes.

Nutrient Value Per Serving: 64 calories, 4 g fat (2 g saturated), 1 g protein, 7 g carbohydrate, 2 g fiber, 210 mg sodium, 10 mg cholesterol.

Sesame Broccoli

MAKES: 8 servings

Steam 1 pound broccoli flowerets (about 4 cups) and 1 medium-size sweet red pepper, cored, seeded, and cut into ¼-inch-wide strips, in steamer basket over ¾ inch water until crisp-tender, 5 to 7 minutes. Meanwhile, in small nonstick skillet, heat 2 teaspoons vegetable oil and 1 teaspoon dark Asian sesame oil over medium-high heat. Add 1 clove garlic, minced, and 1 piece (1 inch) fresh ginger, peeled and cut into thin slivers; stir-fry until fragrant, 30 seconds. Stir in 3 tablespoons reduced-sodium teriyaki sauce and 1 teaspoon fresh lemon juice; heat through. Toss steamed vegetables with sauce to coat. Garnish with 1 tablespoon toasted sesame seeds.

Nutrient Value Per Serving: 42 calories, 2 g fat (0 g saturated), 2 g protein, 5 g carbohydrate, 2 g fiber, 130 mg sodium, 0 mg cholesterol.

Sautéed Grape Tomatoes

MAKES: 6 servings

In medium-size bowl, toss together ½ pound yellow grape tomatoes, rinsed and each halved, ½ pound red grape tomatoes, rinsed and each halved, ¼ teaspoon dried herbes de Provence, ¼ teaspoon salt, and ⅛ teaspoon black pepper. Heat 1 tablespoon vegetable or olive oil in large nonstick skillet over high heat until hot. Add tomato mixture to skillet; cook over high heat until tomatoes just start to soften, about 2 minutes. Serve immediately.

Nutrient Value Per Serving: 36 calories, 3 g fat (0 g saturated), 1 g protein, 4 g carbohydrate, 1 g fiber, 104 mg sodium, 0 mg cholesterol.

Green Bean Packets

MAKES: 8 servings

Cook ¾ pound trimmed fresh green beans in medium-size pot of boiling water until crisp-tender, about 5 minutes. Drain. In medium-size bowl, toss beans with ⅛ teaspoon salt, ⅛ teaspoon black pepper, ¼ teaspoon dried Italian herb seasoning and 2 tablespoons grated Parmesan cheese. Heat oven to 425°. Spread 8 thin slices prosciutto onto a cutting board. Place 7 to 8 beans on each slice; roll up prosciutto to enclose beans. Transfer to large rimmed baking sheet. Bake in 425° oven for 15 minutes or until prosciutto is lightly crisped.

Nutrient Value Per Serving: 56 calories, 3 g fat (3 g saturated), 5 g protein, 3 g carbohydrate, 1 g fiber, 433 mg sodium, 11 mg cholesterol.

Sweet and Sour Cabbage

MAKES: 8 servings

Cook 4 slices turkey bacon in large nonstick pot over high heat until crisp, 5 minutes. Crumble bacon into small pieces and reserve. Heat 1 teaspoon vegetable oil in same pot over medium heat. Add 1 large onion, thinly sliced; cook, stirring frequently, until softened, about 10 minutes. Add 1 medium-size red cabbage (2 pounds), shredded; cook, stirring frequently, 10 minutes. Stir in ¾ cup apple cider, ¼ cup cider vinegar, 4 teaspoons sugar, ½ teaspoon salt, and 1 large McIntosh apple, peeled, cored, and cut into 1-inch pieces. Bring to a boil over high heat. Reduce heat to low; cover and simmer, stirring occasionally, until cabbage is softened, about 1 hour. Remove from heat; stir in bacon.

Nutrient Value Per Serving: 86 calories, 2 g fat (1 g saturated), 3 g protein, 16 g carbohydrate, 3 g fiber, 252 mg sodium, 6 mg cholesterol.

Wine-Marinated Grilled Sirloin

MAKES: 16 servings
PREP: 15 minutes
REFRIGERATE: 4 hours or overnight
GRILL: about 12 minutes

2 cups dry red wine

1 cup water

1 red onion, finely chopped

3 tablespoons Worcestershire sauce

2 teaspoons chili powder

1 teaspoon dried oregano

½ teaspoon liquid hot-pepper sauce

1 boneless sirloin steak (about 3 pounds), 1 inch thick

Chili-Horseradish Glaze:

3 tablespoons bottled chili sauce

2 tablespoons dry red wine

1 tablespoon bottled grated horseradish

½ teaspoon salt

1 Stir together wine, water, onion, Worcestershire, chili powder, oregano, and pepper sauce in medium-size bowl. Place steak in glass baking dish; pour marinade over top. Cover and refrigerate 4 hours or overnight.

2 Glaze: Combine chili sauce, wine, horseradish, and salt in small dish. Set aside.

3 Prepare grill with hot coals, or heat gas grill to high (see broiler method, below). Remove steak from marinade; discard marinade.

4 Grill steak 4 minutes. Turn over and grill 2 minutes. Spread glaze over top of steak. Grill 5 minutes for medium-rare or longer for desired doneness. Let meat rest 10 minutes before slicing thin.

Broiler Method: Heat broiler. Coat broiler-pan rack with cooking spray. Place steak on rack. Broil about 4 inches from heat for 4 minutes. Turn over; broil 2 minutes. Spread glaze over top of steak. Broil 5 minutes.

Nutrient Value Per Serving: 132 calories, 5 g fat (2 g saturated), 19 g protein, 1 g carbohydrate, 0 g fiber, 210 mg sodium, 56 mg cholesterol.

Steak Fajitas

MAKES: 8 servings (2 fajitas per serving)
PREP: 20 minutes
REFRIGERATE: 2 hours
BROIL OR GRILL: 12 to 15 minutes
COOK: 10 minutes

½ cup Worcestershire sauce

½ cup cider vinegar

½ teaspoon ground cumin

4 cloves garlic, finely chopped

1 teaspoon black pepper

1 teaspoon salt

½ teaspoon red-pepper flakes

1 flank steak (1½ pounds)

4 teaspoons chili powder

1 tablespoon vegetable oil

2 large sweet red peppers, cored, seeded, and cut into thin strips

2 medium-size onions, halved and thinly sliced crosswise

¾ pound white mushrooms, sliced

2 medium-size zucchini (1 pound), cut into matchsticks

16 (6-inch) corn tortillas, warmed following package directions

1 Combine Worcestershire, vinegar, cumin, garlic, black pepper, salt, and pepper flakes in plastic food-storage bag. Add steak; seal. Turn to coat. Refrigerate 2 hours.

2 Heat oven broiler, or prepare outdoor grill with hot coals, or heat gas grill to hot.

3 Drain marinade from steak into 2-cup measuring cup; add chili powder and oil.

4 Grill or broil meat for 12 to 15 minutes, turning once, for medium-rare or longer for desired doneness. Remove to cutting board; let stand 10 minutes.

5 Meanwhile, place large nonstick skillet over medium-high heat. Add marinade mixture; heat until sizzling. Add sweet red peppers and onions; cook 3 minutes. Add mushrooms and zucchini; cook 6 minutes or until softened.

6 Thinly slice steak across grain. Add steak to vegetables in skillet; toss to coat. Remove from heat. Use to fill tortillas, dividing equally.

Nutrient Value Per Serving: 310 calories, 10 g fat (3 g saturated), 23 g protein, 31 g carbohydrate, 5 g fiber, 313 mg sodium, 44 mg cholesterol.

Beef and Broccoli Stir-Fry

MAKES: 6 servings
PREP: 15 minutes
REFRIGERATE: 30 minutes
COOK: 20 minutes

1 small boneless sirloin steak (1 pound)

1 tablespoon cornstarch

1 tablespoon olive oil

1 large clove garlic, minced

1 teaspoon grated peeled fresh ginger

¼ teaspoon salt

⅛ teaspoon black pepper

1 bunch broccoli (about 1¼ pounds)

1 cup uncooked white rice

½ pound shiitake mushrooms, stems removed and caps cut into ¼-inch-thick slices

⅓ cup bottled teriyaki sauce

2 tablespoons salted cashews, chopped

1 Cut beef into ¼-inch-thick strips, about
2½ inches long. Combine with cornstarch, oil,
garlic, ginger, salt, and pepper in large bowl.
Cover and refrigerate 30 minutes.

2 Cut broccoli stalks from head. Peel stalks
to remove tough skin. Slice stalks ¼-inch
thick. Cut head into flowerets. Cook flowerets
and stalks in pot of boiling salted water for
2 minutes; drain; transfer to clean bowl.

3 Cook rice following package directions. When
almost cooked, coat large skillet with cooking
spray. Place over medium-high heat. Add
mushrooms; cook until wilted, about 5 minutes.
Add to broccoli.

4 Increase heat to high. Add beef to skillet; stir-
fry 2 to 3 minutes. Add broccoli, mushrooms,
and teriyaki sauce; heat through. Sprinkle with
cashews. Serve with rice.

*Nutrient Value Per Serving: 337 calories, 8 g fat
(2 g saturated), 24 g protein, 42 g carbohydrate,
4 g fiber, 789 mg sodium, 50 mg cholesterol.*

Curried Pepper Steak
with Sweet Potatoes

MAKES: 6 servings

PREP: 10 minutes

COOK: 20 minutes

1 pound beef top-round steak, cut across
grain into ¼-inch-thick slices

1¼ teaspoons salt

1¼ teaspoons curry powder

3 sweet green peppers, cored, seeded, and cut
into 1-inch pieces

1¼ pounds sweet potatoes (about 3 small),
peeled, quartered lengthwise, and cut
crosswise into ¼-inch-thick slices

1 large onion, halved and thinly sliced
crosswise

½ teaspoon ground ginger

⅛ teaspoon cayenne

¾ cup water

¼ cup bottled mango chutney

1 Coat large nonstick skillet with cooking spray.
Place over high heat. Season steak with ¼
teaspoon salt and ¼ teaspoon curry powder.
Add steak to skillet; brown, about 2 minutes
each side. Remove; keep warm.

2 Coat skillet again with cooking spray. Add
peppers, potatoes, and onion; sauté until onion
is softened, about 6 minutes. Add remaining
1 teaspoon curry powder, the ginger, cayenne,
and remaining 1 teaspoon salt; sauté 2 minutes.
Add water. Cover; cook 8 minutes or until
potatoes are tender; stir occasionally.

3 Add meat and chutney to skillet; cook until
heated through. Serve.

*Nutrient Value Per Serving: 244 calories, 3 g fat
(1 g saturated), 20 g protein, 34 g carbohydrate,
4 g fiber, 535 mg sodium, 47 mg cholesterol.*

Marinated Flank Steak with Pineapple Rice

MAKES: 6 servings
PREP: 5 minutes
REFRIGERATE: 2 hours or overnight
COOK: 20 minutes
BROIL OR GRILL: 10 minutes

Flank Steak:

3 tablespoons teriyaki sauce

3 tablespoons red-wine vinegar

2 tablespoons brown sugar

Juice from 8-ounce can pineapple chunks (reserve pineapple for rice, below)

½ teaspoon red-pepper flakes

1 flank steak (1½ pounds)

Pineapple Rice:

1 large shallot, finely chopped

1 tablespoon plus 1½ cups water

1 teaspoon salt

¾ cup basmati rice

¾ cup frozen green peas, thawed

Drained pineapple chunks from 8-ounce can, chopped

2½ tablespoons finely chopped pecans

¼ teaspoon cayenne

1 Flank Steak: Combine teriyaki, vinegar, sugar, pineapple juice, and pepper flakes in plastic food-storage bag. Add flank steak; seal; turn to coat. Refrigerate at least 2 hours or overnight.

2 Pineapple Rice: When ready to serve, coat 3-quart saucepan with cooking spray. Place over medium heat. Add shallot and 1 tablespoon water; cook until softened, about 4 minutes. Add remaining 1½ cups water and salt. Bring to a boil. Add rice; lower heat. Cover; simmer 15 minutes.

3 Meanwhile, heat oven broiler, or prepare outdoor grill with hot coals, or heat gas grill to hot.

4 Remove steak from bag; drain marinade into small saucepan.

5 Broil or grill steak 4 inches from heat 5 minutes each side for medium-rare or longer for desired doneness. Let steak stand 5 minutes; keep warm.

6 Meanwhile, bring marinade to a boil; boil 3 minutes.

7 When rice has finished cooking, stir in peas and pineapple. Heat through. Just before serving, stir in pecans and cayenne.

8 Thinly slice steaks across grain. Serve with marinade and rice.

Nutrient Value Per Serving: 348 calories, 12 g fat (4 g saturated), 28 g protein, 33 g carbohydrate, 2 g fiber, 829 mg sodium, 59 mg cholesterol.

Spicy Beef
in Lettuce Rolls

MAKES: 6 servings
PREP: 20 minutes
REFRIGERATE: 1 to 12 hours
BROIL: 6 minutes
COOK: 3 minutes

½ cup reduced-sodium soy sauce

2 tablespoons sugar

2 tablespoons rice vinegar

4 cloves garlic, finely chopped

4 teaspoons dark Asian sesame oil

¼ teaspoon red-pepper flakes

1½ pounds top-round steak for London broil
(1½ inches thick)

1 bunch scallions, trimmed

1½ cups bean sprouts

2 sweet red peppers, cored, seeded,
and thinly sliced

1 head Boston or leaf lettuce, trimmed

1 In large bowl, whisk together soy
sauce, sugar, vinegar, garlic, sesame
oil, and pepper flakes. Slice beef along
grain into 2-inch-wide strips. Add beef
to soy marinade. Cover and refrigerate
1 hour or up to 12 hours.

2 Cut scallions into 2-inch lengths.
Thinly slice each piece lengthwise.
Place scallions, bean sprouts, and sweet
red peppers in separate serving bowls.
Separate lettuce leaves; flatten core
ends slightly with side of broad knife,
if necessary. Place lettuce in separate
serving bowl.

3 Heat oven to broil. Transfer beef to broiler-pan
rack; pour marinade into small saucepan.

4 Broil beef 4 inches from heat for 3 minutes.
Turn beef over. Broil just until meat is slightly
pink in center, 2 to 3 minutes.

5 Meanwhile, bring marinade to a boil; boil
3 minutes. Pour into small serving bowl; let cool.

6 To serve, thinly slice beef strips on diagonal
and arrange on plate. To make rolls, arrange
a few pieces of beef and a few pieces of each
vegetable on a lettuce leaf; drizzle with a little
reserved marinade. Roll up, tucking in ends of
lettuce as you go. Eat rolls out of hand.

*Nutrient Value Per Serving: 225 calories, 7 g fat
(2 g saturated), 28 g protein, 11 g carbohydrate,
2 g fiber, 1,257 mg sodium, 71 mg cholesterol.*

Onion-Pepper Braciole

MAKES: 6 servings
PREP: 25 minutes
COOK: about 15 minutes
BAKE: at 350° for hour

6 pieces round steak (about 18 ounces total), pounded to ¼-inch thickness

½ teaspoon salt

¼ teaspoon black pepper

¼ teaspoon dried Italian herb seasoning

1 large onion, chopped

1 large sweet green pepper, cored, seeded, and chopped

Sauce:

2 large onions, thinly sliced

1 package (4 ounces) sliced fresh mushroom mix

4 cloves garlic, chopped

1 can (28 ounces) crushed tomatoes

¼ cup dry red wine

¼ cup water

½ teaspoon salt

¼ teaspoon red-pepper flakes

¼ teaspoon dried Italian herb seasoning

4½ cups hot cooked shaped pasta, such as rotini

1 Lay steaks out flat; season with salt, pepper, and Italian seasoning. Evenly distribute onion and green pepper over each steak. Roll up each steak from a narrow end. Tie at both ends with kitchen string.

2 Coat large nonstick skillet with cooking spray. Place over medium-high heat. Add meat; cook until lightly browned, about 2 minutes on each side. Remove to plate.

3 Heat oven to 350°.

4 Sauce: Coat large, deep heavy pot with cooking spray. Place over medium-high heat. Add onions; cook, stirring frequently to prevent scorching, until softened, about 6 minutes. Add mushrooms and garlic; cook 2 minutes, stirring frequently. Stir in tomatoes, red wine, water, salt, pepper flakes, and Italian seasoning. Bring to a simmer. Add meat braciole. Cover pot.

5 Bake braciole 60 minutes; turn meat over halfway through cooking.

6 Serve braciole with sauce and cooked pasta.

Nutrient Value Per Serving: 342 calories, 4 g fat (1 g saturated), 29 g protein, 47 g carbohydrate, 6 g fiber, 634 mg sodium, 53 mg cholesterol.

Picadillo with Rice

MAKES: 6 servings
PREP: 10 minutes
COOK: 40 minutes

   1 large onion, finely chopped

   2 cloves garlic, finely chopped

   1½ teaspoons ground cinnamon

   1 teaspoon dried oregano

   1 teaspoon ground cumin

   1 pound extra-lean ground beef

   1 can (14.5 ounces) recipe-ready diced tomatoes in juice

   2 tablespoons tomato paste

   ¼ cup dark seedless raisins

   ⅓ cup stuffed green olives, sliced

   ½ teaspoon salt

   3 cups hot cooked brown or white rice

1 Lightly coat large nonstick skillet with cooking spray. Place over medium heat. Add onion; cook until softened, about 3 minutes. Add garlic, cinnamon, oregano, and cumin; cook 30 seconds. Add beef; cook, stirring to break up clumps of meat, until beef is lightly browned, about 3 minutes.

2 Stir in tomatoes with juice, tomato paste, raisins, olives, and salt. Heat to a boil over medium-high heat, stirring occasionally. Lower heat; cover and simmer, stirring occasionally, for 30 minutes. Serve over rice.

Nutrient Value Per Serving: 301 calories, 9 g fat (3 g saturated), 20 g protein, 35 g carbohydrate, 4 g fiber, 619 mg sodium, 28 mg cholesterol.

Meat and Veggie Stir-Fry

MAKES: 6 servings
PREP: 10 minutes
COOK: 11 minutes

   ½ pound ground beef

   ½ pound ground pork

   2 cups snow peas, trimmed (12 ounces)

   1½ cups shredded peeled carrots

   3 medium-size ribs celery, cut into matchsticks

   1 sweet red pepper, cored, seeded, and cut into matchsticks

   ¾ cup bottled stir-fry sauce

   2 tablespoons water

   2 teaspoons reduced-sodium soy sauce

   3 cups hot cooked white rice

1 Coat wok or large nonstick skillet with cooking spray. Place over medium-high heat. Add beef and pork; stir-fry, leaving in chunks, until no longer pink, about 5 minutes. Remove meat to plate; keep warm.

2 Add peas, carrots, celery, and red pepper to wok; stir-fry 5 minutes or until crisp-tender. Mix in stir-fry sauce, water, and soy sauce. Return meat to wok; stir until heated through, about 1 minute.

3 Serve over hot cooked rice.

Nutrient Value Per Serving: 313 calories, 9 g fat (3 g saturated), 20 g protein, 37 g carbohydrate, 4 g fiber, 1,203 mg sodium, 37 mg cholesterol.

Garden Meat Loaf

MAKES: 8 servings
PREP: 10 minutes
COOK: 5 minutes
BAKE: at 350° for 1 hour

   1 teaspoon vegetable oil

   2 cups packed coleslaw mix

   1 pound extra-lean ground beef round or sirloin

   ½ pound lean ground pork

   3 large egg whites

   ½ cup packaged seasoned bread crumbs

   1 cup canned stewed tomatoes or crushed tomatoes

   1 teaspoon celery salt

   ¼ teaspoon black pepper

   Good Gravy (recipe follows)

1 Heat oven to 350°. Lightly oil 12 x 8 x 2-inch baking pan.

2 Place large nonstick skillet over high heat. Add oil; swirl to coat. Add coleslaw mix; brown well without stirring, about 3 minutes. Then cook, stirring, 2 minutes longer, adding 2 tablespoons water after 1 minute. Let cool slightly.

3 Crumble beef and pork into large bowl. Add browned vegetables, egg whites, bread crumbs, tomatoes, celery salt, and pepper. Gather together. Place in prepared pan. Shape into 10 x 5-inch loaf.

4 Bake for 1 hour. Carefully drain off drippings; reserve for Good Gravy (recipe follows). Let meat loaf stand 10 minutes before slicing.

Nutrient Value Per Serving: 176 calories, 7 g fat (3 g saturated), 18 g protein, 10 g carbohydrate, 1 g fiber, 574 mg sodium, 45 mg cholesterol.

Good Gravy: Melt 1 tablespoon butter in saucepan over medium heat. Stir in 2 tablespoons all-purpose flour; cook 1 minute (mixture will be dry). Stir in ¼ teaspoon each thyme and celery salt. Stir in 1¾ cups chicken broth and any degreased drippings reserved from Garden Meat Loaf. Cook, stirring, until slightly thickened and simmering, 1 to 2 minutes. Stir together ¼ cup dry white wine and 1 tablespoon cornstarch in cup until smooth. Add to gravy with 2 teaspoons soy sauce; stir until thickened and simmering, 1 to 2 minutes. Serve hot. Makes 2 cups.

Nutrient Value Per ¼ Cup: 37 calories, 2 g fat (1 g saturated), 1 g protein, 3 g carbohydrate, 0 g fiber, 342 mg sodium, 5 mg cholesterol.

Classic Ground Beef Tacos

MAKES: 8 servings (2 tacos per serving)
PREP: 15 minutes
COOK: about 15 minutes

   1 tablespoon olive oil

   1 medium-size onion, thinly sliced

   1½ pounds extra-lean ground beef

   1 tablespoon chili powder

   ¾ teaspoon salt

   ¼ teaspoon ground cumin

   ⅛ teaspoon cayenne

   1 can (8 ounces) tomato sauce

   16 (6-inch) white corn tortillas

1½ cups shredded iceberg lettuce

1 cup cherry tomatoes, each cut into quarters

½ cup shredded cheddar cheese

1 small onion, finely diced

½ cup bottled taco sauce

1 Heat oil in large nonstick skillet over medium-high heat. Add onion; sauté until onion is softened, about 3 minutes. Add beef; cook, stirring with wooden spoon to break up clumps, until beef is no longer pink, 5 to 7 minutes.

2 Add chili powder, salt, cumin, and cayenne; cook, stirring, 1 minute. Stir in tomato sauce. Bring to a boil. Lower heat to medium; cook 5 minutes, stirring occasionally.

3 Heat tortillas following package directions.

4 Serve warm tortillas with meat mixture (about ¼ cup per tortilla), lettuce, tomatoes, cheese, diced onion, and taco sauce.

Nutrient Value Per Serving (2 tacos):
297 calories, 12 g fat (4 g saturated), 19 g protein,
26 g carbohydrate, 4 g fiber, 593 mg sodium,
33 mg cholesterol.

Upside-Down Pizza

MAKES: 8 servings
PREP: 15 minutes
COOK: 12 minutes
BAKE: at 400° for 30 minutes

1 medium-size onion, chopped

1 sweet red sweet pepper, cored, seeded, and chopped

½ pound sweet or hot Italian-style turkey sausage, casings removed

1 pound extra-lean ground beef

¾ teaspoon dried Italian herb seasoning

¾ teaspoon garlic salt

1½ cups prepared tomato pasta sauce with mushrooms

1½ cups shredded part-skim mozzarella cheese

2 large eggs

1 cup nonfat milk

2 teaspoons olive oil

¼ teaspoon salt

1¼ cups all-purpose flour

2 tablespoons shredded Parmesan cheese

1 Heat oven to 400°. Coat 11 x 7 x 2-inch glass baking dish with cooking spray.

2 Coat large nonstick skillet with cooking spray. Place over medium-high heat. Add onion and red pepper; cook until softened, about 5 minutes. Add turkey sausage and ground beef; cook, breaking up clumps with a wooden spoon, until meat is no longer pink, 7 to 8 minutes. Remove skillet from heat. Stir in Italian seasoning, salt, and pasta sauce. Spoon into prepared baking dish. Sprinkle with mozzarella.

3 Whisk together eggs, milk, oil, and salt in medium-size bowl. Whisk in flour to form smooth batter. Spread batter over mixture in baking dish. Sprinkle with Parmesan.

4 Bake for 30 minutes or until top is lightly browned. Let cool 10 minutes before cutting into 8 servings.

Nutrient Value Per Serving: 335 calories, 13 g fat
(5 g saturated), 28 g protein, 25 g carbohydrate,
3 g fiber, 809 mg sodium, 104 mg cholesterol.

Pork Tenderloin with Mustard Sauce

MAKES: 6 servings
PREP: 10 minutes
MARINATE: 15 minutes
BROIL: 30 minutes
COOK: 7 minutes

5 tablespoons Dijon mustard

2 tablespoons dry white wine

½ teaspoon salt

¼ teaspoon black pepper

2 small pork tenderloins (about 1½ pounds total)

1 package (10 ounces) white mushrooms, sliced

1 small onion, chopped

1¼ cups milk

2 tablespoons all-purpose flour

1 Combine 2 tablespoons mustard, wine, ¼ teaspoon salt, and ⅛ teaspoon pepper in plastic food-storage bag. Add pork; seal; turn to coat. Marinate at room temperature for 15 minutes.

2 Heat broiler.

3 Broil pork 5 inches from heat 30 minutes, turning every 10 minutes, until lightly browned and cooked through.

4 Meanwhile, coat large skillet with cooking spray. Place over medium-high heat. Add mushrooms and onion; cook until onion is softened, about 5 minutes. In small bowl, stir together milk and flour until smooth. Stir in remaining 3 tablespoons mustard, salt, and pepper.

5 Return to heat; simmer, stirring, 2 minutes or until sauce is thickened. Remove from heat; keep warm.

6 Let pork stand 5 minutes. Slice and serve with mustard sauce.

Nutrient Value Per Serving: 291 calories, 16 g fat (5 g saturated), 29 g protein, 10 g carbohydrate, 2 g fiber, 595 mg sodium, 85 mg cholesterol.

Pork Adobo

MAKES: 8 servings
PREP: 5 minutes
REFRIGERATE: 4 to 12 hours
ROAST: at 450° for 1 hour
COOK: 20 minutes

3 large cloves garlic, finely chopped

1 cup water

½ cup distilled white vinegar

¼ cup soy sauce

⅛ teaspoon black pepper

1 center-cut boneless pork loin roast

4 cups hot cooked brown rice

6 cups steamed spinach

4 roasted sweet red peppers

8 wedges fresh pineapple, roasted if desired

1 In large bowl, combine garlic, water, vinegar, soy sauce, and pepper. Add pork roast, fat side up. Cover and refrigerate for at least 4 hours or up to 12 hours.

2 Heat oven to 450°. Place roast, fat side up, in roasting pan. Pour ¼ cup marinade into pan; pour remaining marinade into small saucepan.

3 Roast pork for 50 to 60 minutes, basting occasionally with marinade in roasting pan. If pan gets too dry, add ¼ cup water. Let pork stand 10 minutes before thinly slicing.

4 Meanwhile, bring marinade in saucepan to a boil; reduce heat and simmer for 20 minutes.

5 Drizzle sliced pork with warm marinade sauce. Serve with rice, spinach, red peppers, and pineapple.

Nutrient Value Per Serving: 348 calories, 10 g fat (3 g saturated), 32 g protein, 34 g carbohydrate, 6 g fiber, 610 mg sodium, 69 mg cholesterol.

Apricot-Glazed Pork Skewers with Cucumber Salad

MAKES: 8 servings
PREP: 15 minutes
BROIL: 6 minutes

Cucumber Salad:

- 1 tablespoon rice vinegar
- 2 teaspoons dark Asian sesame oil
- 1 teaspoon sugar
- ¼ teaspoon salt
- 1 large seedless cucumber
- 1 sweet red pepper, cored, seeded, and cut into matchstick-thin strips

Pork Skewers:

- ¾ cup apricot preserves
- 2 scallions, chopped
- 1 clove garlic, finely chopped
- 3 tablespoons Dijon mustard
- 1 tablespoon reduced-sodium soy sauce
- 1 teaspoon salt
- 1 teaspoon black pepper
- 2 pork tenderloins (about 1½ pounds total)

1 **Salad:** Whisk together vinegar, sesame oil, sugar, and salt in medium-size bowl. Peel cucumber. Run vegetable peeler lengthwise down cucumber to make long shavings. Add cucumber shavings and red pepper to dressing in bowl; toss to coat. Chill until ready to serve.

2 Heat broiler, or prepare outdoor grill with hot coals, or heat gas grill to hot.

3 **Pork Skewers:** Whisk together preserves, scallions, garlic, mustard, soy sauce, and ½ teaspoon each salt and pepper in small bowl.

4 Thinly slice pork on diagonal. Thread pork on 8 10-inch metal skewers. Season with remaining salt and pepper.

5 Broil or grill pork 6 inches from heat for 3 minutes per side, brushing with glaze. Transfer skewers to platter and serve with cucumber salad.

Nutrient Value Per Serving: 209 calories, 5 g fat (1 g saturated), 19 g protein, 23 g carbohydrate, 1 g fiber, 555 mg sodium, 50 mg cholesterol.

Moo Shu Pork

MAKES: 10 rolls
PREP: 20 minutes
COOK: about 17 minutes

- 1 tablespoon dark Asian sesame oil
- ¾ pound boneless pork chops, cut into thin strips (1½ x ⅛ x ⅛ inch)
- 3 large cloves garlic, minced
- 8 scallions, sliced
- 1 bag (8 ounces) shredded carrots
- 1 bag (10 ounces) shredded coleslaw
- ½ cup hoisin sauce, plus more for brushing tortillas
- 3 tablespoons reduced-sodium soy sauce
- 10 (6-inch) flour tortillas

1 Heat oil in large nonstick skillet over medium-high heat. Add pork and half the garlic; sauté until pork is cooked through, about 3 minutes. Transfer pork and garlic to medium-size bowl.

2 Wipe out skillet with paper toweling. Coat skillet with cooking spray. Place over medium-high heat. Add scallions, carrots, slaw, and remaining garlic; cook, stirring occasionally, 8 minutes or until vegetables are softened. Add hoisin sauce and soy sauce; heat through, about 2 minutes. Add pork; gently heat through, about 2 minutes.

3 Heat tortillas following package directions. Brush each with extra hoisin sauce. Spoon pork mixture down center of each. Roll up and serve.

Nutrient Value Per Roll: 231 calories, 9 g fat (2 g saturated), 11 g protein, 27 g carbohydrate, 2 g fiber, 728 mg sodium, 18 mg cholesterol.

Mustard-Dill Pork Chops with Pumpernickel Stuffing

MAKES: 4 servings
PREP: 15 minutes
BAKE: at 400° for 15 minutes
COOK: 10 minutes

4 boneless center-cut loin pork chops (1 pound), flattened to ½-inch thickness

¼ teaspoon salt

⅛ teaspoon black pepper

1 tablespoon Dijon mustard

1 tablespoon chopped fresh dill OR 1 teaspoon dried

1 teaspoon olive oil

1 clove garlic, finely chopped

1 tablespoon packaged unseasoned bread crumbs

Stuffing:

1 small onion, chopped

2 ribs celery, chopped

2 medium-size carrots, peeled and shredded

1 can (14.5 ounces) chicken broth

¾ teaspoon garlic salt

⅛ teaspoon black pepper

5 slices (1 ounce each) stale pumpernickel bread, cut into small cubes

1 Heat oven to 400°.

2 Season chops with salt and pepper. Place in baking dish.

3 Stir together mustard, dill, olive oil, and garlic in small bowl. Spread evenly over chops. Sprinkle evenly with bread crumbs.

4 Bake chops for 15 minutes or until cooked through. If desired, run under broiler until lightly browned, about 1 minute.

5 Stuffing: Meanwhile, coat large nonstick skillet with cooking spray. Place over medium-high heat. Add onion, celery, and carrots; cook, stirring frequently, until softened, about 8 minutes. Add chicken broth, garlic salt, and pepper. Bring to a boil. Lower heat; simmer 2 minutes. Remove from heat. Gently fold in the bread cubes. Cover; let stand 5 to 10 minutes. Fluff with fork before serving.

6 Serve each chop with 1 cup pumpernickel stuffing.

Nutrient Value Per Serving: 317 calories, 12 g fat (3 g saturated), 26 g protein, 27 g carbohydrate, 5 g fiber, 1,350 mg sodium, 59 mg cholesterol.

Pan BBQ Pork Chops

MAKES: 4 servings
PREP: 10 minutes
COOK: 30 minutes

4 center-cut boneless pork chops, ¾-inch thick
(1¼ pounds total)

½ teaspoon salt

⅛ teaspoon black pepper

1 large onion, sliced

2 small Italian frying peppers, cored, seeded,
and cut into matchsticks

2 zucchini, cut into matchsticks

½ teaspoon dried oregano

¼ teaspoon dried thyme

¼ cup prepared barbecue sauce

1 Coat large nonstick skillet with cooking spray.
Place over medium heat. Season both sides of
pork with salt and pepper. Place in skillet; lightly
brown, about 5 minutes per side. Remove from
skillet to plate.

2 Coat same skillet with cooking spray. Place
over medium heat. Add onion and frying
peppers; cook 1 minute. Add ¼ cup water; cook,
stirring, until softened, about 10 minutes.

3 Add zucchini, oregano, thyme, and barbecue
sauce to skillet; stir to combine. Return pork
chops to skillet. Cover and reduce heat to low;
cook 5 minutes. Uncover and cook 5 minutes or
until pork is cooked through.

*Nutrient Value Per Serving: 250 calories, 7 g fat
(3 g saturated), 30 g protein, 16 g carbohydrate,
3 g fiber, 494 mg sodium, 71 mg cholesterol.*

Pork 'n' Potato Kabobs

MAKES: 6 servings
PREP: 25 minutes
REFRIGERATE: 1 hour
MICROWAVE: 10 minutes
BROIL: 7 to 8 minutes

¼ cup reduced-sodium soy sauce

3 tablespoons roasted peanut oil

2 tablespoons red-wine vinegar

2 tablespoons fresh lemon juice

2 tablespoons Worcestershire sauce

1 tablespoon chopped fresh parsley

2 teaspoons dry mustard

1 teaspoon black pepper

1 center-cut boneless pork loin
(about 1½ pounds), cut into ¾-inch cubes

18 ounces small red-skin potatoes

Assorted grilled vegetables, for garnish
(optional)

1 Add soy sauce, oil, vinegar, lemon juice,
Worcestershire, parsley, mustard, and pepper
to plastic food-storage bag. Add pork; refrigerate
1 hour, turning frequently.

2 Place potatoes in microwave-safe dish. Add
water to ¼-inch depth; cover with plastic wrap,
venting on one side. Microwave at high power
(100%) for 10 minutes or until fork-tender. (Or
cook in saucepan of boiling water until fork-
tender.) Let cool. Cut potatoes in half.

3 Heat broiler. Coat broiler-pan rack with
cooking spray.

4 Remove pork from marinade; thread on
6 metal skewers (or rosemary branches),
alternating with potatoes. Baste with marinade.

5 Broil skewers 3 inches from heat 7 to
8 minutes or until lightly browned and cooked
through; halfway through cooking turn skewers
over and baste with marinade. Discard

remaining marinade, if any. Serve with grilled
vegetables if desired.

*Nutrient Value Per Skewer: 223 calories, 8 g fat
(2 g saturated), 25 g protein, 12 g carbohydrate,
2 g fiber, 165 mg sodium, 57 mg cholesterol.*

Beef and Pork Basics

Even though meat has gotten somewhat of a bad rep based on fat content, some lean cuts actually compare quite favorably to skinless chicken breasts and thighs and ground turkey. To keep yourself on the straight and narrow, incorporate the following choices—all of which appear in our recipes—into your daily menu planning. (All portions are based on a 3-ounce cooked serving, and the numbers are from the U.S. Department of Agriculture.)

	Calories	Total Fat (g)
Ground Beef (95% lean)	139	5.0
Pork Tenderloin	139	4.1
Top Beef Round	153	4.2
Top Beef Sirloin	166	6.1
Boneless Pork Loin Roast	168	7.0
Top Pork Loin Chop	173	6.6
Ground Beef (90% lean)	173	9.1
Beef Tenderloin (filet mignon)	175	8.1
Ground Beef (85% lean)	197	11.9
Skinless Chicken Breast	140	3.0
Skinless Chicken Thigh	178	9.2
Ground Turkey	200	11.2

- Look for the words "loin" or "round" in the name to select a lean cut of beef.

- Trim any visible fat before cooking.

- Cook less tender cuts, such as beef round, using a moist method like braising or stewing.

- Prepare the tender cuts such as tenderloin or ground meat using low-fat cooking methods, like broiling, pan-broiling, grilling, roasting, and stir-frying with a minimal amount of cooking oil.

- Use marinades to tenderize less tender cuts and add flavor. All marinades contain an acid ingredient, such as citrus juice, vinegar, wine, or tomato. You can add a little oil to help the liquid adhere to the meat, but it's not necessary. Figure about ¼ to ½ cup of marinade for each 1 to 2 pounds of meat. Always marinate in the refrigerator rather than at room temperature. Turn the meat occasionally so all sides get exposed to the marinade.

- Do not overcook lean meats. The USDA recommends the following temperatures as measured by an instant-read thermometer inserted into the thickest part: pork, all cuts including ground, 160°; beef steaks, roasts, 145° for medium-rare; ground beef, 160°.

Apple-Marinated Pork Tenderloin

MAKES: 8 servings
PREP: 20 minutes
REFRIGERATE: 4 hours or overnight
COOK: 6 minutes
ROAST: at 425° for 30 minutes

Pork:

1 can (6 ounces) frozen apple juice concentrate, thawed

¼ cup maple syrup

3 tablespoons cider vinegar

1 tablespoon Worcestershire sauce

1 teaspoon salt

½ teaspoon ground cinnamon

½ teaspoon black pepper

2 pork tenderloins (about 2 pounds total)

Roast Sweet Potatoes:

1 tablespoon olive oil

1½ pounds sweet potatoes, peeled, and cut into 1-inch chunks

4 Granny Smith apples (about 2 pounds), peeled, cored, and cut into 1½-inch chunks

1 large red onion, cut into 1-inch chunks

½ teaspoon salt

½ teaspoon dried sage

¼ teaspoon ground cinnamon

¼ teaspoon black pepper

Sauce:

1 tablespoon cornstarch

1 tablespoon water

1 Pork: In bowl, combine juice concentrate, maple syrup, vinegar, Worcestershire, salt, cinnamon, and pepper. Place in large plastic food-storage bag with tenderloins. Refrigerate 4 hours or overnight, turning occasionally.

2 Roast Sweet Potatoes: Place oil in roasting pan. Place pan in oven. Heat oven to 425°.

3 In large bowl, toss together sweet potatoes, apples, and onion. Sprinkle with salt, sage, cinnamon, and pepper; toss to coat. Carefully remove hot roasting pan from oven. Add sweet potato mixture; pan should sizzle. Return to oven. Roast 10 minutes.

4 Remove pork from marinade; reserve marinade. Coat large skillet with cooking spray. Place over medium-high heat. Add pork; sear both pieces of pork on all sides until nicely browned, about 6 minutes.

5 Once sweet potatoes have roasted for 10 minutes, place tenderloins on top. Roast pork and potatoes 20 minutes or until pork is cooked through and potatoes are tender. Remove from oven; let stand 5 minutes.

6 Sauce: Meanwhile, place reserved marinade in medium-size saucepan. Simmer 5 minutes. In small cup, stir together cornstarch and water. Stir into marinade. Gently boil 1 minute or until thickened.

7 Thinly slice pork across grain. Serve with sauce and sweet potato mixture.

Nutrient Value Per Serving: 348 calories, 6 g fat (2 g saturated), 26 g protein, 48 g carbohydrate, 5 g fiber, 519 mg sodium, 67 mg cholesterol.

Red Cabbage with Pork and Apples

MAKES: 6 servings
PREP: 15 minutes
COOK: about 40 minutes

1 tablespoon vegetable oil

1 onion, sliced

3 boneless pork chops (about ¾ pound total), sliced into 1½ x 1-inch strips

1 head red cabbage (2 pounds), thinly sliced

1 cup chicken broth

1 apple, cored, seeded, and cubed

¼ cup plus 2 tablespoons white-wine vinegar

½ teaspoon caraway seeds

¼ cup plus 2 tablespoons sugar

¾ teaspoon salt

⅛ teaspoon black pepper

1½ pounds all-purpose potatoes, peeled and sliced ½-inch thick

1 Heat oil in large nonstick skillet over medium heat. Add onion; sauté for 3 minutes. Add pork; sauté 2 minutes. Add cabbage; sauté until slightly wilted, about 7 minutes. Add chicken broth, apple, vinegar, caraway seeds, sugar, salt, and pepper. Cover; cook for 30 minutes, stirring occasionally.

2 Meanwhile, cook potatoes in pot of lightly salted simmering water until tender, 12 to 15 minutes. Drain; transfer to plate and keep warm.

3 Spoon potatoes on each of 6 dinner plates. Top with pork-cabbage mixture.

Nutrient Value Per Serving: 276 calories, 6 g fat (1 g saturated), 16 g protein, 42 g carbohydrate, 6 g fiber, 719 mg sodium, 29 mg cholesterol.

Pork Fried Rice

MAKES: 8 servings
PREP: 15 minutes
COOK: 35 minutes

1¼ pounds boneless pork chops, about ¾-inch thick

2 sweet green peppers, cored, seeded, and thinly sliced

1 medium-size red onion, thinly sliced

3 large eggs, lightly beaten

2 boxes (6.2 ounces each) fried-rice-flavored rice mix

1 tablespoon butter

1 can (8 ounces) sliced water chestnuts, drained

2 tablespoons reduced-sodium soy sauce

2 tablespoons hoisin sauce

1 teaspoon Asian chile paste

1 Coat large nonstick skillet with cooking spray. Place over medium-high heat. Add pork chops; cook 3 to 4 minutes per side or until cooked through. Cut chops into ½-inch cubes.

2 Wipe out skillet. Coat with cooking spray. Place over medium-high heat. Add sweet peppers and onion; stir-fry 6 to 7 minutes or until crisp-tender. Remove vegetables from skillet to bowl.

3 Wipe out skillet again. Coat with cooking spray. Add eggs; cook without scrambling until set, about 2 minutes. Remove egg disk to cutting board. Cut into thin strips.

4 Prepare rice mixture following package directions, using 1 tablespoon butter and 1 seasoning packet from rice mix. After 12 minutes, stir in reserved pork, vegetables, egg strips, water chestnuts, soy sauce, hoisin sauce, and chile paste; cook, stirring occasionally, until heated through, about 6 minutes. Serve.

Nutrient Value Per Serving: 325 calories, 9 fat (3 g saturated), 20 g protein, 41 g carbohydrate, 4 g fiber, 1,165 mg sodium, 119 mg cholesterol.

Spicy Sausage Pizza

MAKES: 6 servings
PREP: 15 minutes
COOK: 10 minutes
BAKE: at 425° for 10 minutes

½ pound hot Italian sausage links

1 ready-to-use thin crust Italian pizza bread shell (10 ounces)

1 can (8 ounces) tomato sauce

¾ teaspoon dried Italian herb seasoning

2 tablespoons grated Parmesan cheese

½ red onion, thinly sliced

½ sweet red pepper, cored, seeded, and thinly sliced

½ sweet green pepper, cored, seeded, and thinly sliced

2 ounces reduced-fat Monterey Jack cheese, shredded (about ¾ cup)

Fresh basil, for garnishing

1 Place oven rack in lowest position. Heat oven to 425°. Coat 12-inch pizza pan with cooking spray.

2 Cook sausage in nonstick skillet over medium heat for 10 minutes. Remove and let cool. Slice into thin rounds.

3 Place pizza crust on prepared pan. Spread with tomato sauce. Sprinkle with Italian seasoning and Parmesan.

4 Arrange sliced sausage, onion, and sweet peppers over sauce. Sprinkle shredded Jack cheese over pizza, leaving a 1- to 2-inch border around edge.

5 Bake on lowest rack for 10 minutes or until heated through. Garnish with fresh basil. To serve, cut into 6 slices.

Nutrient Value Per Serving: 245 calories, 10 g fat (4 g saturated), 14 g protein, 25 g carbohydrate, 2 g fiber, 779 mg sodium, 23 mg cholesterol.

New Potato and Lamb Casserole

MAKES: 8 servings
PREP: 20 minutes
COOK: about 12 minutes
BAKE: at 350° for 40 minutes

1 medium-size onion, chopped

1 pound ground lamb OR other ground meat

¾ teaspoon salt

2 cloves garlic, chopped

1 teaspoon chopped fresh rosemary OR
½ teaspoon dried

1 package (10 ounces) frozen tender tiny peas

1 package (10 ounces) frozen baby carrots

1 can (14.75 ounces) beef broth

Pinch cayenne

1¼ pounds small new potatoes with skins,
scrubbed and cut into ⅛-inch-thick slices

3 tablespoons cornstarch

3 tablespoons water

1 tablespoon grated Parmesan cheese

1 Heat oven to 350°. Coat shallow 2½-quart baking dish with cooking spray.

2 Coat large skillet with cooking spray. Place over medium heat. Add onion; cook until softened, about 5 minutes. Add ground lamb and ½ teaspoon salt; cook, breaking up clumps with wooden spoon, until no longer pink, about 3 minutes. Add garlic and rosemary; cook 2 minutes. Stir in peas, carrots, beef broth, remaining ¼ teaspoon salt, and the cayenne. Bring to a simmer.

3 Meanwhile, place sliced potatoes in medium-size saucepan. Cover with cold water and lightly salt. Bring to a boil; boil 2 minutes. Drain; let cool.

4 When lamb filling mixture begins to simmer, stir together cornstarch and water in small cup. Stir into lamb mixture; simmer until very thick, about 2 minutes. Remove from heat.

5 Spread one third of potato slices over bottom of prepared baking dish, reserving thinnest slices for top layer. Top with half the lamb filling mixture. Repeat layering with second third of potatoes and the remaining filling. Decoratively fan remaining thin potato slices on top. Sprinkle with Parmesan.

6 Bake for 40 minutes or until potatoes are knife-tender. Let cool 10 minutes before serving.

Nutrient Value Per Serving: 272 calories, 12 g fat (5 g saturated), 19 g protein, 21 g carbohydrate, 4 g fiber, 563 mg sodium, 56 mg cholesterol.

Marinated Rib Lamb Chops

MAKES: 4 servings
PREP: 5 minutes
REFRIGERATE: 2 hours
BROIL: about 10 minutes

3 tablespoons fresh lemon juice

2 tablespoons water

1 tablespoon extra-virgin olive oil

3 cloves garlic, chopped

Grated rind of 1 lemon

1 teaspoon dried herbes de Provence OR ½ teaspoon dried basil plus ½ teaspoon dried rosemary

½ teaspoon salt

½ teaspoon cracked black pepper

8 rib lamb chops (1 pound total)

2 large tomatoes, cut in half crosswise

1 Whisk together lemon juice, water, oil, garlic, rind, herbs, salt, and pepper in small bowl. Reserve 1 tablespoon to brush on tomato halves.

2 Place chops in shallow glass dish. Pour marinade over chops; turn to coat both sides of chops. Cover with plastic wrap and marinate in refrigerator for at least 2 hours; turn chops over a few times.

3 Heat broiler. Broil chops about 4 inches from heat for 3 minutes. Turn over; broil 3 or 4 minutes for medium-rare or longer for desired doneness. Remove chops from broiler. Let rest 5 minutes before serving.

4 Brush reserved marinade over cut side of tomatoes. Broil, cut sides up, for 3 to 4 minutes or until warmed through. Serve with the broiled chops.

Nutrient Value Per Serving: 160 calories, 9 g fat (2 g saturated), 16 g protein, 5 g carbohydrate, 1 g fiber, 123 mg sodium, 48 mg cholesterol.

Butterflied Leg of Lamb with Minted Bulgur Salad

MAKES: 12 servings
SOAK: 30 minutes
PREP: 10 minutes
REFRIGERATE: 1 hour
BROIL OR GRILL: lamb for 30 minutes

Minted Bulgur Salad:

4 cups boiling water

2 cups bulgur

⅔ cup fresh lemon juice

¼ cup olive oil

1 teaspoon ground cumin

1½ teaspoons salt

½ teaspoon black pepper

¼ teaspoon ground cinnamon

4 tomatoes (2½ pounds), halved, seeded, and diced

6 scallions, thinly sliced

½ cup chopped fresh mint

6 tablespoons chopped fresh parsley

Spiced Leg of Lamb:

4 cloves garlic, minced

2 tablespoons chopped fresh mint

2 tablespoons chopped fresh parsley

1 tablespoon grated lemon rind

1½ teaspoons salt

1 teaspoon ground cumin

½ teaspoon ground cinnamon

½ teaspoon black pepper

1 boneless leg of lamb (3 pounds), trimmed and butterflied

1 Minted Bulgur Salad: Pour boiling water over bulgur in medium-size heatproof bowl; let soak for 30 minutes. Strain in sieve; press bulgur gently with back of spoon to remove excess water.

2 Whisk together lemon juice, oil, cumin, salt, pepper, and cinnamon in medium-size bowl. Add bulgur, tomatoes, scallions, mint, and parsley. Cover and refrigerate.

3 Lamb: Heat broiler, or prepare outdoor grill with hot coals, or heat gas grill to hot. In small bowl, combine garlic, mint, parsley, lemon rind, salt, cumin, cinnamon, and black pepper. Rub over both sides of lamb.

4 Broil or grill lamb 6 inches from heat for about 15 minutes on each side for medium-rare or longer for desired doneness. Remove lamb from heat. Let stand 10 minutes before slicing.

Nutrient Value Per Serving: 308 calories, 12 g fat (3 g saturated), 27 g protein, 25 g carbohydrate, 6 g fiber, 654 mg sodium, 73 mg cholesterol.

9 DELICIOUS DESSERTS IN NO TIME

WE ALL KNOW THE FEELING: the urge, uncontrollable and ferocious, for something sweet. That's why there are forty-two luscious desserts on the *Eat What You Love & Lose* plan. Because no matter how disciplined you may be, the craving for sugar is natural. Our bodies need it, and as important, our emotions need it. To help ease the desire, make it a habit to reach for a piece of fruit every day. You'll be surprised at what a lift it gives.

In fact, many of our desserts are based on fruits because of their built-in sweetness. Our Whole Berry Cobbler (page 167) features honey-drenched blueberries—or for that matter, any berry—simmering under a crunchy crust; a cool orange filling tops a chocolate cookie bottom in our heavenly Orange Bavarian Tart (page 170); and slices of mango and strawberry adorn Lime Mini Tarts (page 173). You can enjoy four—yes, four!—of these little jewels for only 180 calories.

Can't tame a temptation for chocolate? No problem. Have a guilt-free slice of our Choco-Mocha Angel Food Cake (page 182). White chocolate and cocoa and espresso powder give it an absolutely sublime taste. For something chewier, indulge in one of the Chocolate-Walnut Squares (page 190), a decadent mix of chocolate chips, coffee, brown sugar, and sour cream.

Cookies make the list too. Everything from molasses and ginger (page 194) to brownies (page 187) to blondies (page 188). For something really irresistible, try Jumbo Island Cookies (page 192). Coconut, chocolate chips, and macadamias make these unforgettable, but a clever alchemy keeps them diet-smart.

Trim Toppers (page 175) offers a trio of suggestions for sauces that make a scoop of frozen yogurt taste even better. Yummm.

Choco-Mocha Angel Food Cake (page 182).

Strawberry Parfait

MAKES: 6 servings
PREP: 15 minutes
REFRIGERATE: 30 minutes or overnight

1 tablespoon unflavored gelatin

2 tablespoons orange juice

2 containers (8 ounces each) low-fat strawberry yogurt

2 cups frozen fat-free nondairy whipped topping, thawed

1 tablespoon grated orange rind

4 cups sliced fresh strawberries

2 tablespoons sugar

1 Sprinkle gelatin over juice in small cup; let stand until softened, 5 minutes. Place cup in small saucepan of simmering water; stir to dissolve gelatin.

2 Fold together yogurt, whipped topping, rind, and dissolved gelatin in bowl. Refrigerate 30 minutes or overnight.

3 Meanwhile, combine strawberries and sugar in large bowl. In 6 parfait glasses, layer equal amounts of berries and yogurt mixture; each glass should contain ⅔ cup berries and ⅔ cup mousse, total. Garnish with whipped topping, if desired.

Nutrient Value Per Serving: 169 calories, 1 g fat (0 g saturated), 5 g protein, 35 g carbohydrate, 3 g fiber, 56 mg sodium, 7 mg cholesterol.

Sweet-Tart Plums

MAKES: 6 servings
PREP: 15 minutes

2 medium-size black plums (about ½ pound total), pitted and sliced

2 medium-size red plums (about ½ pound total), pitted and sliced

4 sweet green or gold plums (about 1¼ pounds total), pitted and sliced

2 tablespoons honey

2 tablespoons cider vinegar OR other sweet vinegar

1 teaspoon sugar

Small pinch white pepper

1 In medium-size bowl, combine plum slices.

2 In small bowl, whisk together honey, vinegar, sugar, and pepper until smooth. Drizzle over plums. Serve immediately, or let stand, covered, for 1 hour to mellow flavors.

Nutrient Value Per Serving: 113 calories, 1 g fat (0 g saturated), 1 g protein, 28 g carbohydrate, 2 g fiber, 0 mg sodium, 0 mg cholesterol.

Whole Berry Cobbler

MAKES: 8 servings

PREP: 20 minutes

BAKE: at 350° for 30 minutes

¾ cup plus 2 tablespoons all-purpose flour

½ teaspoon baking soda

1 tablespoon confectioners' sugar

⅛ teaspoon salt

3 tablespoons unsalted butter, chilled

3 tablespoons liquid egg substitute

2 tablespoons low-fat (1%) milk

1½ tablespoons plus 1½ teaspoons granulated sugar

1 teaspoon ground cinnamon

¼ teaspoon crystallized ginger

1 teaspoon cornstarch

5 cups fresh blueberries

2 tablespoons honey

1 Heat oven to 350°. Coat 8 x 8 x 2-inch-square baking pan with cooking spray.

2 Combine flour, baking soda, confectioners' sugar, and salt in food processor; pulse to combine. Add butter; pulse until mixture resembles coarse meal. (Or, by hand, mix dry ingredients in medium-size bowl. Cut in butter with pastry blender or 2 knives held scissors fashion.)

3 Stir together egg substitute and milk in small cup; reserve 1 tablespoon. With food processor running, add egg-milk mixture to flour mixture and process until dough forms. Transfer to plastic wrap or plastic food-storage bag; flatten dough into disk; seal. Place in freezer while continuing with recipe.

4 Stir together the 1½ tablespoons sugar, cinnamon, ginger, and cornstarch in small bowl. Stir together berries and honey in large bowl; add sugar mixture; toss. Scrape into pan.

5 Remove dough from freezer. On well-floured surface, roll dough out to ¼-inch thickness. Cut diagonally across dough into ¾-inch wide strips. Arrange strips on top of berries. Brush with reserved egg-milk mixture. Sprinkle with the 1½ teaspoons sugar.

6 Bake for 30 minutes or until filling is bubbly and topping is browned. Serve warm, with fat-free nondairy whipped topping, if desired.

Nutrient Value Per Serving: 179 calories, 5 g fat (3 g saturated), 3 g protein, 32 g carbohydrate, 3 g fiber, 134 mg sodium, 12 mg cholesterol.

Berry Shortcake

MAKES: 8 servings
PREP: 20 minutes
BAKE: at 425° for 15 minutes

2 cups reduced-fat biscuit and all-purpose baking mix

¼ cup sugar

1 tablespoon grated orange rind

⅔ cup low-fat (1%) milk

2 teaspoons orange extract

3 cups assorted berries, such as raspberries, blueberries, and sliced strawberries

2 tablespoons all-fruit strawberry spread

1½ cups frozen fat-free nondairy whipped topping, thawed

Fresh mint sprigs, for garnish

1 Heat oven to 425°.

2 Stir together baking mix, sugar, and orange rind in large bowl. Stir in milk and 1 teaspoon orange extract until soft dough forms.

3 With lightly floured hands, press mixture into ungreased 9-inch-round cake pan.

4 Bake for 15 minutes or until toothpick inserted in center comes out clean. Remove cake to wire rack; let cool completely.

5 Meanwhile, prepare fruit: Reserve a few berries for garnish. Combine remaining berries, fruit spread, and remaining 1 teaspoon orange extract in large bowl. Let stand 15 minutes.

6 Carefully split shortcake horizontally in half with long serrated knife. Place bottom half, cut side up, on serving plate.

7 Cover with 1 cup whipped topping. Top with berries. Place top cake half, cut side down, on berries. Spoon remaining ½ cup whipped topping in center of shortcake. Garnish with berries and mint sprigs.

Nutrient Value Per Serving: 200 calories, 2 g fat (1 g saturated), 3 g protein, 40 g carbohydrate, 3 g fiber, 368 mg sodium, 1 mg cholesterol.

Fruit Crêpes

MAKES: 4 servings
PREP: 15 minutes
REFRIGERATE: 15 minutes

1 package (1 ounce) sugar-free, fat-free instant vanilla pudding

2 cups nonfat milk

4 tablespoons light pancake syrup

1½ cups sliced strawberries

1 cup blueberries

1 cup raspberries

4 ready-to-use refrigerated crêpes

½ cup all-fruit apricot spread

1 teaspoon confectioners' sugar, for serving

1 Stir together vanilla pudding, milk, and 2 tablespoons of light pancake syrup in small bowl. Refrigerate until thickened, about 15 minutes.

2 Combine strawberries, blueberries, raspberries, and remaining 2 tablespoons light pancake syrup in large bowl.

3 Place crêpes on individual serving plates. Spread one-fourth of pudding mixture into center of each crêpe. Top each with one-fourth of the berry mixture. Roll up, jelly-roll fashion.

4 Top each crêpe with 2 tablespoons all-fruit apricot spread. Sprinkle with confectioners' sugar.

Nutrient Value Per Serving: 199 calories, 1 g fat (0 g saturated), 6 g protein, 42 g carbohydrate, 5 g fiber, 456 mg sodium, 2 mg cholesterol.

One-Crust Fresh Peach Pie

MAKES: 10 servings
PREP: 20 minutes
BAKE: at 375° for 45 to 50 minutes

Peach Filling:

2½ pounds fresh peaches, peeled, pitted, and sliced (about 6 cups) OR 2 bags (20 ounces each) frozen peaches, thawed

1 cup fresh raspberries

⅔ cup sugar

3 tablespoons all-purpose flour

1 teaspoon ground cinnamon

1 teaspoon almond extract

Crust:

1 cup all-purpose flour

¼ teaspoon salt

3 tablespoons olive oil

3 to 4 tablespoons water

1 Heat oven to 375°. Coat 10-inch deep-dish pie plate with cooking spray.

2 Peach Filling: Gently fold together peaches, raspberries, sugar, flour, cinnamon, and almond extract in large bowl.

3 Crust: Toss together with a fork the flour, salt, and olive oil in medium-size bowl until mixture resembles coarse crumbs. Add water, a tablespoon at a time, tossing with fork until mixture forms a ball. Place ball between 2 sheets of waxed paper; flatten. Using a rolling pin, roll out into 11-inch round.

4 Spoon peach filling into prepared pie plate. Place crust on top; crimp edges. Cut 2-inch round hole in center.

5 Bake for 45 to 50 minutes or until filling is bubbly and crust is golden. If crust browns too quickly, tent crust with aluminum foil. Remove to wire rack; let cool.

Nutrient Value Per Serving: 187 calories, 4 g fat (1 g saturated), 2 g protein, 36 g carbohydrate, 3 g fiber, 59 mg sodium, 0 mg cholesterol.

Peaches and Cream Tart

MAKES: 10 servings
PREP: 20 minutes
BAKE: crust at 375° for 5 to 7 minutes
COOK: 3 minutes
REFRIGERATE: 2½ hours

Crust:

1½ cups graham cracker crumbs

6 tablespoons reduced-calorie margarine

1 teaspoon ground cinnamon

Filling:

¼ cup sugar

3 tablespoons all-purpose flour

1 envelope unflavored gelatin

¼ teaspoon salt

1½ cups nonfat milk

1 large egg

1 teaspoon vanilla extract

½ cup frozen fat-free nondairy whipped topping, thawed

2 medium-size ripe peaches, pitted and thinly sliced

2 tablespoons peach jam, melted

1 Heat oven to 375°.

2 Crust: Combine crumbs, margarine, and cinnamon in small bowl until blended. Press mixture over bottom and up sides of 9-inch tart pan with removable bottom.

3 Bake crust for 5 to 7 minutes or until lightly colored. Transfer tart pan to wire rack; let cool.

4 Filling: Stir together sugar, flour, gelatin, and salt in medium-size saucepan. Whisk in milk and egg. Cook over medium heat, stirring constantly, until mixture coats back of spoon, about 3 minutes. Do not boil or mixture may curdle; remove from heat. Stir in vanilla.

5 Place saucepan in large bowl filled with ice cubes and water. Refrigerate until mixture mounds when dropped from spoon, about 30 minutes. Fold in whipped topping. Spoon mixture into cooled crust. Refrigerate until firm, about 2 hours.

6 Arrange sliced peaches in concentric circles on top of tart. Brush with melted jam. Serve immediately.

Nutrient Value Per Serving: 163 calories, 6 g fat (1 g saturated), 4 g protein, 24 g carbohydrate, 1 g fiber, 279 mg sodium, 22 mg cholesterol.

Orange Bavarian Tart

MAKES: 10 servings
PREP: 15 minutes
BAKE: crust at 375° for 7 minutes
COOK: 8 minutes
REFRIGERATE: 2⅓ hours

Crust:

1½ cups chocolate graham cracker crumbs (about 11 boards)

6 tablespoons reduced-calorie margarine

Filling:

¼ cup sugar

3 tablespoons all-purpose flour

1 envelope unflavored gelatin

¼ teaspoon salt

1 cup low-fat (1%) milk

1 large egg

½ cup orange juice

1 teaspoon vanilla extract

½ cup frozen light nondairy whipped topping, thawed

3 navel oranges

1 Heat oven to 375°.

2 Crust: Combine chocolate graham cracker crumbs and margarine in small bowl until well blended. Press mixture over bottom and up sides of 9-inch tart pan with removable bottom (or use a 9-inch pie plate).

3 Bake crust for 7 minutes. Transfer tart pan to wire rack; let cool completely.

4 Filling: Stir together sugar, flour, gelatin, and salt in medium-size saucepan. Whisk in milk and egg. Cook over medium heat, stirring constantly, until mixture coats back of spoon, about 8 minutes. Remove saucepan from heat. Stir in orange juice and vanilla.

5 Place saucepan in large bowl filled with ice cubes and water. Refrigerate for 20 minutes or until mixture mounds when dropped from spoon. Fold in whipped topping. Spoon mixture into cooled crust. Refrigerate until firm, about 2 hours.

6 To serve: Cut peel from oranges. Cut oranges into segments, discarding membranes. Drain segments on paper toweling. Arrange segments on top of the tart around outer edge. Arrange a few segments in center. Serve tart immediately.

Nutrient Value Per Serving: 189 calories, 7 g fat (2 g saturated), 4 g protein, 29 g carbohydrate, 2 g fiber, 219 mg sodium, 23 mg cholesterol.

Pear Tart

MAKES: 10 servings
PREP: 10 minutes
BAKE: at 400° for 40 minutes

1 refrigerated ready-to-use folded pie crust

1 large egg white, lightly beaten

1 cup fat-free sour cream

2 large eggs

¼ cup granulated sugar

½ teaspoon vanilla extract

2 tablespoons light brown sugar

2 tablespoons cake crumbs OR graham cracker crumbs

2 teaspoons butter

2 ripe pears

1 Place baking sheet in oven. Heat oven to 400°.

2 Unfold pie crust; ease into 9-inch tart pan with removable bottom. Trim overhang to fit. Brush bottom with egg white.

3 Stir together sour cream, eggs, granulated sugar, and vanilla in small bowl. Crumble together brown sugar, crumbs, and butter in second small bowl.

4 Peel, halve, and core pears. Cut lengthwise into ¼-inch-thick slices. Arrange slices in crust in 2 concentric rings, overlapping slightly.

5 Pour sour cream mixture over pears. Sprinkle with crumb topping.

6 Bake tart on heated baking sheet for 40 minutes or until cream is set and top is lightly golden.

Nutrient Value Per Serving: 199 calories, 8 g fat (3 g saturated), 4 g protein, 28 g carbohydrate, 1 g fiber, 127 mg sodium, 51 mg cholesterol.

Very Berry Tart

MAKES: 8 servings
PREP: 20 minutes
BAKE: at 425° for 10 minutes
COOK: 4 minutes

¼ cup pecans

¾ cup all-purpose flour

2 tablespoons sugar

¼ teaspoon salt

3 tablespoons vegetable oil

1 teaspoon low-fat (1%) milk

2 ounces semisweet chocolate

6 strawberries, hulled and halved lengthwise

½ cup blueberries

1 cup raspberries

2 tablespoons strawberry jelly

1 teaspoon water

1 Heat oven to 425°.

2 Place pecans in food processor; pulse until ground. Add flour, sugar, and salt. Pulse to combine. With processor running, add oil; pulse until oil is incorporated. Add milk; pulse until dough forms.

2 Press dough over bottom and up sides of 9-inch tart pan with removable bottom. If dough is too soft, chill to firm, about 30 minutes.

3 Bake for 10 minutes or until lightly colored. Let cool on wire rack.

4 Melt chocolate in glass measuring cup in microwave oven following manufacturer's directions, or place cup in saucepan of simmering water. Spread chocolate evenly over bottom of cooled tart shell. Arrange strawberries, cut side down, in decorative pattern over chocolate. Surround strawberries with blueberries. Fill in remaining open areas with raspberries.

5 Melt jelly with water in small saucepan. Brush glaze over berries. Let set, about 5 minutes.

Nutrient Value Per Serving: 191 calories, 10 g fat (2 g saturated), 2 g protein, 25 g carbohydrate, 3 g fiber, 77 mg sodium, 0 mg cholesterol.

Coconut Dream Pie

MAKES: 12 servings
PREP: 30 minutes
BAKE: at 425° for 10 to 11 minutes
COOK: 8 minutes
REFRIGERATE: 2 hours

1½ cups corn flake crumbs

5 tablespoons butter, melted

1 tablespoon honey

¼ cup granulated sugar

¼ cup cornstarch

1 envelope unflavored gelatin

1 can (about 11.8 ounces) sweetened coconut milk

1 teaspoon coconut extract

1 container (8 ounces) frozen light nondairy whipped topping, thawed

3 tablespoons sweetened flaked coconut, toasted

1 Heat oven to 425°.

2 Stir together corn flake crumbs, melted butter, honey, and 1 tablespoon of the sugar in medium-size bowl. Press crumb mixture evenly over bottom and up sides of 10-inch round pie plate.

3 Bake crust for 10 to 11 minutes or until slightly golden around edges. Remove pie plate to wire rack; let cool.

4 Meanwhile, stir together remaining 3 tablespoons sugar, cornstarch, and gelatin in medium saucepan. Stir in coconut milk. Cook over medium heat until thickened, clear, and bubbly, 8 minutes. Stir in extract. Let cool to room temperature, about 15 minutes.

5 Once cooled, fold in whipped topping. Spread filling evenly in prepared pie shell. Garnish with toasted coconut. Refrigerate 2 hours or until set.

Nutrient Value Per Serving: 180 calories, 8 g fat (6 g saturated), 2 g protein, 25 g carbohydrate, 0 g fiber, 115 mg sodium, 13 mg cholesterol.

Lime Mini Tarts

MAKES: 45 mini tarts
PREP: 15 minutes
COOK: 6 minutes
REFRIGERATE: 2 hours or up to 6 hours

Lime Curd Filling:

3 large eggs

¾ cup sugar

½ teaspoon ground ginger

½ cup fresh lime juice

1 tablespoon grated lime rind

Tart Shells and Garnish:

3 packages (2.1 ounces each) mini phyllo pastry shells (15 baked shells per package, 45 shells total)

1 firm-ripe mango, peeled, pitted, sliced and cut into 1 x ¼-inch pieces

1 cup sliced strawberries

1 Lime Curd: In heavy-bottom medium-size saucepan, whisk together eggs, sugar, ginger, and lime juice. Cook over medium heat, whisking constantly, just until boiling and mixture is thickened, about 6 minutes (mixture should register 160° on instant-read thermometer). Transfer to medium-size bowl; stir in lime rind. Cover surface with plastic wrap; refrigerate 2 hours or until chilled.

2 Tart Shells and Garnish: Spoon 1½ teaspoons Lime Curd into each phyllo shell; top with piece of mango and strawberry slice. Serve immediately or refrigerate up to 4 hours. Garnish with additional grated lime rind, if desired.

Nutrient Value Per Mini Tart: 45 calories, 1 g fat (0 g saturated), 1 g protein, 7 g carbohydrate, 0 g fiber, 14 mg sodium, 14 mg cholesterol.

Mocha Sorbet

MAKES: 12 servings
PREP: 5 minutes
COOK: 5 minutes
FREEZE: 5 hours

4 cups water

1 cup sugar

½ cup light corn syrup

¾ cup unsweetened cocoa powder

1 tablespoon instant espresso powder

2 squares (1 ounce each) semisweet chocolate, chopped

1 Combine water, sugar, corn syrup, cocoa powder, espresso powder, and chocolate in medium-size saucepan. Simmer until sugar dissolves, about 5 minutes.

2 Pour into 13 x 9 x 2-inch metal baking pan. Place in freezer for 2½ hours or until partially frozen.

3 Working in batches, spoon chocolate mixture into food processor or blender. Process 1 minute or until smooth; do not overprocess. Pour back into baking pan. Freeze 1 hour.

4 Repeat Step 3. Freeze for 1½ hours or until firm.

Nutrient Value Per Serving: 140 calories, 2 g fat (1 g saturated), 1 g protein, 33 g carbohydrate, 3 g fiber, 20 mg sodium, 0 mg cholesterol.

Cinnamon Coffee Custard

MAKES: 10 servings
PREP: 20 minutes
BAKE: at 350° for 35 minutes
REFRIGERATE: 4 hours or overnight

3 cups low-fat (1%) milk

1 cup brewed coffee, cooled

2 tablespoons instant coffee powder

½ teaspoon ground cinnamon

3 large whole eggs

3 large egg whites

½ cup sugar

¼ teaspoon salt

1 Heat oven to 350°.

2 Heat milk, coffee, instant coffee powder, and cinnamon in heavy-bottom 2-quart saucepan over medium heat just until bubbles form around edge of pan. Remove from heat; let cool slightly.

3 Beat together whole eggs and egg whites in large bowl until blended. Beat in sugar and salt until blended. Gradually stir in hot milk mixture. Pour into ten 6-ounce custard cups. Place custard cups in 13 x 9 x 2-inch baking pan and 8 x 8 x 2-inch square baking pan. Place pans on oven rack. Fill pans with hot water to come halfway up sides of cups.

4 Bake for 35 minutes or until knife inserted in centers comes out clean. Remove cups from water.

5 Refrigerate, covered, to chill, 4 hours or overnight. Garnish with thawed frozen light nondairy whipped topping and coffee beans, if desired.

Nutrient Value Per Serving: 103 calories, 2 g fat (1 g saturated), 6 g protein, 15 g carbohydrate, 0 g fiber, 134 mg sodium, 68 mg cholesterol.

TRIM TOPPERS

Frozen yogurt is a terrific dessert option, and our slimmed-down toppings make a scoop even more special. Start with a ½ cup serving of nonfat frozen yogurt for about 80 calories, then spoon on one of these treats—and still stay below a 200 calorie tally.

Cinnamon-Berry

MAKES: 4 servings (1½ cups total)

In small saucepan, combine 1 pound strawberries, rinsed, hulled, and quartered, 2 tablespoons sugar, 1 tablespoon butter, 1 tablespoon lemon juice, and ½ teaspoon ground cinnamon. Bring to a boil over medium heat; cover and cook 3 minutes, breaking up berries with a spoon. Remove from heat. Spoon about ⅓ cup over frozen yogurt. Top with a total of 2 tablespoons toasted shredded coconut.

Nutrient Value Per Serving (with coconut): 98 calories, 4 g fat (3 g saturated), 1 g protein, 16 g carbohydrate, 9 mg sodium, 8 mg cholesterol.

Choco-Berry

MAKES: 6 servings (1½ cups total)

In food processor, puree two 6-ounce containers fresh raspberries with ¼ cup packed brown sugar. Force through sieve into small saucepan. Add 3 tablespoons mini semisweet chocolate chips. Heat over medium heat, stirring until chocolate is melted. Remove from heat. Stir in another 6-ounce container raspberries. Spoon ¼ cup over frozen yogurt.

Nutrient Value Per Serving: 101 calories, 2 g fat (1 g saturated), 1 g protein, 22 g carbohydrate, 4 mg sodium, 0 mg cholesterol.

Minty Fudge

MAKES: 6 servings (⅔ cup total)

In small saucepan over medium-low heat, heat ¼ cup fat-free half-and-half, 1 tablespoon butter, 3 tablespoons granulated sugar, ¼ cup packed brown sugar, ¼ cup unsweetened cocoa powder, and 1 ounce semisweet chocolate, stirring, until smooth and sugars are melted, about 8 minutes. Remove from heat. Stir in ¼ teaspoon mint extract. Spoon about 2 tablespoons over frozen yogurt.

Nutrient Value Per Serving: 115 calories, 4 g fat (2 g saturated), 1 g protein, 21 g carbohydrate, 15 mg sodium, 5 mg cholesterol.

Irish Pots de Crème

MAKES: 6 servings
PREP: 15 minutes
BAKE: at 325° for 35 minutes
REFRIGERATE: 3 hours or overnight

6 large egg yolks

¼ cup sugar

1¾ cups milk

¼ cup Irish cream liqueur

½ teaspoon vanilla extract

⅛ teaspoon ground nutmeg

1 Heat oven to 325°.

2 Whisk together egg yolks and sugar in medium-size bowl until mixture is well blended. Heat milk gently in small saucepan just until it reaches simmering. Remove saucepan from heat.

3 Whisk small amount of hot milk into yolk mixture; then whisk yolk mixture into hot milk in saucepan. Stir in liqueur and vanilla. Pour milk mixture through fine-mesh sieve into 4-cup glass measure to remove any cooked pieces of egg.

4 Pour milk mixture into six 4-ounce ramekins or custard cups, dividing equally. Sprinkle tops of custards with nutmeg.

5 Place ramekins in 9 x 9 x 2-inch baking dish. Place baking dish on middle rack in oven. Carefully pour enough hot water, about 4 cups, into baking dish to come halfway up the sides of ramekins.

6 Bake for 35 minutes or until centers are just set. Remove baking dish from oven; remove ramekins from water bath to wire racks. Refrigerate until thoroughly chilled, 3 hours or overnight.

Nutrient Value Per Serving: 170 calories, 9 g fat (4 g saturated), 5 g protein, 14 g carbohydrate, 0 g fiber, 52 mg sodium, 224 mg cholesterol.

Ginger Cupcakes

MAKES: 12 cupcakes
PREP: 15 minutes
BAKE: at 350° for 20 to 25 minutes

1½ cups all-purpose flour

⅓ cup granulated sugar

⅓ cup packed light-brown sugar

3 tablespoons finely chopped candied ginger

1½ teaspoons ground cinnamon

1¼ teaspoons baking powder

½ teaspoon ground cloves

½ teaspoon salt

¼ cup light molasses

¼ cup Prune Puree (recipe follows) OR bottled prune puree

¼ cup low-fat (1%) milk

3 tablespoons olive oil

2 large egg whites

1 large whole egg

1 Heat oven to 350°. Line twelve 2½-inch muffin-pan cups with paper cupcake liners.

2 Stir together flour, granulated sugar, brown sugar, ginger, cinnamon, baking powder, cloves, and salt in medium-size bowl.

3 Whisk together molasses, prune puree, milk, olive oil, egg whites, and whole egg in large bowl. Fold in flour mixture just until moistened. Spoon batter into muffin-pan cups, dividing equally.

4 Bake for 20 to 25 minutes or until toothpick inserted in centers comes out clean. Remove cupcakes to wire racks; let cool completely.

Nutrient Value Per Cupcake: 178 calories, 4 g fat (1 g saturated), 3 g protein, 33 g carbohydrate, 1 g fiber, 173 mg sodium, 18 mg cholesterol.

Prune Puree

MAKES: 2 cups puree

Puree ½ pound (1⅓ cups) pitted prunes and 1¼ cups water in food processor, about 1 minute. Refrigerate for up to 2 months.

Nutrient Value Per ¼ cup: 64 calories, 0 g fat (0 g saturated), 1 g protein, 17 g carbohydrate, 2 g fiber, 2 mg sodium, 0 mg cholesterol.

Tiramisu

MAKES: 4 servings
PREP: 10 minutes
REFRIGERATE: 1 hour

6 ounces fat-free cream cheese, at room temperature

¼ cup confectioners' sugar

2 tablespoons unsweetened cocoa powder

2 tablespoons low-fat (1%) milk

½ teaspoon ground cinnamon

1 teaspoon vanilla extract

½ cup frozen nondairy nonfat whipped topping, thawed

8 ladyfingers, split into 16 halves

½ cup strong black coffee

1 square (1 ounce) semisweet chocolate, grated

1 Beat together cream cheese, confectioners' sugar, cocoa powder, milk, cinnamon, and vanilla in medium-size bowl until smooth. Fold in ¼ cup of whipped topping.

2 Place 2 ladyfinger halves in bottom of dessert glass. Brush with 1 tablespoon strong black coffee. Top with 2 tablespoons cream cheese mixture, spreading evenly with back of spoon. Top with 2 more ladyfinger halves, coffee, and cheese mixture. Dollop with 1 tablespoon whipped topping. Repeat with remaining ladyfinger halves, coffee, cheese mixture, and whipped topping to make 3 more desserts. Sprinkle chocolate equally over each. Refrigerate at least 1 hour before serving.

Nutrient Value Per Serving: 181 calories, 4 g fat (2 g saturated), 9 g protein, 27 g carbohydrate, 2 g fiber, 263 mg sodium, 56 mg cholesterol.

The Lowdown on Low-Fat Baking

Yes, you can have your cake and eat it, too! While fat, an essential ingredient in baked goods, carries flavor and creates texture, there are a few cheats that you can use to keep desserts under control.

- In cheesecakes, replace some of the cream cheese with pureed cottage cheese and light cream cheese. Just experiment with different proportions until you're pleased. Use low-fat granola to make the crusts and fruit spreads for a glaze. Stir in unsweetened cocoa powder—low in fat—to add chocolate-y oomph.

- Choose ingredients that signal "richness." For instance, bananas or caramel are often paired with rich treats such as cream pie or custard. Pour a little caramel over low-fat frozen yogurt or vanilla pudding, and your taste buds will fill in the missing fat.

- Consider using fruit purees as a fat replacement. Mashed bananas, applesauce, or prune and other fruit purees can replace at least part of the fat in recipes. They ensure moist, light texture in baked goods— from breakfast breads to brownies. You do the math: a cup of butter holds about 180 grams of fat and 1,600 calories; a cup of applesauce, no fat and 100 calories. You can buy a bottled version of prune puree, sometimes called lekvar, or you can make your own (recipe, page 177). Though there are no hard-and-fast rules for substituting fruit for butter, oil, or other fats, here are a few general guidelines for using fruit purees when it comes to baking.

  1. Start by switching a puree for half the butter called for in a recipe. In some cases you can use a puree for all the fat; this is a trial and error process.

  2. Use cake flour (not self-rising) for some or all of the regular flour. Because fruit purees tend to be dense, using the finer flour results in a lighter product.

  3. When you cut fat, you need to increase the amount of sugar to improve texture. Start by adding ¼ cup more sugar per recipe, then more as desired. But keep in mind that additional sugar means additional calories.

  4. Buttermilk, yogurt, and low-fat sour cream can be substituted for the liquid in the recipe, resulting in a more tender product.

  5. Increase the amount of spices and other flavorings to compensate for the lack of fat, which carries flavor.

Cappuccino Cupcakes

MAKES: 18 cupcakes
PREP: 10 minutes
BAKE: at 350° for 17 to 20 minutes

2 cups all-purpose flour

1½ cups sugar

½ cup unsweetened cocoa powder

1 teaspoon baking soda

½ teaspoon salt

½ cup bottled prune puree OR
Prune Puree (see page 177)

¼ cup vegetable oil

2 large eggs

¼ cup instant espresso powder, dissolved
in ½ cup warm water

2 teaspoons vanilla extract

1½ cups frozen light nondairy whipped
topping, thawed

1 teaspoon unsweetened cocoa powder,
for dusting

1 Heat oven to 350°. Lightly coat 18 standard-size muffin-pan cups with cooking spray.

2 Whisk together flour, sugar, cocoa powder, baking soda, and salt in small bowl.

3 Stir together prune puree, oil, eggs, dissolved espresso powder, and vanilla in large bowl. Stir in flour mixture until blended. Spoon batter evenly into prepared muffin cups, filling each cup about halfway full.

4 Bake for 17 to 20 minutes or until tops spring back when lightly touched. Let cupcakes cool in pan for 3 minutes. Turn cupcakes out onto wire rack; let cool completely.

5 Just before serving, frost each cupcake with a tablespoonful of whipped topping. Dust with cocoa powder through fine-mesh sieve.

Nutrient Value Per Cupcake: 180 calories, 5 g fat (1 g saturated), 3 g protein, 32 g carbohydrate, 1 g fiber, 143 mg sodium, 24 mg cholesterol.

Chocolate Peppermint Frappe

MAKES: 4 servings
PREP: 5 minutes

3 small round peppermint candies
(¾ ounce total)

4 ice cubes, crushed

1½ cups frozen nonfat coffee yogurt OR
frozen nonfat chocolate yogurt

2 cups cold nonfat milk

¼ cup chocolate syrup

Peppermint sticks, for garnish (optional)

1 Whirl candies in blender until pulverized fine. Add crushed ice, frozen coffee yogurt, milk, and chocolate syrup. Pulse until mixture is thick and smooth.

2 Pour into 4 chilled tall glasses and serve. Garnish each drink with a peppermint stick, if desired.

Nutrient Value Per Serving: 193 calories, 1 g fat (1 g saturated), 9 g protein, 38 g carbohydrate, 2 g fiber, 120 mg sodium, 3 mg cholesterol.

Apple-Spice Bundt Cake

MAKES: 16 slices
PREP: 15 minutes
BAKE: at 400° for 30 to 35 minutes

1¼ cups all-purpose flour

1 cup whole-wheat flour

1 teaspoon baking soda

½ teaspoon ground cinnamon

¼ teaspoon ground nutmeg

2 large egg whites

½ cup packed light-brown sugar

1 jar (16 ounces) applesauce

2 tablespoons canola oil

1 apple, peeled, cored, and chopped

½ cup golden seedless raisins

¼ cup walnuts, chopped

1 Heat oven to 400°. Coat 6-cup bundt pan with cooking spray.

2 Stir together all-purpose flour, whole-wheat flour, baking soda, cinnamon, and nutmeg in large bowl.

3 Beat together egg whites, brown sugar, applesauce, and oil in separate bowl until well blended. Fold egg white mixture into flour mixture along with apple, raisins, and walnuts until combined. Scrape batter into prepared pan.

4 Bake 30 to 35 minutes or until toothpick comes out clean. Transfer pan to wire rack; let cool 10 minutes. Unmold cake onto rack; let cool.

Nutrient Value Per Slice: 144 calories, 3 g fat (0 g saturated), 3 g protein, 28 g carbohydrate, 2 g fiber, 90 mg sodium, 0 mg cholesterol.

Angelic Chocolate Cupcakes

MAKES: 24 mini cupcakes
PREP: 20 minutes
BAKE: at 350° for 15 to 20 minutes

⅓ cup all-purpose flour

3 tablespoons unsweetened cocoa powder

¼ teaspoon ground cinnamon

5 large egg whites

½ teaspoon cream of tartar

¾ cup superfine sugar

Topping:

¼ cup semisweet chocolate chips

3 tablespoons heavy cream

1 Heat oven to 350°.

2 Into medium-size bowl, sift together flour, cocoa powder, and cinnamon.

3 In large bowl, beat together whites and cream of tartar on medium-high speed until frothy peaks form. Gradually beat in sugar, 1 tablespoon at a time, until shiny stiff peaks form, about 5 minutes.

4 Sift half the flour mixture over beaten egg whites; gently fold in. Repeat 2 more times, until all the flour mixture is incorporated. Spoon into large pastry bag without a tip on end. Or spoon into large plastic food-storage bag; snip off one corner.

5 Pipe egg white mixture up to tops of indentations in two 12-cup mini cupcake pans.

6 Bake until dry to touch and puffy, 15 to 20 minutes. Transfer pans to wire racks; let cool in pans. Gently pull edge of cupcakes from sides of cups. Remove cupcakes and transfer to wire rack.

7 Topping: Heat together chocolate chips and heavy cream in microwave-safe bowl at high power for 1 minute, or in small saucepan over low heat. Stir until smooth, using whisk, if necessary.

8 Carefully dip tops of cupcakes into topping, scraping off excess. Set mini cupcakes upright on waxed paper. Let stand until set. Keep refrigerated in airtight container for up to 1 week.

Nutrient Value Per Mini Cupcake: 50 calories, 1 g fat (1 g saturated), 1 g protein, 9 g carbohydrate, 0 g fiber, 12 mg sodium, 3 mg cholesterol.

Carrot Cake

MAKES: 12 servings
PREP: 15 minutes
BAKE: at 350° for 30 minutes

1½ cups cake flour (not self-rising)

½ cup granulated sugar

1 teaspoon baking powder

1 teaspoon baking soda

1 teaspoon ground cinnamon

½ teaspoon salt

½ cup canned crushed pineapple, drained

¼ cup olive oil

2 large eggs

¼ cup packed light-brown sugar

1 cup shredded carrot

¼ cup orange juice

¼ cup dark seedless raisins

Lemon Icing (recipe follows)

1 Heat oven to 350°. Coat 9-inch-round cake pan with cooking spray. Dust with flour; tap out excess.

2 Sift together flour, granulated sugar, baking powder, baking soda, cinnamon, and salt into medium-size bowl.

3 Whirl pineapple in food processor until pureed, about 1 minute.

4 Beat together at medium speed olive oil, eggs, and brown sugar in medium-size bowl. Stir in carrot, pineapple puree, and orange juice. Stir in flour mixture until blended. Stir in raisins. Scrape batter into prepared cake pan.

5 Bake for 30 minutes or until toothpick inserted in center comes out clean. Let cake cool in pan on wire rack for 10 minutes. Remove cake from pan to wire rack; let cool completely. Spread with Lemon Icing.

Lemon Icing: Beat together 4 ounces ⅓-less-fat cream cheese, ¼ cup confectioners' sugar, and 1 tablespoon fresh lemon juice in small bowl until smooth.

Nutrient Value Per Serving: 200 calories, 7 g fat (2 g saturated), 3 g protein, 31 g carbohydrate, 1 g fiber, 287 mg sodium, 41 mg cholesterol.

Choco-Mocha Angel Food Cake

MAKES: 12 servings
PREP: 15 minutes
BAKE: at 350° for 45 minutes

1 cup cake flour (not self-rising)

½ cup unsweetened cocoa powder

2 tablespoons instant espresso powder

1 teaspoon ground cinnamon

14 large egg whites, at room temperature

1½ teaspoons cream of tartar

1½ cups sugar

2 ounces white baking chocolate, melted

1 Place oven rack in lowest position. Heat oven to 350°.

2 Sift together flour and cocoa powder into medium-size bowl. Stir in espresso powder and cinnamon.

3 Beat egg whites in medium-size bowl on medium speed until frothy. Beat in cream of tartar. Beat in sugar, 2 tablespoons at a time, until soft, glossy peaks form.

4 Fold flour mixture, in thirds, into whites. Spoon batter into ungreased 10-inch tube pan; gently smooth surface.

5 Bake on bottom rack for 45 minutes or until top of cake is dry and cracked. Invert cake pan and slip center tube over top of a bottle so pan is elevated. Let cool 1 hour. Gently remove cake from pan. Drizzle with melted chocolate.

Nutrient Value Per Serving: 184 calories, 2 g fat (1 g saturated), 6 g protein, 37 g carbohydrate, 1 g fiber, 71 mg sodium, 1 mg cholesterol.

Chocolate-Almond Soufflé

MAKES: 8 servings
PREP: 15 minutes
COOK: 10 minutes
REFRIGERATE: 15 minutes
BAKE: at 350° for 40 minutes

½ cup plus 2 teaspoons granulated sugar

¼ cup unsweetened cocoa powder

3 tablespoons all-purpose flour

1 envelope unflavored gelatin

¼ teaspoon salt

1½ cups low-fat (1%) milk

1 large egg yolk

1 teaspoon almond extract

6 large egg whites

½ teaspoon cream of tartar

1 teaspoon confectioners' sugar, for sprinkling

1 Combine ¼ cup of the sugar, the cocoa powder, flour, gelatin, and salt in medium-size saucepan.

2 Whisk together milk and egg yolk in small bowl. Gradually stir milk mixture into cocoa mixture in saucepan. Cook over low heat, stirring constantly, until mixture coats back of spoon, about 10 minutes.

3 Remove saucepan from heat. Stir in almond extract. Spoon mixture into small bowl. Place into larger bowl filled with ice. Refrigerate until mixture mounds when dropped from spoon, 15 to 20 minutes.

4 Heat oven to 350°. Coat 2-quart soufflé dish with cooking spray. Sprinkle inside with 2 teaspoons of the sugar to coat completely.

5 Beat together egg whites and cream of tartar in large bowl on high speed until soft peaks form. Gradually beat in remaining ¼ cup sugar, 2 tablespoons at a time, until stiff, glossy peaks form.

6 Stir ¼ cup egg white mixture into cooled cocoa mixture to lighten. Gently fold remaining cocoa mixture into beaten egg whites just until blended. Spoon into soufflé dish.

7 Bake for 40 minutes or until puffed and browned. Lightly sprinkle with confectioners' sugar. Serve immediately.

Nutrient Value Per Serving: 117 calories, 2 g fat (1 g saturated), 6 g protein, 20 g carbohydrate, 1 g fiber, 141 mg sodium, 29 mg cholesterol.

Pineapple Cheesecake

MAKES: 12 servings
PREP: 15 minutes
BAKE: at 325° for 1 hour
STAND: 1 hour in oven

Crust:

½ cup low-fat granola

Filling:

1 container (1 pound) low-fat (1%) cottage cheese

1 package (8 ounces) ⅓-less-fat cream cheese, at room temperature

¼ cup plus 2 tablespoons all-purpose flour

1¼ cups granulated sugar

¼ teaspoon salt

4 large egg whites

1 teaspoon vanilla extract

1 cup canned unsweetened crushed pineapple, drained

1 Heat oven to 325°.

2 Crust: Whirl granola in food processor until slightly ground. Coat 8-inch springform pan with cooking spray. Coat inside of pan with granola.

3 Filling: Process cottage cheese and cream cheese in food processor until smooth. Add flour, sugar, salt, egg whites, and vanilla. Whirl until well blended. Stir in pineapple. Pour into prepared pan. Place pan on baking sheet.

4 Bake for 1 hour. Turn oven off. Let cheesecake stand in oven with door slightly open for 1 hour. Remove pan to wire rack; let cool completely. Remove sides of pan. Refrigerate.

Nutrient Value Per Serving: 198 calories, 5 g fat (3 g saturated), 9 g protein, 30 g carbohydrate, 1 g fiber, 309 mg sodium, 15 mg cholesterol.

Marble Cheesecake

MAKES: 12 servings
PREP: 15 minutes
BAKE: at 325° for 50 minutes
STAND: 1 hour in oven

Crust:

½ cup low-fat granola

Filling:

1 container (1 pound) low-fat (1%) cottage cheese

1 package (8 ounces) ⅓-less-fat cream cheese, at room temperature

¼ cup plus 2 tablespoons all-purpose flour

1¼ cups sugar

¼ teaspoon salt

4 large egg whites

1 teaspoon vanilla

2 tablespoons unsweetened cocoa powder

1 tablespoon low-fat (1%) milk

1 Heat oven to 325°.

2 Crust: Whirl granola in food processor until slightly ground. Coat 8-inch springform pan with cooking spray. Coat inside of pan with granola.

3 Filling: Process together cottage cheese and cream cheese in food processor until smooth.

4 Add flour, 1 cup and 2 tablespoons of sugar, the salt, egg whites, and vanilla. Whirl until well blended. Remove ⅓ cup of filling to small bowl; stir in cocoa powder, remaining 2 tablespoons sugar, and milk. Pour plain mixture into prepared pan. Spoon chocolate mixture into mounds over top. With small knife, gently swirl chocolate mixture into plain batter to make marble pattern. Place pan on baking sheet.

5 Bake for 50 minutes. Turn oven off. Let cheesecake stand in oven with door slightly open for 1 hour. Remove pan to wire rack; let cool completely. Remove sides of pan. Refrigerate.

Nutrient Value Per Serving: 193 calories, 5 g fat (3 g saturated), 9 g protein, 29 g carbohydrate, 1 g fiber, 281 mg sodium, 19 mg cholesterol.

Lemon Cheesecake with Apricot Glaze

MAKES: 12 servings
PREP: 15 minutes
BAKE: at 325° for 50 minutes
STAND: 1 hour in oven

Crust:

⅓ cup low-fat granola

Filling:

1 container (1 pound) low-fat (1%) cottage cheese

1 package (8 ounces) light cream cheese, softened

¼ cup plus 2 tablespoons all-purpose flour

1¼ cups sugar

¼ teaspoon salt

4 large egg whites

1 tablespoon grated lemon rind

1 tablespoon fresh lemon juice

Glaze:

¼ cup apricot preserves

1 Heat oven to 325°.

2 Crust: Whirl granola in food processor until slightly ground. Coat 8-inch springform pan with cooking spray. Coat inside of pan with granola.

3 Filling: Process together cottage cheese and cream cheese in food processor until smooth. Whirl in flour, sugar, salt, egg whites, lemon rind, and juice. Pour into prepared pan. Place pan on a baking sheet.

4 Bake for 50 minutes. Turn off oven. Let cheesecake stand in oven with door slightly open for 1 hour. Remove pan to wire rack to cool completely. Gently loosen sides. Remove sides of pan.

5 Glaze: Melt preserves in small saucepan over medium heat. When cool enough to touch, brush over top of cake. Refrigerate.

Nutrient Value Per Serving: 199 calories, 4 g fat (2 g saturated), 9 g protein, 33 g carbohydrate, 0 g fiber, 272 mg sodium, 82 mg cholesterol.

Citrus Roll

MAKES: 10 servings
PREP: 20 minutes
BAKE: at 400° for 8 to 10 minutes

Sponge Cake:

¾ cup all-purpose flour

½ teaspoon salt

¼ teaspoon baking powder

¼ teaspoon baking soda

4 large eggs, separated into yolks and whites

½ cup granulated sugar

1 teaspoon grated orange rind

1 tablespoon confectioners' sugar

Orange Cream Filling:

1 container (8 ounces) frozen light nondairy whipped topping, thawed

1 teaspoon orange extract

1 cup chopped peeled orange segments (from 1 to 2 large navel oranges)

Garnish (optional):

Orange slices

Fresh mint leaves

1 Heat oven to 400°. Coat 15½ x 10½ x 1-inch jelly-roll pan with cooking spray. Line with waxed paper. Coat paper with spray.

2 Cake: Sift together flour, salt, baking powder, and baking soda into medium-size bowl.

3 Beat egg whites in medium-size bowl on high speed until fluffy. Gradually beat in sugar until mixture forms stiff, glossy peaks.

4 Beat together yolks and rind in large bowl until fluffy. Gently fold in ½ cup beaten whites. Fold in remaining whites alternately along with flour mixture in 2 more additions. Spread batter evenly in prepared pan.

5 Bake for 8 to 10 minutes or until golden and top springs back when lightly pressed with fingertip.

6 Loosen cake around edges with small spatula. Invert pan carefully onto paper toweling or clean kitchen towel dusted with 1 tablespoon confectioners' sugar. Peel off waxed paper. Starting at a short end, roll up cake and towel together; place, seam side down, on wire rack; let cool.

7 Filling: Fold together whipped topping and orange extract in medium-size bowl just until extract is blended in. Set aside 1 cup for topping. Stir chopped orange into larger portion remaining in bowl.

8 Unroll cooled cake. Spread cake evenly with filling. Reroll from short end, using towel as a guide. Spread reserved 1 cup whipped topping mixture over cake roll. Refrigerate until ready to serve. Garnish with orange slices and mint, if desired.

Nutrient Value Per Serving: 171 calories, 5 g fat (4 g saturated), 4 g protein, 26 g carbohydrate, 1 g fiber, 183 mg sodium, 85 mg cholesterol.

Banana Bread

MAKES: 12 slices

PREP: 15 minutes

BAKE: at 350° for 45 minutes

2 cups cake flour (not self-rising)

¾ cup sugar

1 teaspoon baking powder

¼ teaspoon baking soda

1 teaspoon salt

1 large egg, lightly beaten

1½ cups banana puree (3 small ripe bananas)

½ cup buttermilk

1 teaspoon vanilla extract

½ cup golden seedless raisins

1 Heat oven to 350°. Coat 8½ x 4 x 3-inch loaf pan with cooking spray.

2 Stir together flour, sugar, baking powder, baking soda, and salt in medium-size bowl.

3 Stir together egg, banana puree, buttermilk, vanilla, and raisins in separate bowl.

4 Gradually stir flour mixture into buttermilk mixture until well blended. Scrape batter into prepared pan, spreading evenly.

5 Bake for 45 minutes or until toothpick inserted in center comes out clean. Transfer pan to wire rack; let cool 15 minutes. Remove loaf from pan to rack; let cool completely.

Nutrient Value Per Slice: 144 calories, 1 g fat (0 g saturated), 3 g protein, 32 g carbohydrate, 1 g fiber, 268 mg sodium, 18 mg cholesterol.

Brownies

MAKES: 16 brownies

PREP: 15 minutes

COOK: 3 minutes

BAKE: at 375° for 30 to 35 minutes

3 ounces unsweetened chocolate, cut into 1-inch pieces

½ cup Prune Puree (see page 177) OR bottled prune puree

3 large egg whites

1¾ cups sugar

1 teaspoon salt

¼ cup low-fat (1%) milk

1 teaspoon vanilla extract

1 cup cake flour (not self-rising), sifted

3 tablespoons unsweetened cocoa powder

1 Heat oven to 375°. Coat 9 x 9 x 2-inch square baking pan with cooking spray.

2 Melt chocolate, stirring occasionally, in top of double boiler over simmering water. Scrape chocolate into medium-size bowl.

3 Beat prune puree, egg whites, sugar, salt, milk, and vanilla into melted chocolate.

4 Sift together flour and cocoa powder into chocolate mixture; stir to combine. Spread evenly in prepared pan.

5 Bake for 30 to 35 minutes or until top is springy to touch. Let cool in pan on wire rack. Cut in sixteen 2¼-inch squares.

Nutrient Value Per Brownie: 150 calories, 3 g fat (2 g saturated), 2 g protein, 31 g carbohydrate, 2 g fiber, 159 mg sodium, 0 mg cholesterol.

Berry Blondies

MAKES: 16 blondies
PREP: 20 minutes
BAKE: at 325° for 45 to 50 minutes

6 ounces fine-quality or premium white baking chocolate, chopped

5 tablespoons unsalted butter, cut into pieces

2 large eggs

⅔ cup sugar

1 teaspoon vanilla extract

1⅓ cups all-purpose flour

1 teaspoon baking powder

½ teaspoon salt

1 cup fresh raspberries

1 cup fresh blueberries

1 Heat oven to 325°. Line 9 x 9 x 2-inch square baking pan with foil; coat with cooking spray.

2 In metal bowl set over saucepan of barely simmering water, melt together white chocolate and butter, stirring until smooth. Let cool to room temperature.

3 In large bowl, beat together eggs, sugar, and vanilla on medium speed until thickened and pale, 3 minutes. On low speed, gradually beat in chocolate mixture.

4 Into a bowl, sift together flour, baking powder, and salt. Beat into chocolate mixture until combined. Spread evenly in prepared pan. Sprinkle with berries.

5 Bake until top is very lightly browned but center still soft when lightly pressed, 45 to 50 minutes. Let cool completely in pan on rack. (Blondies are easiest to cut if chilled, but serve at room temperature for best flavor.)

Nutrient Value Per Blondie: 181 calories, 8 g fat (5 g saturated), 3 g protein, 25 g carbohydrate, 1 g fiber, 124 mg sodium, 39 mg cholesterol.

Cakey Pineapple Bars

MAKES: 16 bars
PREP: 10 minutes
BAKE: at 350° for 30 to 40 minutes

2 cups all-purpose flour

2½ cups confectioners' sugar

2 large eggs, lightly beaten

1 can (20 ounces) crushed pineapple in syrup

2 teaspoons baking soda

½ teaspoon salt

1 Heat oven to 350°. Coat 13 x 9 x 2-inch nonstick baking pan with cooking spray.

2 In large bowl, stir together flour, 2 cups of the confectioners' sugar, eggs, pineapple with syrup, baking soda, and salt until combined; stir for 2 minutes. Spoon batter into prepared pan.

3 Bake for 30 to 40 minutes or until top is lightly browned and springs back when lightly touched. Let cake cool completely in pan on wire rack.

4 Cut cake into 16 bars.

5 In small bowl, stir together remaining ½ cup confectioners' sugar with 2 teaspoons water until smooth. Drizzle over bars. Let stand at room temperature for 30 minutes to set before serving.

Nutrient Value Per Bar: 155 calories, 1 g fat (0 g saturated), 3 g protein, 35 g carbohydrate, 1 g fiber, 239 mg sodium, 27 mg cholesterol.

Rich Cocoa Bars

MAKES: 28 bars
PREP: 20 minutes
BAKE: at 350° for 25 minutes

Bars:

1¼ cups cake flour (not self-rising)

⅔ cup granulated sugar

½ cup unsweetened cocoa powder

1¼ teaspoons baking soda

¾ teaspoon baking powder

½ teaspoon salt

1 cup nonfat milk

**1 cup Prune Puree (see page 177) OR
1 cup bottled prune puree**

1 large egg

1 large egg white

2 teaspoons vanilla extract

Frosting:

3 cups confectioners' sugar

6 tablespoons butter or margarine, at room temperature

7 to 8 teaspoons milk

Pinch salt

1 square (1 ounce) semisweet chocolate, melted

1 Heat oven to 350°. Coat 15½ x 10 x 1-inch jelly-roll pan with cooking spray.

2 Bars: Stir together flour, sugar, cocoa powder, baking soda, baking powder, and salt in medium-size bowl.

3 Beat together milk, prune puree, egg, egg white, and vanilla in large bowl on low speed just until eggs are beaten. Slowly beat in flour mixture. Pour into prepared pan.

4 Bake for 25 minutes or until toothpick inserted in center comes out clean. Remove pan to wire rack; let cool.

5 Frosting: Beat together confectioners' sugar, butter, 7 teaspoons milk, and salt in medium-size bowl until smooth and good spreading consistency. Beat in another teaspoon milk, if needed.

6 Spread frosting over bar. Drizzle with melted chocolate. Let stand until chocolate sets. Cut into bars.

Nutrient Value Per Bar: 123 calories, 3 g fat (2 g saturated), 2 g protein, 23 g carbohydrate, 1 g fiber, 132 mg sodium, 15 mg cholesterol.

Chocolate-Walnut Squares

MAKES: about 3 dozen squares
PREP: 20 minutes
BAKE: at 350° for 30 minutes

1 tablespoon freeze-dried coffee granules

1 tablespoon hot water

½ cup (1 stick) unsalted butter,
at room temperature

1¼ cups packed dark-brown sugar

¼ cup dark corn syrup

2 large eggs

2 teaspoons vanilla extract

2 cups all-purpose flour

1 teaspoon baking powder

1½ teaspoons ground cinnamon

¼ teaspoon salt

½ cup sour cream

¾ cup mini chocolate chips

1½ cups walnuts, chopped

1 can (1 pound) chocolate frosting

1 Heat oven to 350°. Coat 15½ x 10½ x 1-inch jelly-roll pan with cooking spray. Line with waxed paper; coat paper with spray. Dissolve coffee granules in water in small bowl.

2 Beat together butter and sugar at medium speed in large bowl until combined, 3 minutes. Add corn syrup; beat until smooth. Beat in eggs, coffee mixture, and vanilla.

3 Stir together flour, baking powder, cinnamon, and salt in medium-size bowl. On low speed, beat flour mixture alternately with sour cream into butter mixture, ending with flour mixture. Fold in chips and walnuts. Spread in prepared pan.

4 Bake for 30 minutes or until center is set. Let cool in pan on wire rack. Spread with prepared chocolate frosting. Cut into 2-inch squares and serve.

Nutrient Value Per Square: 196 calories, 10 g fat (4 g saturated), 2 g protein, 26 g carbohydrate, 1 g fiber, 62 mg sodium, 20 mg cholesterol.

Lemon-Blueberry Cookie-Tart

MAKES: 10 servings
PREP: 20 minutes
BAKE: at 350° for 15 to 20 minutes

1 box (7.75 ounces) 50%-less-fat creme sandwich cookies (18 cookies)

5 tablespoons yellow cornmeal

1 large egg

½ cup frozen light nondairy whipped topping, thawed

¼ cup bottled lemon curd

1 tablespoon grape jelly

1½ cups fresh blueberries

1 Heat oven to 350°.

2 Break apart sandwich cookies into food processor. Add cornmeal. Process until cookie pieces are finely crushed. Add egg; pulse until evenly moistened and crumbs stick together.

3 Between 2 sheets of plastic wrap, roll "dough" out to 12 x 8-inch rectangle. Press over bottom and up sides of 11 x 7 x 1-inch rectangular tart pan with removable bottom (see Note, below).

4 Bake crust until dry to the touch and lightly browned around edge, 15 to 20 minutes. Transfer pan to wire rack; let cool.

5 With sharp knife, release edge of crust from pan. Remove side of pan. Transfer to serving platter (you may leave pan bottom in place to help support).

6 In small bowl, stir together whipped topping and lemon curd. In small saucepan, heat grape jelly until melted. Remove from heat. Add blueberries; toss to coat.

7 Spread lemon filling evenly in crust. Top with blueberries. Serve immediately, or refrigerate, loosely covered, for up to 2 hours.

Note: If you do not have a rectangular tart pan, you can use a 9-inch round tart pan with removable bottom pan and roll dough out to 10-inch circle.

Nutrient Value Per Serving: 158 calories, 4 g fat (1 g saturated), 2 g protein, 32 g carbohydrate, 1 g fiber, 93 mg sodium, 21 mg cholesterol.

Jumbo Devil's Food Cookies

MAKES: 3 dozen
PREP: 10 minutes
REFRIGERATE: 15 minutes
BAKE: at 350° for 13 to 14 minutes

1 box (18.25 ounces) Devil's food cake mix

⅓ cup unsweetened cocoa powder

¼ cup water

¼ cup (½ stick) butter, melted

2 large eggs

1 cup crispy rice cereal

1 cup fluffy marshmallow topping

1 Heat oven to 350°. Butter and flour 2 large light-colored baking sheets (not nonstick).

2 Place cake mix, cocoa powder, water, melted butter, and eggs in large bowl. On low speed, beat until combined, about 1 minute. On medium speed, beat 2 minutes. Add cereal. On low speed, beat just until combined. Lightly stir in marshmallow topping, leaving mixture marbled. Refrigerate, covered, 15 minutes.

3 Using greased tablespoon, spoon slightly heaping tablespoons of dough, spacing about 2 inches apart, onto prepared baking sheets. Refrigerate remaining dough in between batches.

4 Bake for 13 to 14 minutes or until cookies are puffed and set in center. Let cool on baking sheet 1 minute. With metal spatula, carefully remove cookies to wire rack; let cool completely.

5 Clean baking sheets. Butter and flour sheets; repeat shaping and baking with remaining dough.

Nutrient Value Per Cookie: 108 calories, 4 g fat (2 g saturated), 2 g protein, 18 g carbohydrate, 1 g fiber, 139 mg sodium, 24 mg cholesterol.

Jumbo Island Cookies

MAKES: about 2 dozen
PREP: 15 minutes
BAKE: at 375° for 10 to 12 minutes

1²⁄₃ cups all-purpose flour

¾ teaspoon baking powder

½ teaspoon baking soda

½ teaspoon salt

¼ teaspoon ground nutmeg

6 tablespoons (¾ stick) unsalted butter,
at room temperature

¾ cup packed light-brown sugar

⅓ cup granulated sugar

1 cup mashed ripe banana

1 large egg

1 teaspoon vanilla extract

2 cups or 1 bag (12 ounces) semisweet
chocolate chips

1 cup sweetened flaked coconut

¼ cup chopped macadamia nuts

1 Heat oven to 375°. Sift together flour, baking
powder, baking soda, salt, and nutmeg into
medium-size bowl.

2 On medium-high speed, beat butter in large
bowl until creamy about 2 minutes. Add sugars
and mashed banana; beat until light and fluffy,
about 3 minutes. Beat in egg and vanilla.

3 On low speed, beat flour mixture into butter
mixture. Stir in chocolate chips, coconut, and
macadamia nuts. Drop batter, 3 tablespoons for
each cookie, spacing about 2 inches apart, onto
ungreased baking sheets (a total of 24 cookies).

4 Bake for 10 to 12 minutes or until lightly
golden. Let cookies cool on sheet on wire rack
for 1 to 2 minutes. Transfer cookies to wire rack;
let cool completely.

*Nutrient Value Per Cookie: 197 calories, 10 g fat
(5 g saturated), 2 g protein, 29 g carbohydrate,
2 g fiber, 102 mg sodium, 17 mg cholesterol.*

Sugar Daisies

MAKES: 3½ dozen
PREP: 15 minutes
BAKE: at 350° for 12 to 14 minutes

2½ cups all-purpose flour

½ teaspoon salt

½ cup (1 stick) unsalted butter, at room
temperature

1 cup granulated sugar

2 large eggs

1 teaspoon vanilla extract

Colored crystallized sugar, for decorating

1 Heat oven to 350°. Coat large baking sheet
with cooking spray.

2 Stir together flour and salt in medium-size
bowl.

3 Beat together butter, sugar, eggs, and vanilla
in large bowl until light and fluffy, 3 minutes.
Stir flour mixture into butter mixture.

4 Spoon dough into cookie press fitted with
"flower" disk. Press out cookies about 1 inch
apart onto ungreased baking sheets. Sprinkle
tops with colored crystallized sugar.

5　Bake for 12 to 14 minutes or until edges are lightly golden. Transfer to wire racks; let cool. Store airtight at room temperature up to 1 week.

Nutrient Value Per Daisy: 69 calories, 3 g fat (1 g saturated),1 g protein, 11 g carbohydrate, 0 g fiber, 31 mg sodium, 16 mg cholesterol.

Chocolate Meringue Drops

MAKES: 28 drops
PREP: 15 minutes
BAKE: at 350° for 10 minutes

　2 large egg whites

　1¼ cups confectioners' sugar

　3 tablespoons unsweetened cocoa powder

　1 tablespoon all-purpose flour

　1 teaspoon finely ground coffee beans (optional)

　½ tablespoon water

　½ cup pecans, finely ground

1　Heat oven to 350°. Line 2 baking sheets with parchment or waxed paper.

2　Beat egg whites in medium-size bowl on medium-speed until frothy. Add sugar, cocoa powder, flour, coffee if using, and water. Beat on low speed to combine. Increase speed to high; beat until thick like marshmallow topping, 3 minutes. Fold in pecans. Drop by heaping teaspoonfuls onto baking sheets.

3　Bake for 10 minutes or until tops crack. Let cool on baking sheets on wire rack.

Nutrient Value Per Drop: 33 calories, 1 g fat (0 g saturated), 1 g protein, 5 g carbohydrate, 0 g fiber, 4 mg sodium, 0 mg cholesterol.

Orange Madeleines

MAKES: 12 madeleines
PREP: 15 minutes
BAKE: at 400° for 10 minutes

　2 large eggs, separated into whites and yolks

　⅛ teaspoon salt

　⅓ cup granulated sugar

　⅓ cup all-purpose flour

　1 tablespoon grated orange rind

　1 tablespoon olive oil

　1 teaspoon orange extract

　1 teaspoon confectioners' sugar, for sprinkling

1　Heat oven to 400°. Coat one madeleine pan (twelve 2 x 3⅜-inch shells) with cooking spray.

2　Beat together egg whites and salt in medium-size bowl on high speed until stiff, glossy peaks form.

3　Beat together egg yolks and sugar in large bowl until pale yellow, about 1 minute. Stir in flour, orange rind, oil, and orange extract until blended. Gently fold in beaten egg whites just until blended; do not overfold. Spoon batter into each shell, dividing equally.

4　Bake for 10 minutes or until golden. Immediately remove madeleines from pan to wire rack; let cool completely. Just before serving, sift confectioners' sugar over madeleines.

Nutrient Value Per Madeleine: 58 calories, 2 g fat (0 g saturated), 1 g protein, 9 g carbohydrate, 0 g fiber, 35 mg sodium, 35 mg cholesterol.

Ginger Crackles

MAKES: 4 dozen cookies
PREP: 20 minutes
REFRIGERATE: 1 hour
BAKE: at 350° for 12 minutes

½ cup (1 stick) butter, at room temperature

1 cup granulated sugar

¼ cup molasses

1 large egg

2 cups all-purpose flour

¾ teaspoon baking soda

¼ teaspoon salt

1 tablespoon ground ginger

½ teaspoon ground cinnamon

¼ teaspoon white pepper

1 tablespoon crystallized ginger, chopped

¾ cup confectioners' sugar

1 In large bowl, beat together butter, sugar, and molasses on medium speed until blended. Beat in egg until blended, scraping down side of bowl.

2 Sift together flour, baking soda, salt, ginger, cinnamon, and white pepper into medium-size bowl. Add to butter mixture; beat on low speed until blended. Stir in crystallized ginger. Cover; refrigerate 1 hour.

3 Heat oven to 350°. Lightly coat 2 large baking sheets with cooking spray.

4 Place confectioners' sugar in small bowl. Dust hands lightly with flour. Roll pieces of dough into 1-inch balls, using about 2 teaspoons per ball. Roll dough in confectioners' sugar to completely coat. Transfer to prepared baking sheets, spacing at least 2 inches apart.

5 Bake for 12 minutes or until cookies have expanded and flattened; the tops will be covered with cracks. Let cookies cool on baking sheets on wire rack 2 minutes. Transfer cookies directly to racks; let cool completely. Cookies can be stored in airtight container at room temperature for up to 1 week.

Nutrient Value Per Cookie: 66 calories, 2 g fat (1 g saturated), 1 g protein, 11 g carbohydrate, 0 g fiber, 35 mg sodium, 10 mg cholesterol.

Jumbo Oatmeal Cookies

MAKES: 2 dozen cookies
PREP: 20 minutes
BAKE: at 375° for 15 minutes

3 cups old-fashioned rolled oats

¾ cup all-purpose flour

½ teaspoon ground cinnamon

¼ teaspoon ground allspice

¼ teaspoon ground cloves

Pinch salt

½ cup (1 stick) butter, at room temperature

1 cup packed light-brown sugar

2 large egg whites

1 teaspoon vanilla extract

¾ cup cinnamon chips

½ cup sweetened dried cranberries, chopped

Drizzle:

⅓ cup confectioners' sugar

1¼ to 1½ teaspoons water

1 Heat oven to 375°. In medium-size bowl, stir together oats, flour, cinnamon, allspice, cloves, and salt.

2 In large bowl, beat butter until smooth. Add brown sugar; beat until well mixed. Beat in egg whites, one at a time, scraping down side of bowl. Beat in vanilla extract.

3 Stir oat mixture into butter mixture, along with cinnamon chips and cranberries.

4 Lightly coat baking sheets with cooking spray. Using large spoon (about 3 tablespoons), drop batter into mounds on sheets, 6 per sheet, about 24 total. Flatten mounds slightly to form 3-inch rounds.

5 Bake until lightly golden around edges, about 15 minutes. Let cookies cool on baking sheet 2 minutes. Transfer cookies to wire rack; let cool completely.

6 Drizzle: In small bowl, stir together confectioners' sugar and just enough water until smooth and good drizzling consistency. Transfer to small plastic food-storage bag. Place cookies close together on sheet of waxed paper. Snip off small corner of plastic bag; drizzle over cookies. Let stand until drizzle sets, about 15 minutes. Store in airtight container at room temperature for up to 2 weeks.

Nutrient Value Per Cookie: 175 calories, 7 g fat (4 g saturated), 3 g protein, 27 g carbohydrate, 1 g fiber, 27 mg sodium, 10 mg cholesterol.

10

THE BREAKFAST
& LUNCH BUNCH

TURNS OUT OUR MOTHERS WERE RIGHT ALL ALONG. They were always nudging us to eat a good breakfast, and according to nutritionists, this meal is absolutely essential. Breakfast gets your metabolism kicking, a factor that's especially crucial if you want to shed pounds. It also fuels your energy, which revs up your willpower to make the right food choices throughout the day. Our collection spotlights portable goodies like Apple-Raisin Muffins (page 208)—egg whites are the fat-cutting secret in these —and a fruit-laden Tropical Smoothie (page 209), as well as some scrumptious egg dishes worthy of serving to friends for brunch.

Some of the glorious choices here include a Broccoli-Cheese Quiche (page 198) updated with goat cheese, a lovely, light Cheddar-Chive Soufflé (page 202) and a Potato-Bacon Frittata (page 203) that's rich, but still diet-right. Tex-Mex classic Huevos Rancheros (page 199)—a layering of eggs, cheese, and tortilla topped with salsa—fills you up but won't fatten you up. Also in the morning mix are Blueberry Cottage Cheese Pancakes (page 204), Spiced French Toast (page 206), and Banana-Pecan Waffles (page 205) that taste almost like dessert.

Although you can find lots of lunch options in the preceding chapters, we also created some recipes for die-hard sandwich lovers. BBQ Pork Melts (page 212) are a savory combination of red peppers, relish, pulled pork, and cheddar plus homemade coleslaw on a toasted French baguette. Equally tasty is a good-for-you Falafel (page 211) and a Red Pepper Panini (page 213) topped with olive spread, mozzarella, basil, and red peppers.

And, since they never go out of style, chicken, egg, tuna, and seafood salads (page 210), done the low-fat way.

Blueberry Cottage Cheese Pancakes (page 204).

Broccoli-Cheese Quiche

MAKES: 8 servings
PREP: 15 minutes
BAKE: at 400° for 35 minutes

½ of 15-ounce box refrigerated ready-to-use folded pie crust (1 crust)

4 large eggs

1½ cups fat-free half-and-half

1 small onion, grated (about 2 tablespoons)

½ teaspoon salt

¼ teaspoon black pepper

⅛ teaspoon ground nutmeg

1 package (10 ounces) frozen chopped broccoli, thawed, drained, and squeezed dry

4 ounces goat cheese

1 Place baking sheet in oven. Heat oven to 400°. Unfold pie crust; gently fit into bottom and up sides of 10-inch tart pan with removable bottom.

2 In large bowl, whisk together eggs, half-and-half, onion, salt, pepper, and nutmeg. Scatter broccoli over bottom of pie crust. Crumble goat cheese on top; carefully pour in egg mixture. Place on heated baking sheet in oven.

3 Bake for 35 minutes or until knife inserted in center comes out clean and top is slightly golden. Let cool in pan on wire rack 15 minutes. Remove side of pan. Place quiche on serving platter. Serve warm or at room temperature.

Nutrient Value Per Serving: 247 calories, 14 g fat (7 g saturated), 10 g protein, 20 g carbohydrate, 1 g fiber, 401 mg sodium, 122 mg cholesterol.

Crustless Artichoke Quiche

MAKES: 6 servings
PREP: 15 minutes
COOK: 6 minutes
BAKE: at 350° for 30 minutes

2 tablespoons packaged unseasoned bread crumbs

Filling:

4 scallions, cut into 1-inch pieces

1 package (9 ounces) frozen artichoke hearts, thawed

½ teaspoon dried tarragon

4 large eggs

1½ cups fat-free half-and-half

⅓ cup grated Parmesan cheese

¼ teaspoon salt

¼ teaspoon black pepper

⅛ teaspoon ground nutmeg

1 cup shredded reduced-fat Swiss cheese (4 ounces)

1 Heat oven to 350°. Sprinkle bread crumbs over bottom of 9-inch pie plate.

2 Filling: Chop scallions in food processor. Add artichokes; pulse just until chopped.

3 Coat medium-size skillet with cooking spray. Place over medium heat. Add artichoke mixture and tarragon; cook 6 minutes or until tender. Remove from heat.

4 Combine eggs, half-and-half, Parmesan, salt, pepper, and nutmeg in food processor. Whirl 30 seconds or until blended.

5 Spoon artichoke mixture into prepared pie plate. Sprinkle with Swiss cheese. Place dish on baking sheet. Pour in egg mixture.

6 Bake quiche for 30 minutes or until set in center. Transfer to wire rack; let cool 15 minutes or until firm in center.

Nutrient Value Per Serving: 178 calories, 6 g fat (3 g saturated), 15 g protein, 14 g carbohydrate, 2 g fiber, 522 mg sodium, 151 mg cholesterol.

Huevos Rancheros

MAKES: 4 servings
PREP: 10 minutes
BAKE: at 350° for 5 minutes
COOK: about 8 minutes

8 (6-inch) corn tortillas

1 teaspoon vegetable oil

1 teaspoon chili powder

¼ teaspoon coarse salt

1 can (16 ounces) fat-free refried beans

1 can (4 ounces) chopped green chiles

4 large eggs

1 tablespoon water

1 cup bottled salsa

1 tablespoon chopped fresh cilantro, for garnish (optional)

1 Heat oven to 350°.

2 Brush 4 tortillas lightly with oil; sprinkle with chili powder and salt. Cut each of the 4 tortillas into 4 wedges; place on baking sheet along with 4 whole tortillas, lightly brushed with oil.

3 Bake for 5 minutes.

4 Meanwhile, stir together beans and chiles in small skillet. Cook over medium heat until heated through, 3 to 4 minutes.

5 Coat 10-inch nonstick skillet with cooking spray. Heat over medium heat just until hot enough that a drop of water sprinkled on surface sizzles. Break eggs and slip gently into pan, without breaking yolks. Immediately reduce heat to low. Cook until edges turn white. Add the tablespoon water. Cover pan to hold in steam. Cook until whites are completely set and yolks begin to thicken, but are not hard, 3 to 4 minutes.

6 Spread ½ cup of bean mixture on each of the remaining whole tortillas. Place 1 tortilla on each plate. Top with cooked egg. Spoon salsa over top. Serve with chili chips. Garnish with cilantro, if desired.

Nutrient Value Per Serving: 279 calories, 7 g fat (2 g saturated), 15 g protein, 39 g carbohydrate, 9 g fiber, 1,075 mg sodium, 213 mg cholesterol.

Sausage-and-Apple Strata

MAKES: 8 servings
PREP: 10 minutes
BAKE: at 425° for 25 minutes

8 large egg whites

4 large whole eggs

1½ cups low-fat (1%) milk

2 tablespoons Dijon mustard

¾ teaspoon salt

½ teaspoon black pepper

6 slices low-calorie, high-fiber multigrain bread, cut into cubes

½ pound fully-cooked reduced-fat chicken sausage, casings removed and meat crumbled OR turkey meatballs

½ teaspoon dried sage

2 Granny Smith apples, peeled, cored, and cut into ½-inch cubes

1½ cups shredded cheddar cheese

1 Heat oven to 425°. Coat 13 x 9 x 2-inch baking pan with cooking spray.

2 Lightly beat together egg whites and whole eggs in medium-size bowl. Stir in milk, mustard, salt, and pepper.

3 Toss together bread, sausage, and sage in large bowl. Spread in prepared baking dish. Top with apples. Slowly pour egg mixture into baking dish. Sprinkle with cheese. Cover with foil. Let stand 10 minutes or refrigerate for up to 10 hours. If refrigerated, remove strata to counter for 30 minutes before baking.

4 Bake, covered, for 10 minutes. Uncover; bake 15 minutes or until set and top is lightly browned. Let stand 10 minutes.

Nutrient Value Per Serving: 250 calories, 12 g fat (6 g saturated), 20 g protein, 16 g carbohydrate, 3 g fiber, 775 mg sodium, 163 mg cholesterol.

Frittata Squares

MAKES: 8 servings
PREP: 5 minutes
COOK: 7 minutes
BAKE: at 400° for 20 minutes

2 teaspoons olive oil

3 cups frozen O'Brien potatoes, slightly thawed

½ cup diced lean ham (2 ounces)

2 containers (4 ounces each) liquid egg substitute

2 tablespoons nonfat sour cream

½ teaspoon salt

⅛ teaspoon cayenne

½ cup shredded low-fat Swiss cheese or other low-fat cheese (2 ounces)

1 Heat oven to 400°. Coat 11 x 7 x 2-inch baking dish with cooking spray.

2 Heat olive oil in skillet over medium-high heat. Add potatoes; sauté until browned, 5 to 7 minutes. Transfer to medium-size bowl. Add ham.

3 Whisk together egg substitute, sour cream, salt, and cayenne in small bowl until well blended. Stir into potato mixture. Pour into prepared baking dish. Sprinkle with shredded cheese.

4 Bake for 20 minutes or until golden.

Nutrient Value Per Serving: 114 calories, 3 g fat (1 g saturated), 8 g protein, 14 g carbohydrate, 1 g fiber, 378 mg sodium, 6 mg cholesterol.

German Pancake

MAKES: 8 servings
PREP: 5 minutes
BAKE: at 400° for 20 minutes

6 large eggs

1 cup milk

1 cup all-purpose flour

⅓ cup sugar

½ teaspoon salt

2 tablespoons butter

1 to 2 tablespoons confectioners' sugar, for dusting

1 Heat oven to 400°.

2 Whisk together eggs, milk, flour, sugar, and salt in large bowl.

3 Melt butter in ovenproof skillet, preferably 10-inch cast-iron pan, over medium heat. Using pot holder, remove skillet from heat. Pour egg mixture into hot skillet.

4 Carefully transfer hot skillet to oven. Bake for 20 minutes or until pancake is golden and puffed.

5 Sift confectioners' sugar over top of pancake and serve immediately.

Nutrient Value Per Serving: 192 calories, 8 g fat (4 g saturated), 7 g protein, 23 g carbohydrate, 0 g fiber, 208 mg sodium, 171 mg cholesterol.

Cheddar-Chive Soufflé

MAKES: 8 servings
PREP: 20 minutes
COOK: 5 minutes
HEAT: oven to 400°
BAKE: at 375° for 30 to 35 minutes

3 tablespoons plus ⅓ cup grated Parmesan cheese

1½ cups low-fat (1%) milk

¼ cup all-purpose flour

1½ cups shredded reduced-fat cheddar cheese (6 ounces)

1½ teaspoons Dijon mustard

½ teaspoon salt

¼ cup snipped fresh chives

4 large eggs, separated into yolks and whites

2 large egg whites

¼ teaspoon cream of tartar

1 Heat oven to 400°. Coat 10-cup soufflé dish with cooking spray. Coat with the 3 tablespoons Parmesan.

2 Whisk together milk and flour in medium-size saucepan. Bring to simmering over medium-high heat, whisking occasionally, until thickened, about 5 minutes. Remove from heat. Whisk in remaining ⅓ cup Parmesan, the cheddar, mustard, salt, and chives.

3 Place egg yolks in medium-size bowl; whisk small amount of hot milk mixture into yolks. Whisk in almost half of milk mixture; whisk yolk mixture back into milk mixture in saucepan. Pour into large bowl.

4 In clean bowl, beat together egg whites and cream of tartar on medium speed until foamy. Increase to high speed; beat until stiff peaks form. Fold half of whites into yolk mixture; fold in remaining whites.

Flavor Without Fat

To jazz up egg dishes with a distinctive smoky flavor and add personality to sandwiches, roast some sweet peppers (any color will do) for an easy-to-fix, no-fat accent. Bottled are available, but homemade are better.

- Heat an oven broiler, or prepare an outdoor grill with hot coals, or heat a gas grill to high.

- Coat broiler-pan rack or grill grid with cooking spray. Place whole sweet peppers on rack or grid. Broil or grill 4 to 6 inches from heat, turning occasionally with long tongs, until peppers are black and blistered all over, about 15 minutes.

- Transfer peppers to brown paper bag and seal, or place in a bowl and cover with plastic wrap.

- Let stand until the skins loosen from the peppers as they cool.

- Transfer peppers to cutting board. Cut in half through stem end. Remove stem, seeds, and inner membranes. Peel off skin and discard, using fingers and small paring knife. Cut peppers into thin strips or small dice or any other shape you fancy, and add to the recipe.

5 Scrape into prepared soufflé dish; smooth top. To make "top hat" on soufflé, hold spoon upright and with back side of tip, make circle around mixture, 1 inch from edge of pan.

6 Place soufflé in oven; reduce temperature to 375°. Bake for 30 to 35 minutes or until lightly golden, puffy, and lightly set in center. Serve immediately.

Nutrient Value Per Serving: 175 calories, 10 g fat (5 g saturated), 14 g protein, 6 g carbohydrate, 0 g fiber, 540 mg sodium, 128 mg cholesterol.

Potato-Bacon Frittata

MAKES: 6 servings
PREP: 5 minutes
COOK: about 10 minutes
BAKE: at 375° for 30 minutes
STAND: 10 minutes

4 slices turkey bacon, chopped

1 sweet green pepper, cored, seeded, and chopped (1 cup)

1¼ cups water

1¼ cups fat-free half-and-half

⅛ teaspoon dried thyme

1 tablespoon all-purpose flour

Pinch cayenne

1 box (5.25 ounces) au gratin potatoes

4 large eggs

2 large egg whites

1 can (14.5 ounces) chopped tomatoes, drained

½ cup shredded reduced-fat cheddar cheese

1 Heat oven to 375°. Coat fluted quiche pan with cooking spray.

2 Cook bacon in medium-size nonstick skillet over medium-high heat until crisp, 5 minutes. Remove bacon to paper toweling. Add green pepper to skillet; cook until slightly softened, about 2 minutes. Remove green pepper.

3 Bring water, half-and-half, thyme, flour, cayenne, and seasoning from packaged potatoes to a boil in medium-size saucepan. Lightly beat together whole eggs and egg whites in large bowl. Gradually whisk hot liquid from saucepan into eggs. Stir in potatoes, tomatoes, cheese, and reserved bacon and green pepper. Pour into quiche pan.

4 Bake, covered, for 15 minutes. Uncover; bake 15 minutes or until center is set and edges begin to brown. Let stand 10 minutes.

Nutrient Value Per Serving: 235 calories, 7 g fat (3 g saturated), 14 g protein, 31 g carbohydrate, 3 g fiber, 923 mg sodium, 152 mg cholesterol.

Salsa-Topped Omelet for Two

MAKES: 2 servings
PREP: 10 minutes
COOK: 12 minutes

  1 red potato with skin, diced

  1 onion, chopped

  ½ cup reduced-sodium chicken broth

  ¼ teaspoon salt

  ⅛ teaspoon black pepper

  1 ounce fully-cooked Canadian bacon, chopped

  3 large egg whites

  2 large whole eggs

  1 tablespoon grated Parmesan cheese

  ½ cup bottled salsa

1 Lightly coat 10-inch nonstick skillet with cooking spray. Place over medium-high heat. Add potato and onion; cook, stirring often, for 2 minutes or until lightly browned. Add broth, ⅛ teaspoon salt, and the pepper. Reduce heat to medium; cover; cook 5 minutes. Uncover; cook until liquid evaporates, 3 to 5 minutes longer. Stir in bacon.

2 Meanwhile, beat together egg whites, whole eggs, remaining ⅛ teaspoon salt, and the Parmesan cheese in medium-size bowl until well blended.

3 Transfer potato mixture to small bowl; cover and set aside. Wipe out skillet with paper toweling. Coat skillet with cooking spray.

4 Place skillet over medium heat. Add egg mixture; cook 30 seconds or until bottom is just set. Tilt skillet and lift edge of cooked egg and fill open space with uncooked egg. Spoon potato filling over half of omelet; fold other half of omelet over to cover filling. Cut in half. Slide each half onto separate plates.

5 Add salsa to skillet; heat 1 minute. Divide equally between omelet halves.

Nutrient Value Per Serving: 228 calories, 7 g fat (2 g saturated), 19 g protein, 23 g carbohydrate, 3 g fiber, 1,031 mg sodium, 220 mg cholesterol.

Blueberry Cottage Cheese Pancakes

MAKES: 18 (4-inch) pancakes
PREP: 5 minutes
COOK: about 8 minutes per batch

  1¼ cups all-purpose flour

  ⅓ cup sugar

  1 teaspoon baking soda

  ½ teaspoon salt

  1 cup fat-free sour cream

  1 cup reduced-fat (1% fat) cottage cheese

  2 large eggs

  1 teaspoon vanilla extract

  2 cups fresh blueberries

  1 tablespoon butter, for griddle

Toppings (optional):

  Lite pancake syrup

  Berries

  Citrus wedges

1 Stir together flour, sugar, baking soda, and salt in medium-size bowl.

2 Stir together sour cream, cottage cheese, eggs, and vanilla in large bowl. Add flour mixture; stir just until combined. Gently stir in blueberries.

3 Heat oven to 200°. Heat griddle over medium heat. Lightly butter griddle.

4 Spoon scant ¼ cup batter onto griddle for each pancake; spread to diameter of 4 inches. Batter will be very thick. Cook until light brown on bottom and bubbles begin to form on top, 5 to 6 minutes. Turn pancakes over with wide spatula. Cook until set in center, about 2 minutes.

5 Transfer to baking sheet and keep warm in oven until ready to serve. Repeat with remaining batter. Serve with light pancake syrup and garnish with berries and citrus wedges, if desired.

Nutrient Value Per Pancake: 91 calories, 2 g fat (1 g saturated), 4 g protein, 15 g carbohydrate, 1 g fiber, 155 mg sodium, 27 mg cholesterol.

Banana-Pecan Waffles

MAKES: 8 waffles
PREP: 20 minutes
COOK: 3 to 4 minutes per waffle

1¾ cups all-purpose flour

1 tablespoon sugar

½ teaspoon baking powder

½ teaspoon baking soda

½ teaspoon ground cinnamon

¼ teaspoon salt

¾ cup mashed banana (2 small)

2 large egg whites

1 large whole egg

1 tablespoon vegetable oil

1 cup buttermilk

1 teaspoon vanilla extract

¼ cup pecans, toasted and finely chopped

Toppings (optional):

Butter, maple syrup, sliced bananas, chopped pecans

1 Heat nonstick Belgian or standard waffle iron.

2 Stir together flour, sugar, baking powder, baking soda, cinnamon, and salt in large bowl.

3 Beat together banana, egg whites, and whole egg in medium-size bowl. Beat in oil, buttermilk, vanilla, and pecans.

4 Make well in center of flour mixture. Add banana mixture to well, stirring quickly, just until flour mixture is evenly moistened.

5 Coat waffle iron with cooking spray. Spoon slightly rounded ⅓ cup batter for each 4-inch waffle onto hot iron, quickly spreading to cover entire surface. Cook following manufacturer's instructions.

6 Serve waffles hot with an assortment of desired toppings.

Nutrient Value Per Waffle: 193 calories, 6 g fat (1 g saturated), 6 g protein, 30 g carbohydrate, 2 g fiber, 230 mg sodium, 28 mg cholesterol.

Spiced French Toast

MAKES: 6 servings

PREP: 15 minutes

SOAK: 10 minutes

COOK: about 12 minutes

1 loaf (about 12 ounces, 25 inches long) French bread

6 large whole eggs

3 large egg whites

⅔ cup fat-free half-and-half

3 tablespoons dark rum

1 teaspoon vanilla extract

¼ teaspoon salt

Pinch ground allspice

Pinch ground cinnamon

1 tablespoon confectioners' sugar

6 tablespoons light pancake syrup

1 Slice ends off loaf. Slice loaf diagonally into 18 equal slices, about ¾ inch thick.

2 In large bowl, whisk together whole eggs, egg whites, half-and-half, rum, vanilla, salt, allspice, and cinnamon. In 13 x 9 x 2-inch baking dish, place half the bread slices in single layer. Pour half of egg mixture over bread. Let soak 10 minutes, turning occasionally.

3 Meanwhile, coat large nonstick skillet or griddle with cooking spray. Heat skillet or griddle over medium-high heat. Transfer soaked bread to hot griddle. Place remaining bread in baking dish and add remaining egg mixture.

Sensible Starters

Even if you're running behind in the A.M., do have breakfast. Pick up an English muffin, a piece of fruit, and skim milk and eat them at your desk or before you start out on the car pool. Or have a cup of low or nonfat yogurt, flavored with cut-up fruit or maple syrup. Here are some tips to get you going.

- Picking a truly low-calorie breakfast cereal is simple. It's just a matter of reading. Skip over the banners on the packaging that scream out "low-fat" or "healthy" or "whole grain." Go directly to the nutrition panel on the side of the box to check out the calorie count per serving. Aim to keep a serving under 120 calories and 3 grams of fat, and serve with fat-free milk.

- Granola is classically high in fat. If you must include it for breakfast, stir ¼ cup low-fat granola into fat-free plain yogurt.

- Look for high-fiber cereals to help keep you feeling full without investing in a lot of calories. Other high-fiber options include whole-grain bread, English muffins, and whole-grain waffles.

- If you love eggs for breakfast and the rest of your diet is low in saturated fat (not much red meat, chicken skin, or creamy foods), then feel free to indulge occasionally. Even though eggs are high in cholesterol—213 mg each—health experts say that we should be more concerned with the total fat and, in particular, the saturated fat in our diet. An egg has only 5 grams total fat and 2 grams saturated, so we can afford to eat them a couple of times a week. And since all the fat is in the yolks, consider making omelets or scrambled eggs from a mix of whole eggs and whites.

4 Cook first batch of bread until golden brown, about 2 to 3 minutes per side (instant-read thermometer inserted in center of a slice should register 160°). Transfer French toast to serving platter; cover with foil.

5 Cook second batch of French toast. Place on top of first batch. Dust with confectioners' sugar, if desired. Serve immediately with 1 tablespoon syrup per serving.

Nutrient Value Per Serving: 296 calories, 7 g fat (2 g saturated), 14 g protein, 42 g carbohydrate, 2 g fiber, 596 mg sodium, 213 mg cholesterol.

Pumpkin Spice Muffins

MAKES: 12 muffins
PREP: 10 minutes
BAKE: at 375°F for 25 minutes

2 cups all-purpose flour

¾ cup packed light-brown sugar

1 tablespoon baking powder

1 teaspoon ground cinnamon

1 teaspoon ground ginger

¾ teaspoon salt

¼ teaspoon ground allspice

3 tablespoons unsalted butter, cut into pieces and chilled

¼ cup liquid egg substitute

¾ cup plus 2 tablespoons canned solid-pack pumpkin puree (not pie filling)

⅔ cup nonfat milk

1 teaspoon vanilla

2 tablespoons chopped pecans

1 Heat oven to 375°F. Coat 12 standard-size muffin-pan cups with cooking spray, coating muffin-pan top around cups as well.

2 In large bowl, stir together flour, brown sugar, baking powder, cinnamon, ginger, salt, and allspice. With pastry blender or 2 knives used scissors fashion, cut in butter until mixture resembles fine crumbs.

3 In small bowl, beat together egg substitute, pumpkin, milk, and vanilla until blended. Stir egg mixture into flour mixture just until blended. Spoon batter into muffin cups, dividing equally. Sprinkle pecans over tops of batter.

4 Bake for 25 minutes or until golden and toothpick inserted in centers comes out clean. Remove muffins from pan to wire rack. Let cool slightly. Serve warm.

Nutrient Value Per Muffin: 179 calories, 4 g fat (2 g saturated), 4 g protein, 32 g carbohydrate, 2 g fiber, 291 mg sodium, 8 mg cholesterol.

Orange–Poppy Seed Muffins

MAKES: 12 muffins
PREP: 15 minutes
BAKE: at 350° for 25 minutes

½ cup honey

2 tablespoons orange juice

2 teaspoons fresh lemon juice

1¾ cups all-purpose flour

1 tablespoon baking powder

¾ teaspoon salt

3 tablespoons unsalted butter, cut into pieces and well chilled

1¼ tablespoons poppy seeds

1 tablespoon grated orange rind

⅔ cup mashed banana (1 large)

2 large egg whites

¾ cup nonfat milk

1½ teaspoons orange extract

1 Heat oven to 350°. Coat 12 standard-size muffin-pan cups with cooking spray, coating muffin-pan top around cups as well.

2 Heat 2 tablespoons of the honey, the orange juice, and lemon juice in small saucepan to a boil. Reduce heat to low; cook until thickened slightly, about 5 minutes. Remove pan from heat; let glaze cool.

3 Stir together flour, baking powder, and salt in large bowl. With pastry blender or 2 knives used scissors fashion, cut in butter until mixture resembles fine crumbs. Stir in poppy seeds and rind.

4 Lightly beat together banana, remaining 6 tablespoons honey, egg whites, milk, and orange extract in small bowl. Stir egg mixture into flour mixture just until evenly moistened. Spoon batter into muffin cups, dividing equally.

5 Bake for 25 minutes or until golden and toothpick inserted in centers comes out clean. Remove muffins from pan to wire rack. Brush tops with the orange glaze. Serve warm.

Nutrient Value Per Muffin: 163 calories, 4 g fat (2 g saturated), 3 g protein, 30 g carbohydrate, 1 g fiber, 286 mg sodium, 8 mg cholesterol.

Apple-Raisin Muffins

MAKES: 12 muffins
PREP: 15 minutes
BAKE: at 400° for 25 minutes

2 cups all-purpose flour

½ cup packed dark-brown sugar

1 teaspoon baking powder

½ teaspoon baking soda

½ teaspoon ground cinnamon

½ teaspoon salt

¾ cup buttermilk

½ cup unsweetened applesauce

2 large egg whites

2 tablespoons canola oil

1 cup chopped peeled apple

⅓ cup dark seedless raisins

1 Heat oven to 400°. Coat 12 standard-size muffin-pan cups with cooking spray.

2 Stir together flour, brown sugar, baking powder, baking soda, cinnamon, and salt in large bowl. Make well in center.

3 Stir together buttermilk, applesauce, egg whites, and canola oil in small bowl. Pour buttermilk mixture into well of dry ingredients; stir just until dry ingredients are evenly moistened. Do not overmix. Gently fold in apple and raisins. Divide batter evenly among 12 muffin cups.

4 Bake for 25 minutes or until toothpick inserted in centers of muffins comes out clean. Turn muffins out onto wire rack; let cool.

Nutrient Value Per Muffin: 161 calories, 3 g fat (0 g saturated), 3 g protein, 32 g carbohydrate, 1 g fiber, 221 mg sodium, 1 mg cholesterol.

Tropical Smoothie

MAKES: 4 servings
PREP: 5 minutes

> 1 cup frozen nonfat vanilla yogurt
>
> 1 cup fresh orange juice
>
> 1 mango, pitted, peeled, and chopped
>
> 1 papaya, seeded, peeled, and chopped
>
> 2 cups strawberries, hulled

Place yogurt and orange juice in blender; whirl to combine. Add mango, papaya, and strawberries; whirl until smooth, about 1 minute. Serve chilled.

Nutrient Value Per Serving: 178 calories, 1 g fat (0 g saturated), 5 g protein, 36 g carbohydrate, 3 g fiber, 29 mg sodium, 0 mg cholesterol.

Avoiding the Muffin Trap

Tempted by the fresh-baked goodies at your favorite breakfast stop? Before you take your first bite, consider the fattening facts.

- **SIZE MATTERS** The typical bake-shop muffin is mammoth: at least twice the size of a supermarket package product. At 4 ounces, just one is like eating four slices of bread.

- **CALORIES COUNT** But that's not the whole story. With all the fat, sugar, and other add-ins, these muffins bake up more calories than those four bread slices—at least 430 calories versus about 280. Keep those numbers in mind when checking out a "reduced-calorie" treat.

- **FAT FIGURES** Even a "healthy" fruit-flecked or bran muffin can pack in 18 grams of fat. If you choose one chock-full of chocolate chips or nuts, you really up the fat grams. Look for low-fat versions, which can bring you down to 4 grams of fat and 260 calories. But do check the numbers: Some shops may cut fat yet up the amount of sugar, so there isn't much of a dent in calories. Whichever muffin you walk away with, you'll do better by saving half for tomorrow. Even smaller, packaged muffins typically round out at 220 calories, 11 grams of fat, and 12 grams of sugar. The bottom line: If you control the size, sugar, and fat content, homemade takes the cake every time. In the long run, an English muffin might be the best option.

GUILT-FREE SALAD SPREADS

Sometimes, all you want is a tuna salad sandwich. Well, here's a variation on tuna as well as chicken, egg, and seafood salads that keep the calorie counts under control while offering new taste sensations. And look to the following alternatives for bread: 1 small (1-ounce) pita bread, 71 calories; 1 small potato roll, 80 calories; 2 slices light oatmeal bread, 93 calories; 1 low-fat flour tortilla (9 inches), 110 calories; or a small English muffin, 130 calories.

Curried Tuna

MAKES: 4 servings (1⅔ cups total)

In small bowl, combine two 6-ounce cans tuna packed in water, drained, ⅓ cup reduced-fat mayonnaise dressing, ¾ teaspoon curry powder, 1 carrot, peeled and shredded, ¼ cup thinly sliced red onion, ¼ teaspoon salt, and ¼ teaspoon black pepper.

Nutrient Value Per Serving: 144 calories, 3 g fat (1 g saturated), 22 g protein, 6 g carbohydrate, 1 g fiber, 615 mg sodium, 26 mg cholesterol.

In-a-Pickle Chicken

MAKES: 6 servings (4 cups total)

In small bowl, combine ⅓ cup reduced-fat mayonnaise dressing, ⅓ cup chopped sweet gherkin pickles, 3 tablespoons pickle liquid, 1 tablespoon yellow mustard, ¼ teaspoon salt, ¼ teaspoon black pepper, 1 sweet red pepper, diced, and 3 cups cubed cooked chicken.

Nutrient Value Per Serving: 185 calories, 7 g fat (2 g saturated), 21 g protein, 8 g carbohydrate, 1 g fiber, 383 mg sodium, 59 mg cholesterol.

Honey and Dill Egg

MAKES: 4 servings (1⅔ cups total)

Hard-cook 5 eggs and finely chop. In small bowl, stir together 1 teaspoon honey, 1 tablespoon snipped dill, and ⅓ cup reduced-fat mayonnaise dressing. Stir in chopped eggs, ¼ teaspoon salt, ⅛ teaspoon black pepper, ¼ cup finely chopped celery, ¼ cup finely chopped scallion, and ⅛ teaspoon liquid hot-pepper sauce.

Nutrient Value Per Serving: 139 calories, 9 g fat (3 g saturated), 8 g protein, 6 g carbohydrate, 0 g fiber, 406 mg sodium, 265 mg cholesterol.

Tarragon-Seafood

MAKES: 4 servings (2 cups total)

In small bowl, break up 8 ounces imitation crabmeat (surimi) into small pieces. Stir in ¼ cup light mayonnaise, 2 chopped scallions (including some of green), 1 teaspoon distilled white vinegar, 1 teaspoon sugar, and ⅓ teaspoon tarragon.

Nutrient Value Per Serving: 117 calories, 6 g fat (1 g saturated), 9 g protein, 8 g carbohydrate, 0 g fiber, 203 mg sodium, 22 mg cholesterol

Ham and Scallion Roll

MAKES: 6 servings
PREP: 15 minutes

1 piece flat shepherd's bread, not whole-wheat (from 14-ounce package)

1 container (about 6.5 ounces) spreadable herb cheese

1 sweet red pepper, cored, seeded, and cut into strips

¼ pound thinly sliced deli ham

3 tablespoons mayonnaise-style salad dressing

3 scallions, trimmed

1 Unfold bread. Spread with cheese. Sprinkle pepper strips across center. Top with ham; spread with dressing. Lay scallions across short length of bread.

2 Beginning with short end, roll up bread. Trim ends. Slice into 1½- to 2-inch-thick pinwheels.

Nutrient Value Per Serving: 186 calories, 9 g fat (1 g saturated), 9 g protein, 21 g carbohydrate, 2 g fiber, 518 mg sodium, 27 mg cholesterol.

Falafel

MAKES: 4 servings
PREP: 15 minutes
COOK: 6 minutes

1 can (19 ounces) chickpeas, drained and rinsed

½ onion, coarsely chopped

⅓ cup packaged unseasoned bread crumbs

2 tablespoons chopped flat-leaf Italian parsley

1 teaspoon ground cumin

2 cloves garlic, smashed

½ teaspoon salt

¼ teaspoon black pepper

1 cup nonfat plain yogurt

2 tablespoons tahini (ground sesame paste)

2½ tablespoons fresh lemon juice

1 clove garlic, chopped

½ cucumber, peeled and diced

4 small pita breads

2 cups shredded iceberg lettuce

1 Whirl together chickpeas, onion, bread crumbs, parsley, cumin, garlic, ¼ teaspoon salt, and ⅛ teaspoon pepper in food processor until well blended. Divide into 12 equal portions. Roll each into a ball and flatten slightly.

2 Coat nonstick skillet with cooking spray. Heat over medium heat. Add falafel balls; cook 2 to 3 minutes per side or until lightly browned. Set aside.

3 Whirl together yogurt, tahini, lemon juice, garlic, remaining ¼ teaspoon salt, and remaining ⅛ teaspoon pepper in food processor until smooth. Stir in cucumber.

4 Split each pita bread halfway down side. Put ½ cup lettuce inside each pita; add 3 falafel balls and top with some of the cucumber sauce.

Nutrient Value Per Serving: 347 calories. 8 g fat (1 g saturated), 17 g protein, 57 g carbohydrate, 9 g fiber, 670 mg sodium, 1 mg cholesterol.

Italian Bread Pepperoni Pizza

MAKES: 6 servings
PREP: 15 minutes
BAKE: at 400° for 15 minutes

1 loaf Italian bread (about 14 ounces), split in half horizontally

1½ cups bottled fat-free pasta sauce

¼ pound white mushrooms, thinly sliced

2 ounces turkey pepperoni, finely chopped

1½ cups coarsely shredded part-skim mozzarella (6 ounces)

1 teaspoon dried oregano

Pinch each of salt and black pepper

2 tablespoons grated Parmesan cheese

1 Heat oven to 400°.

2 Place bread halves, cut sides up, on baking sheet. Pull out some of soft bread centers to make loaves slightly concave. Spread each half with ½ cup of pasta sauce. Arrange mushrooms over sauce; sprinkle with pepperoni. Top with mozzarella; sprinkle with oregano, salt, and pepper. Spoon remaining pasta sauce over tops.

3 Bake until lightly browned, about 15 minutes. Sprinkle with Parmesan. Cut on angle into slices. Serve hot.

Nutrient Value Per Serving: 312 calories, 9 g fat (4 g saturated), 18 g protein, 40 g carbohydrate, 3 g fiber, 952 mg sodium, 30 mg cholesterol.

French Bread BBQ Pork Melts

MAKES: 6 servings
PREP: 20 minutes
BAKE: at 400° for 12 minutes

Slaw:

⅓ cup reduced-fat mayonnaise dressing

1 tablespoon fresh lemon juice

1 tablespoon nonfat milk

½ teaspoon sugar

½ teaspoon ground celery seeds

1 bag (16 ounces) shredded coleslaw mix

Pork Melts:

1 crusty baguette (18 inches long, about
6 ounces, or trimmed to weigh 6 ounces)

3 tablespoons sweet pickle relish

1 jar (12 ounces) roasted red peppers, drained

1 container (20 ounces) prepared pulled pork
with barbecue sauce

1 cup shredded reduced-fat cheddar cheese
(4 ounces)

1 Slaw: In small bowl, whisk together
mayonnaise dressing, lemon juice, milk, sugar,
and celery seeds. Place coleslaw mix in medium-
size bowl. Add mayonnaise mixture; toss to
combine. Cover and refrigerate until serving.

2 Pork Melts: Heat oven to 400°. Slice baguette
into 3 equal pieces, each about 5½ inches long.
Slice each piece of bread in half horizontally to
make 6 pieces total. Arrange bread, cut sides up,
on a baking sheet.

3 Spread ½ tablespoon relish onto each piece
of bread. Top with roasted peppers, dividing
equally. Divide pulled pork among bread pieces,
about ⅓ cup per sandwich. Sprinkle with
cheddar, about 1½ tablespoons each.

4 Bake sandwiches for 12 minutes or until
barbecued pork is hot and cheese is melted.
Run under the broiler for 2 minutes to crisp
cheese, if desired. Serve warm with coleslaw.

*Nutrient Value Per Serving: 343 calories, 10 g fat
(4 g saturated), 22 g protein, 41 g carbohydrate,
3 g fiber, 1,394 mg sodium, 36 mg cholesterol.*

Red Pepper Panini

MAKES: 4 servings
PREP: 20 minutes

1 tablespoon boiling water

¼ cup dark seedless raisins

1 tablespoon balsamic vinegar

1 teaspoon grated orange rind

¼ cup fresh orange juice

½ cup oil-cured black olives, pitted

1 teaspoon dried oregano

¼ teaspoon black pepper

2 (6-inch) focaccia, tomato or plain

⅔ cup shredded mozzarella cheese

1 jar (7 ounces) roasted red peppers, drained
and cut into strips

8 to 10 fresh basil leaves (optional)

1 Pour 1 tablespoon boiling water over raisins in
1-cup measure. Stir in balsamic vinegar. Cover
with plastic wrap; let stand 15 minutes to plump
raisins. Add orange rind and juice.

2 Combine olives, raisin mixture, oregano, and
pepper in food processor or blender. Whirl until
almost smooth.

3 Split each focaccia horizontally into 2 equal
halves. Spread 1½ tablespoons of olive mixture
over one bottom half of focaccia. Top with ⅓
cup cheese, half the red-pepper strips, and half
the basil leaves, if using. Replace top. Repeat
with other focaccia and remaining ingredients.
Divide each focaccia into quarters.

*Nutrient Value Per Serving: 299 calories, 13 g fat
(4 g saturated), 8 g protein, 40 g carbohydrate,
2 g fiber, 989 mg sodium, 15 mg cholesterol.*

11 WEEKEND WARRIORS

WEEKEND. WHAT A GLORIOUS WORD. Time to relax with family and friends, to kick up your heels, to pursue your personal passion. But weekends can be a weight-loss challenge. A more fluid agenda opens up all sorts of fat traps, and restaurants and get-togethers can lure even the most dedicated dieter astray.

To the rescue: sixteen delectable dips and other hors d'oeuvres for diet-wise partying, plus a few strategies for dining out without scaling up.

Consider for instance, our stuffed tomatoes. We have two versions: one filled with cheddar (page 216), the other with broccoli (page 216). These nifty morsels are so tasty, your guests will never guess they're diet delights. Our twist on hot artichoke dip (page 220) trims fat but doesn't compromise the hearty flavor. Ditto our Creamy Crab Spread (page 219) made with lemon, red pepper, and crab. Mock Guacamole (page 218) is another winner. Instead of fat-laden avocado, we substitute green peppers and sour cream—and we've heard nothing but compliments on the result.

Calorie-conscious canapés include Shrimp 'n' Sausage Skewers (page 221)—you'll be surprised at how well these opposites attract—Ham 'n' Potato Kabobs (page 222) with garlic mayonnaise, and Sesame Chicken (page 222) with a tart red currant dip.

Got the munchies? Stave the crave with our South-of-the-Border Snack Mix (page 219). Socko spices and Worcestershire sauce give chips, pretzels, and peanuts an explosion of flavor. Or slide some veggies into our pesto spread (page 220), made with cottage cheese, ricotta, light cream cheese, and grated Parmesan.

For more weekend weapons, study out our Diet-Safe Dining-Out Guide (page 228) and Party Survival Primer (page 226).

Clockwise from lower right: Seseme Chicken with Dipping Sauce (page 222),
Ham 'n' Potato Kabobs (page 222), and Tex-Mex Crab-Filled Scoops (page 223).

Cheddar-Stuffed Cherry Tomatoes

MAKES: 36 tomatoes

PREP: 20 minutes

36 cherry tomatoes (about 2 pints)

1 package (8 ounces) ⅓-less-fat cream cheese, at room temperature

1 cup finely shredded reduced-fat cheddar cheese (4 ounces)

1 tablespoon milk

1 small clove garlic, mashed

½ teaspoon salt

¼ teaspoon ground cumin

¼ teaspoon cayenne

¼ teaspoon black pepper

1 Rinse cherry tomatoes; pull off stems. Using sharp knife, cut cone-shaped core from stem end of each. Spoon out center of each tomato using small spoon. Drain tomatoes, upside down, on paper toweling.

2 Cut up cream cheese into bowl. Add cheddar, milk, garlic, salt, cumin, cayenne, and black pepper; mash with fork. Spoon into pastry bag fitted with large plain tip; pipe into tomatoes (or use a spoon).

Nutrient Value Per Tomato: 30 calories, 2 g fat (1 g saturated), 2 g protein, 1 g carbohydrate, 0 g fiber, 88 mg sodium, 7 mg cholesterol.

Stuffed Tomatoes with Broccoli Filling

MAKES: 36 tomatoes

PREP: 20 minutes

COOK: 12 minutes

36 cherry tomatoes (about 2 pints)

3 cups lightly packed broccoli flowerets and sliced stems

½ cup light sour cream

2 tablespoons vegetable oil

1 small onion, finely chopped

2 tablespoons all-purpose flour

½ teaspoon salt

¼ teaspoon cayenne

⅛ teaspoon black pepper

½ cup grated Parmesan cheese

1 tablespoon fresh lemon juice

1 Rinse tomatoes; pull off stems. Using sharp knife, cut out cone-shaped core from stem end of each. Spoon out center of each tomato, using small spoon. Drain tomatoes, upside down, on paper toweling.

2 Bring large saucepan of water to boiling. Add broccoli; boil 5 minutes or until tender. Drain; let cool slightly. Combine broccoli and sour cream in food processor. Whirl to puree.

3 Heat oil in nonstick skillet over low heat. Add onion; sauté for 3 minutes. Add flour; cook, stirring, 2 minutes. Add puree to skillet; cook 2 minutes or until thickened. Remove from heat. Stir in salt, cayenne, and black pepper. Let cool slightly. Stir in Parmesan.

4 Spoon mixture into pastry bag fitted with large plain tip; pipe into tomatoes (or use a spoon).

Nutrient Value Per Tomato: 21 calories, 1 g fat (1 g saturated), 1 g protein, 2 g carbohydrate, 0 g fiber, 65 mg sodium, 2 mg cholesterol.

Double-Deviled Eggs

MAKES: 24 egg halves
PREP: 10 minutes
COOK: about 15 minutes

12 large eggs, at room temperature

¼ cup reduced-fat mayonnaise dressing

4 teaspoons Dijon mustard

2 ounces baked Virginia ham, finely chopped (about ½ cup)

1 teaspoon Worcestershire sauce

Garnish:

Ground paprika

2 tablespoons sliced, pitted black olives

2 tablespoons finely chopped baked Virginia ham

1 Place eggs in large saucepan; add enough cold water to cover eggs. Bring to a boil over high heat. Lower heat to medium; simmer for 10 minutes. Drain eggs in colander; cool under cold running water. Peel. Let cool completely at room temperature.

2 Cut each egg in half lengthwise; carefully remove yolks and place in bowl. Place whites on work surface.

3 Add mayonnaise dressing and mustard to yolks; mash with fork until well blended and smooth. Stir in ham and Worcestershire sauce.

4 Mound scant tablespoon of yolk mixture into hollow of each egg white. Garnish third of eggs with paprika, another third with olives, and remaining third with ham.

Make-Ahead Tip: If not serving immediately, do not garnish. Cover filled eggs with plastic wrap; refrigerate up to 2 days. Garnish when ready to serve.

Nutrient Value Per Egg Half: 47 calories, 3 g fat (1 g saturated), 4 g protein, 1 g carbohydrate, 0 g fiber, 104 mg sodium, 107 mg cholesterol.

Roasted Pepper Hummus Dip

MAKES: 1½ cups
PREP: 5 minutes

1 container (8 ounces) hummus (about 1 cup)

1 bottled roasted red pepper, drained and coarsely chopped (about ½ cup)

¼ teaspoon ground cumin

Pinch cayenne

Combine hummus, roasted pepper, cumin, and cayenne in blender or food processor. Whirl until smooth. Serve at room temperature.

Nutrient Value Per 1 Tablespoon: 16 calories, 1 g fat (0 g saturated), 1 g protein, 1 g carbohydrate, 1 g fiber, 40 mg sodium, 0 mg cholesterol.

Mock Guacamole

MAKES: 1½ cups
PREP: 10 minutes
COOK: about 15 minutes

1 pound sweet green peppers

2 tablespoons finely chopped onion

1 small clove garlic, finely chopped

1 teaspoon salt

½ teaspoon dried oregano

⅛ teaspoon black pepper

2 tablespoons fresh lime juice

6 cilantro stems with leaves

¼ cup light sour cream

Extra cilantro, for garnish (optional)

1 Roast peppers over an open flame on stove top or under broiler, turning occasionally until charred all over, about 15 minutes. Place peppers in brown paper bag; seal; let cool. Remove peppers from bag. Halve peppers lengthwise; remove stems and seeds. Scrape off skins.

2 Blend together peppers, onion, garlic, salt, oregano, black pepper, lime juice, and cilantro in blender or food processor until smooth. Scrape into small bowl. Stir in sour cream. Garnish with cilantro, if desired.

Nutrient Value Per 2 Tablespoons: 18 calories, 0 g fat (0 g saturated), 1 g protein, 4 g carbohydrate, 1 g fiber, 200 mg sodium, 2 mg cholesterol.

Blue-Cheese Dip

MAKES: 2 cups
PREP: 5 minutes
REFRIGERATE: at least 1 hour

1 container (16 ounces) nonfat sour cream

½ cup crumbled blue cheese (2 ounces)

½ cup chopped scallions (about 4)

¼ teaspoon salt

¼ teaspoon coarse black pepper

1 Pulse together sour cream and blue cheese in food processor until creamy (may be slightly lumpy). Remove to bowl. Stir in scallions, salt, and pepper. Refrigerate at least 1 hour.

2 Serve with a selection of vegetables.

Nutrient Value Per 1 Tablespoon: 19 calories, 1 g fat (1 g saturated), 1 g protein, 2 g carbohydrate, 0 g fiber, 57 mg sodium, 2 mg cholesterol.

South-of-the-Border Snack Mix

MAKES: about 12½ cups
PREP: 15 minutes
BAKE: at 250° for 30 minutes

- 4 cups broken baked tortilla chips (bite-size)
- 3 cups multi-bran cereal squares
- 2 cups reduced-fat cheddar cheese nips
- 3 cups mini pretzel twists
- ½ cup dry-roasted unsalted peanuts
- ¼ cup (½ stick) butter or margarine, melted
- 2 tablespoons Worcestershire sauce
- 1 tablespoon chili powder
- 2 teaspoons ground cumin
- 1 teaspoon garlic powder
- 1 teaspoon seasoned salt
- 1 teaspoon cayenne, or to taste

1 Position oven racks in second and third levels in oven. Heat oven to 250°.

2 Toss together broken tortilla chips, cereal squares, cheese nips, pretzel twists, and peanuts in large bowl until well mixed.

3 Stir together melted butter, Worcestershire sauce, chili powder, cumin, garlic powder, seasoned salt, and cayenne in small bowl until well mixed. Pour seasoning mixture over snack mix; toss until snack mix is evenly and lightly moistened with seasoning mixture. Turn snack mix into 2 ungreased 15 x 10 x 1-inch jelly-roll pans.

4 Bake snack mix for 30 minutes or until coating on snack mix begins to darken slightly; stir mix every 10 minutes and rotate the jelly-roll pans halfway through baking.

5 Let snack mix cool completely in pans on wire racks. Store tightly covered at room temperature for up to 5 days.

Nutrient Value Per ¼ Cup Serving: 56 calories, 2 g fat (1 g saturated), 1 g protein, 9 g carbohydrate, 1 g fiber, 132 mg sodium, 3 mg cholesterol.

Creamy Crab Spread

MAKES: 1½ cups
PREP: 10 minutes
REFRIGERATE: 30 minutes or up to 1 day

- 8 ounces ⅓-less-fat cream cheese, at room temperature
- 1 can (6 ounces) crabmeat, drained
- 1 large sweet red pepper, cored, seeded, and diced
- 1 large scallion, chopped (about ¼ cup)
- 1 teaspoon grated lemon rind
- 1 teaspoon fresh lemon juice
- 1 teaspoon Worcestershire sauce
- ¼ teaspoon liquid hot-pepper sauce
- ¼ teaspoon salt
- ¼ teaspoon black pepper

1 Beat cream cheese in medium-size bowl until creamy. Stir in drained crabmeat, red pepper, scallion, lemon rind, and juice, Worcestershire sauce, hot-pepper sauce, salt, and black pepper. Cover bowl tightly with a sheet of plastic wrap. Refrigerate at least 30 minutes or up to 1 day.

2 Spoon spread into small serving bowl. Serve with assortment of crackers for spreading.

Nutrient Value Per 1 Tablespoon: 33 calories, 2 g fat (1 g saturated), 3 g protein, 1 g carbohydrate, 0 g fiber, 91 mg sodium, 13 mg cholesterol.

Pesto Cheese Spread

MAKES: 3 cups
PREP: 10 minutes

   1½ cups low-fat (1%) cottage cheese

   ½ cup part-skim ricotta cheese

   2 tablespoons light cream cheese

   1 tablespoon grated Parmesan cheese

   2 teaspoons fresh lemon juice

   1 cup packed fresh basil leaves

   1 scallion, chopped

   1 clove garlic, finely chopped

   Assorted cut-up vegetables, for dipping

1 Combine cottage cheese, ricotta, cream cheese, Parmesan, and lemon juice in food processor or blender. Whirl until almost smooth.

2 Add basil, scallion, and garlic. Pulse until scallions are finely chopped and evenly distributed.

3 Serve at once, or cover and refrigerate up to 3 days.

Nutrient Value Per 1 Tablespoon: 11 calories, 0 g fat, (0 g saturated), 1 g protein, 0 g carbohydrate, 0 g fiber, 37 mg sodium, 1 mg cholesterol.

Hot Artichoke Dip

MAKES: 5 cups
PREP: 10 minutes
BAKE: at 350° for about 25 minutes

   2 tablespoons butter

   ¼ cup all-purpose flour

   2 cups low-fat (1%) milk

   ¾ teaspoon salt

   ¼ teaspoon black pepper

   Pinch ground nutmeg

   Few drops liquid hot-pepper sauce

   2 cloves garlic

   2 cans (14 ounces each) artichoke hearts, well drained

   1 package (10 ounces) frozen spinach, thawed and well drained

   2 cups shredded reduced-fat Jarlsberg cheese (8 ounces)

1 Melt butter in medium-size saucepan over medium heat. Whisk in flour; cook, stirring, about 1 minute. Slowly whisk in milk. Add salt, pepper, nutmeg, and hot-pepper sauce; cook, stirring, 1 to 2 minutes or until mixture is very thick. Let cool; stir occasionally.

2 Heat oven to 350°.

3 Process garlic, artichoke hearts, and spinach in food processor until very smooth. Stir into cooled sauce. Reserve 3 tablespoons cheese. Stir remaining cheese into mixture. Spoon into 1½-quart baking dish. Sprinkle with remaining cheese.

4 Bake for 25 minutes or until heated through.

Nutrient Value Per 1 Tablespoon: 18 calories, 1 g fat (0 g saturated), 2 g protein, 1 g carbohydrate, 0 g fiber, 66 mg sodium, 2 mg cholesterol.

Goat Cheese–Stuffed Mushrooms

MAKES: about 3 dozen mushroom caps
PREP: 15 minutes
COOK: 16 minutes
BAKE: at 400° for 10 minutes

**36 white mushrooms (about 1½ pounds),
stems removed and chopped**

3 slices bacon, chopped

⅓ cup finely chopped red onion

1 large clove garlic, finely chopped

¼ teaspoon dried thyme

1 thin slice white bread, finely diced

1 tablespoon chopped parsley

3 ounces goat cheese, crumbled

1 Heat oven to 400°.

2 Cook mushroom caps in saucepan of boiling
water until partially cooked, 5 minutes. Drain.
Place, stem side up, on paper towels.

3 Cook bacon in medium-size nonstick skillet
over medium heat for 3 minutes. Add chopped
mushroom stems, onion, garlic, and thyme;
cook, stirring occasionally, for 8 minutes. Scrape
mixture into medium-size bowl. Add bread,
parsley, and goat cheese; mix well.

4 Place mushroom caps on baking pan. Spoon
1 to 2 teaspoons filling into each cap, depending
on size of mushrooms.

5 Bake for 10 minutes or until slightly golden.

*Nutrient Value Per Mushroom Cap: 23 calories,
1 g fat (1 g saturated), 2 g protein, 1 g carbohydrate,
0 g fiber, 40 mg sodium, 2 mg cholesterol.*

Shrimp 'n' Sausage Skewers

MAKES: about 5 dozen skewers
PREP: 15 minutes
SOAK: skewers in water 30 minutes
BROIL: 2 to 4 minutes

60 (6-inch) wooden skewers

½ cup apricot jam

2 tablespoons water

**2 packages (3.25 ounces each) chorizo sausage,
cut into ¼-inch-thick slices (about 60), or
other precooked spicy sausage**

**2 pounds large shrimp (about 60), shelled and
cleaned**

1 Soak wooden skewers in pan of water
overnight.

2 To prepare dipping sauce, heat together jam
and water in small saucepan over medium-low
heat, stirring to mix.

3 Heat broiler.

4 Place 1 slice of chorizo in center part of
cleaned shrimp. Slide a skewer through shrimp
and chorizo. Place on baking sheet. Repeat with
remaining shrimp and chorizo.

5 Broil for 1 to 2 minutes per side or until
shrimp is cooked through. Serve with apricot
dipping sauce.

*Nutrient Value Per Skewer: 30 calories, 1 g fat
(0 g saturated), 3 g protein, 2 g carbohydrate,
0 g fiber, 60 mg sodium, 21 mg cholesterol.*

Ham 'n' Potato Kabobs

MAKES: 18 skewers
PREP: 15 minutes
COOK: 7 minutes
GRILL: 3 minutes

¾ pound red or white new potatoes with skins, quartered

3 cloves garlic, pressed or mashed

¾ cup nonfat mayonnaise

1 teaspoon olive oil

1 tablespoon fresh lemon juice

Pinch salt

Pinch black pepper

1 jar (7 ounces) roasted red peppers, drained

½ pound baked or boiled ham (whole piece), cut into 1-inch cubes

18 bamboo skewers (8 inch)

1 Prepare outdoor grill with hot coals, heat gas grill to hot, or heat oven broiler. Soak bamboo skewers in warm water while preparing food.

2 Place potatoes in medium-size saucepan with enough water to cover. Bring to a boil; cook 7 minutes or until barely tender. Drain; rinse. Let cool so pieces do not split while threading skewers.

3 Prepare Aioli (garlic mayonnaise): Combine garlic, mayonnaise, olive oil, lemon juice, salt, and pepper in food processor or blender. Chop about 3 tablespoons of roasted peppers and add to blender. Puree until smooth and blended.

4 Once potatoes have cooled, remove skewers from soaking liquid. Thread each with 1 ham cube. Slice remaining peppers into 1-inch pieces. Thread onto skewers, followed by potato. (Skewers may be prepared up to this point and refrigerated.)

5 Grill or broil for 3 minutes, turning once, until heated through. Serve skewers with aioli sauce.

Nutrient Value Per Skewer: 44 calories, 1 g fat (0 g saturated), 3 g protein, 6 g carbohydrate, 0 g fiber, 216 mg sodium, 7 mg cholesterol.

Sesame Chicken with Dipping Sauce

MAKES: about 6 dozen
PREP: 20 minutes
MARINATE: 15 minutes
BAKE: at 350° for 20 minutes

2 pounds skinless, boneless chicken breasts, cut into 1-inch cubes

¼ cup bottled teriyaki sauce

½ cup all-purpose flour

1 teaspoon salt

½ teaspoon black pepper

4 large egg whites

1 bottle (2.6 ounces) sesame seeds (about ¾ cup), lightly toasted

Dipping Sauce:

- **½ cup red currant jelly**
- **2 teaspoons soy sauce**
- **1 teaspoon grated fresh ginger**

1 Heat oven to 350°. Coat baking sheet with cooking spray.

2 Combine chicken pieces and teriyaki sauce in medium-size bowl. Let stand 15 minutes.

3 Combine flour, salt, and pepper in large plastic food-storage bag. Lightly beat egg whites in medium-size bowl. Spread out sesame seeds in shallow pan. Add chicken cubes, a few at a time, to flour mixture; seal bag; shake to coat. Dip floured chicken pieces into egg white. Roll in sesame seeds to coat. Place on prepared baking sheet.

4 Bake for about 20 minutes or until golden and cooked through (instant-read thermometer inserted in chicken pieces should register 160°).

5 Sauce: Meanwhile, combine jelly, soy sauce, and ginger in small saucepan. Heat gently until warmed. Serve with chicken.

Nutrient Value Per Chicken Piece: 30 calories, 1 g fat (0 g saturated), 3 g protein, 3 g carbohydrate, 0 g fiber, 89 mg sodium, 7 mg cholesterol.

Tex-Mex Crab-Filled Scoops

MAKES: 60 scoops
PREP: 10 minutes

- **½ pound crabmeat, picked over and cartilage and shell discarded OR imitation crabmeat, finely shredded**
- **⅓ cup light mayonnaise**
- **⅛ teaspoon black pepper**
- **1½ tablespoons sliced pickled bottled jalapeño chiles, chopped**
- **⅔ cup prepared guacamole**
- **⅓ cup fat-free sour cream**
- **60 scoop-shaped corn tortilla chips (from 12-ounce bag)**
- **1 pint grape tomatoes, rinsed and each tomato halved**

1 In medium-size bowl, combine crabmeat, mayonnaise, black pepper, and jalapeño. In second bowl, stir together guacamole and sour cream.

2 Spread the 60 tortilla scoops onto large rimmed baking sheet. Place grape tomato half into bottom of each. Top each cup with 1 teaspoon crab mixture.

3 Just before serving, top with a teaspoon of guacamole–sour cream mixture.

Nutrient Value Per Scoop: 24 calories, 1 g fat (0 g saturated), 1 g protein, 2 g carbohydrate, 0 g fiber, 36 mg sodium, 4 mg cholesterol

Eggplant Crostini

MAKES: 24 crostini
PREP: 10 minutes
COOK: 50 minutes
BAKE: at 350° for 10 minutes

Eggplant caviar:

3 tablespoons olive oil

1 large shallot, finely chopped (about ⅓ cup)

1 large eggplant (about 2 pounds), peeled and cut into ¼-inch dice

¼ teaspoon salt

⅛ teaspoon black pepper

1 tablespoon fresh lemon juice

1 tablespoon balsamic vinegar

Crostini:

1 large loaf crusty Italian bread (about ¾ pound)

1 tablespoon olive oil

2 cloves garlic, peeled

1 Eggplant caviar: In a large heavy-bottom saucepan, heat together olive oil and shallot over medium heat for 1 minute. Add eggplant; cook, uncovered, stirring occasionally to prevent sticking, until smooth, thick, and somewhat dry in texture, about 50 minutes. If mixture becomes too dry, add a little water, a tablespoon at a time.

2 Transfer eggplant mixture to glass bowl. Stir in salt, pepper, lemon juice, and vinegar until well blended. Let mixture cool. Cover bowl tightly with plastic wrap; refrigerate until ready to serve, or up to 1 week.

3 Crostini: While eggplant is cooking, heat oven to 350°. Cut loaf of bread diagonally into ¼-inch-thick slices, for total of 24 slices. Brush one side of each slice with olive oil. Place slices, oil side up, on baking sheet.

4 Bake bread until golden and slightly crispy, about 10 minutes; turn slices over halfway through baking. Rub hot crostini a few times on both sides with peeled garlic cloves. Let crostini cool. Store in airtight container until ready to serve, or up to 2 days.

5 To serve: Spread 1 tablespoon eggplant caviar over each crostini. Serve immediately. Any leftover eggplant can be used as a dip for vegetables.

Nutrient Value Per Crostini: 71 calories, 3 g fat (0 g saturated), 2 g protein, 10 g carbohydrate, 1 g fiber, 109 mg sodium, 0 mg cholesterol

STOCKING THE BEVERAGE SHELF

The weekend has arrived, and now it's time to kick back. And that means, perhaps, a relaxing beverage with family and friends. The good news is that you're allowed; use the alcohol calories in place of snacks. Take a look at our following tips, and remember—everything in moderation.

When it comes to alcohol options, here are the numbers from our Nutrition Data Base. If you are making mixed drinks, keep in mind that 1 jigger is generally 1½ ounces.

	Calories
4 ounces red wine	82
4 ounces white wine	77
12 ounces beer	139
12 ounces light beer	95
1 ounce vodka, gin, or scotch	
94 proof	78
90 proof	75
86 proof	71
80 proof	66

For nonalcoholic beverages, the trick is to keep on eye on the sugar.

- Pass on the empty-calorie beverages, including sugared sodas and flavored juice "drinks," in favor of 100 percent fruit juices, such as orange juice and grapefruit, and vegetable juices.

- For a light change of pace, sample some of the naturally flavored seltzers, such as berry and citrus.

- Switch from whole milk to skim or nonfat, and you can save 70 calories per cup, as well as reducing fat grams.

PARTY SURVIVAL PRIMER

Here's the challenge: You're staring at tables of sumptuous party food and all the alarms are going off! Keep in mind our helpful hints, and you'll get by while still having a good time.

The first rule is not to fast all day in anticipation of the goodies to come. You'll be so hungry when you arrive that you'll eat twice as much. Instead, stick with your all-important breakfast and a light lunch, then turn to our smart strategies and savor the evening.

You're at a Buffet

- Always approach the buffet table with a salad plate, not a dinner plate, to encourage small portions.

- Eat slowly, and sit far from the food to discourage unconscious wandering in search of seconds.

- Look for the boiled shrimp (go skimpy on the dips), smoked salmon, and skinless chicken or turkey.

- Fill up on fresh or steamed vegetables and fruit.

- Salad is good, too, provided it's not covered with calorie-laden dressing.

You're Off to a Cocktail Party

- Make sure you have a light meal beforehand with some protein, such as turkey with lettuce and tomato on whole-grain bread, or plain tuna on a bed of lettuce. This will help regulate your blood sugar during the festivities so you are less susceptible to cravings.

- Stay clear of white dips; they're usually made with mayonnaise, butter, heavy cream, or sour cream.

- Favor red tomato-based cocktail sauce and salsa.

- Feel free to enjoy a drink or two, but remember that alcohol is converted to fat. Cut liquor with your choice of no-calorie mixers such as seltzer, diet tonic, or diet soda. For every alcoholic drink you have, sip one or two glasses of water or seltzer to keep your overall liquor consumption down.

- Prepare your offerings with no-one-will-notice swaps, such as low-fat ricotta and mozzarella in a tray of lasagna or baked ziti.

- Bring the fixin's for a chef's salad: lots of different greens, vegetables, and thin strips of cooked turkey breast, with a low-fat or no-fat dressing on the side and a small container of crumbled, cooked turkey bacon.

HOLIDAY HOW-TOS

Holidays pose a particular challenge to dieters, but there's no need to feel deprived. Quite the opposite. Our sensible swaps will help you out.

- **Serve potato latkes with ¼ cup unsweetened applesauce (232 calories) instead of the same-size serving of full-fat sour cream (329 calories).**

- **Make the wild rice variety of stuffing (166 calories per cup) instead of the traditional bread stuffing (356 calories).**

- **Skip the candied sweet potatoes drowned in butter and marshmallows (240 calories) in favor of plain baked sweet potatoes (117 calories).**

- **Substitute 1 cup French-style green beans (19 calories) for a serving of green bean casserole (121 calories).**

- **Instant cocoa made with sugar substitute instead of sugar (54 calories) will stand in for homemade cocoa prepared with whole milk and sugar (193 calories).**

- **Spread leftover turkey sandwiches with 2 tablespoons cranberry sauce (50 calories) instead of the same amount of full-fat mayonnaise (200 calories).**

- **For a festive drink, have two 4-ounce glasses of champagne (210 calories) instead of a cup of eggnog (343 calories).**

- **Instead of 1 cup of creamed spinach (338 calories), try 2 cups of sautéed spinach accented with garlic (106 calories).**

When we first went on the *Eat What You Love & Lose* plan, we steered clear of restaurants in order to get into a new rhythm of eating. We figured if we stayed away from the temptation of rich sauces and dessert carts, we'd be better off. After a few weeks, however, we felt confident enough to face a menu and win! The trick—and it really isn't tricky—is portion control. "Most places serve a huge plate of pasta!" says Julie. "It's twice as much as you need." The same goes for most other dishes. But since we now know what realistic portions are, it's fairly easy to eat the right amount and leave the rest. Julie's strategy is to divide her meal and ask for a doggie bag before she even starts so there's no confusion (or temptation). "Yes, waiters sometimes look at me oddly, but this technique works," she states.

We also read menu descriptions with vigilance. Some words, like "fried" and "cheesy," are immediately suspect. (For help in decoding terms, see Menu Talk, page 230.) One word of warning: When the waiter says, "Just a touch of cream," we've found it's more like a stream. And, remember, even a harmless-sounding entrée can be full of fat; chefs like to brush chicken and fish with butter or marinate them in an oil-based mixture before grilling or broiling. So see if it's possible to substitute; ask for a baked instead of scalloped potatoes or veggies rather than starch. We discovered it pays to be specific. Keeping in mind how Meg Ryan always ordered in *When Harry Met Sally*, we leave nothing to chance. Caesar salad, dressing on the side, hold the croutons; broiled fish with a slice of lemon, no butter or oil. If the dish doesn't arrive as promised, we don't hesitate to send it back, politely of course. After all, we're paying!

Foreign cuisines are usually good choices because they deliver highly seasoned dishes; we simply work hard to make the right selection (for more advice, see Foreign Intrigue, opposite). Fast-food restaurants, on the other hand, pose a big problem, but they're a fact of life—and a convenient time-saver when you're chauffeuring kids around. Anything labeled supersized, whopper, deluxe, or double is automatically off our list. And we close our eyes to the dessert offerings, since they are generally fat disasters. If you must, opt for low-fat frozen yogurt. (For other tips, see Fast-Food Strategies, page 230.)

Ethnic restaurants offer a wide range of diet-savvy dishes—but weighty ones as well. Here's how to make the best picks from three of the most popular international cuisines.

	CHINESE	ITALIAN	MEXICAN
Order	Broth-based vegetable soups; chop suey or chow mein; steamed or stir-fried dishes; steamed dumplings.	Baked, broiled, or grilled chicken, seafood, or meat; pasta (with marinara or other noncreamy sauces); polenta; vinaigrette dishes.	Baked burritos, black beans, fajitas, gazpacho, salsa, seafood or chicken filling, ceviche, soft tortillas.
Fat Traps	Breaded, battered, crispy, fried, or sweet-and-sour entrées; cashew or peanut dishes; egg or spring rolls; fried rice; lo mein; Peking duck; spareribs; lobster and other premade sauces.	Antipasto platters; baked stuffed clams; cream sauces (and other no-no's from "Menu Talk," following); eggplant (grilled, baked, or fried—it soaks up oil); meatballs; prosciutto (ham); stuffed pastas such as ravioli or tortellini.	Chili con queso; chimichangas; enchiladas; guacamole; nachos; quesadillas; refried beans; sopaipillas (sugary fried dough); tacos.
Tips	Request that stir-fries be made with minimal oil. Stretch 1 cup of a high-fat dish with steamed rice. For a filling meal, order steamed chicken or seafood with veggies, brown rice, and sauce on the side.	Check how dishes are prepared; the veggies in pasta primavera, for example, may be sautéed in oil. Not all tomato sauces are low in fat; those described as "pink" are usually made with cream.	Ask the waiter to bring warm tortillas (not tortilla chips) to the table for munching. Shun high-fat add-ons like sour cream and shredded cheese, but help yourself to salsa—almost no calories!

Menu Talk

These descriptive terms on your bill of fare will tip you off to dishes that do and don't fit into your diet plan. Pick from dishes that suggest little or no fat has been added:

Au jus (cooked in its natural juices)

Baked

Blackened (rubbed with spicy flavorings and cooked in a hot skillet)

Broiled

Grilled or grillé

Marinara (tomato-based sauce)

Poached or poché

Primavera (fresh vegetables)

Roasted or roti

Steamed

Steer clear of selections that translate into high fat due to oil, butter, cheese, or cream:

Alfredo

All'olio

Au gratin

Béarnaise

Béchamel

Beurre blanc

Carbonara

Française, francese

Hollandaise

Marsala

Mornay

Parmigiana

Piccata

Scampi

Fast-Food Strategies

Try these tips to survive life in the fast-food lane.

- Make it plain. Hold the mayo or "special sauce" and substitute ketchup or mustard. Cheese and bacon are other high-fat extras you can do without.

- Check your chicken sandwich. For lowest calorie count, it should be made with broiled or grilled (not breaded or fried) poultry. The same for fishwiches; most are fried and have more calories than a burger!

- Go slow at the salad bar. Choose undressed greens and cut-up raw veggies. Steer clear of mayonnaise or oil-based salads and high-fat add-ons like bacon bits, croutons, nuts, seeds, or cheese cubes. Ask for reduced-fat or fat-free dressing.

- Drink wisely. Ask for low-fat milk. For a vitamin boost, order orange juice instead of soda. But if you spring for soda, make it diet.

12 EAT WHAT YOU LOVE & MAINTAIN

OKAY. WE TOOK IT OFF, NOW WHAT? We're happy to say that the dreaded "maintenance" that follows most diets, didn't faze us. That's not to say we weren't nervous. "I was a wreck," admits Peggy Katalinich. "I loved my new body, but had this fear that if I ate anything extra at all I'd morph into my old self again. Now, six months later, I've kept those 28 pounds off and I'm enjoying every minute of the new, slimmer me."

So, how did we do it? The answer lies in the diet itself.

The *Eat What You Love & Lose* plan was specifically designed to avoid bounce-back pounds. "Since this isn't a super low-cal diet it doesn't require that much readjustment to maintain weight," says Susan McQuillan. "You should continue to keep close to the portion sizes in the menus, but realize you have a little more 'wiggle room.' If you're faced with special occasions you can indulge a bit; if you're stuck in a situation in which you can't make the best choices, relax. A few more calories here and there won't make a big difference as long as you stick to the basic concept."

For example, on days when you feel hungrier than usual, add a snack or have a slightly larger entrée. "The original two-week menus are fashioned so that you learn how to eyeball a plate of food and tell what a healthy portion looks like," adds Susan. "That way, no matter where you are or what you're eating, you're able to make a sensible judgment about how much food to eat." Picking up that all-important skill of sizing up portions is critical. "I can 'eyeball' a steak dinner and estimate my 3 ounces of meat and my allotment of baked potato in two seconds," says Michael Tyrrell. "I know immediately what I can and cannot eat."

"Once you have portion size under control, the rest is pretty easy," says Peggy. "Plus, I now have a better handle on how to cook for my family as well as what to serve company. And nobody is walking away hungry." After all, there are no good or bad foods, just appropriate portions. Even barbecued ribs don't make the endangered list. "When it's grilling season, I know I will indulge," admits Peggy. "But in a few ribs only, not a rack."

Susan also advises to stay on top of your weight. "I'm going to get on that scale every Monday morning," says Diane Mogelever. "If I see I'm slipping, I can correct it right away." Don't wait until you put on five pounds, agrees Susan. "Too many dieters delay until a few pounds becomes five, then ten, then it becomes more of a challenge." Immediately, when you see a pound or two creep up, return to the original plan and work off any gains pronto.

And keep exercising! Numerous studies of people who maintain weight losses have shown that those who stay active, stay slim. One of the most effective activities is walking; all you need are your two feet and a plan. Donna Meadow and Diane walk to and from work each day; Althea Needham heads to a local track at 5:30 A.M. for a 3-mile speed-walk. For a structured approach, consult our Walk Off the Weight workout (page 242). Or take a look at other alternative activities (chart, page 240). As with all new regimens, be sure to consult your doctor before beginning.

Now that the entire team has internalized proper proportions, we can't be fooled. Understanding what a healthy, sensible amount of food constitutes has been one of our biggest lessons. And making the lifelong commitment to taking care of ourselves. "We still love food and restaurants and talking about it and creating new recipes," says Julie Miltenberger. "But there's something extremely satisfying about getting control of your weight. Forever."

Switch and Save Diet Helper

After following the *Eat What You Love & Lose* two-week plan and preparing the recipes throughout this book, making smart food switches will become second nature. But to get you on your way, Mindy Hermann, R.D., has prepared this chart with swaps that keep all the flavor while cutting fat and calories.

INSTEAD OF:	SWITCH TO:	SAVINGS:
cheddar cheese (1 oz), 114 cal/9 g fat	cheddar cheese spread (1 oz), 54 cal/2 g fat	60 cal/7 g fat
butter (1 Tbs), 100 cal/11 g fat	whipped butter (1 Tbs), 65 cal/7 g fat	35 cal/4 g fat
yellow cake with icing (1 slice), 342 cal/8 g fat	angel food cake (1 slice) with low-fat whipped topping (2 Tbs), 138 cal/1 g fat	204 cal/7 g fat
butter, margarine, or oil (½ cup) in a bread, cake, or muffin recipe, 800 cal/91 g fat	applesauce or pureed fruit (½ cup), 53 cal/0 g fat	747 cal/91 g fat
butter or margarine (½ cup) in a brownie recipe, 800 cal/91 g fat	pureed prunes (½ cup), 90 cal/0 g fat	710 cal/91 g fat
egg (1), 75 cal/5 g fat	egg whites (2), 34 cal/0 g fat	41 cal/5 g fat
toast (1 slice) with butter or margarine (1 Tbs), 165 cal/5 g fat	toast (1 slice) with jelly (1 Tbs), 115 cal/1 g fat	50 cal/4 g fat
baking powder biscuit (1), 104 cal/12 g fat	dinner roll (1), 85 cal/2 g fat	19 cal/10 g fat
margarine (1 Tbs), 101 cal/11 g fat	fat-free spread (1 Tbs), 5 cal/0 g fat	96 cal/11 g fat
mayonnaise (1 Tbs), 100 cal/12 g fat	tartar sauce (1 Tbs), 75 cal/8 g fat	25 cal/4 g fat
salad dressing, blue cheese (2 Tbs), 154 cal/16 g fat	nonfat yogurt (1½ Tbs) with crumbled blue cheese (½ Tbs), 27 cal/1 g fat	127 cal/15 g fat
heavy cream (½ cup), 411 cal/44 g fat	evaporated skim milk (½ cup), 100 cal/0 g fat	311 cal/44 g fat
sour cream (1 cup), 493 cal/48 g fat	nonfat plain yogurt (1 cup), 127 cal/0 g fat	366 cal/48 g fat
brownie (1 medium), 139 cal/7 g fat	fat-free devil's food cookies (2), 100 cal/0 g fat	39 cal/7 g fat

INSTEAD OF:	SWITCH TO:	SAVINGS:
pudding, chocolate (½ cup) made with whole milk, 163 cal/4 g fat	pudding, chocolate (½ cup) made with skim milk, 144 cal/0 g fat	19 cal/4 g fat
ice cream, soft-serve (½ cup), 185 cal/11 g fat	fat-free frozen yogurt (½ cup), 110 cal/0 g fat	75 cal/11 g fat
ice cream, strawberry, super premium (½ cup), 188 cal/9 g fat	sherbet, strawberry (½ cup), 154 cal/2 g fat	34 cal/7 g fat
coffee (6 oz) with half-and-half (2 Tbs), 43 cal/3 g fat	coffee (6 oz) with skim milk (2 Tbs), 14 cal/0 g fat	29 cal/3 g fat
cocoa with whole milk, whipped cream (1 cup), 269 cal/15 g fat	cocoa with skim milk and marshmallows (1 cup), 201 cal/1 g fat	68 cal/14 g fat
chicken Kiev (3½ oz), 290 cal/22 g fat	herbed roast chicken breast (3½ oz), 173 cal/5 g fat	117 cal/17 g fat
pizza, sausage (⅛ large pie), 556 cal/22 g fat	pizza, vegetable, with half the usual amount of cheese (⅛ large pie), 425 cal/11 g fat	131 cal/11 g fat
spaghetti (1 cup) with meatballs (2 meatballs with ½ cup sauce), 415 cal/21 g fat	spaghetti (1 cup) with red clam sauce (2 oz clams with ½ cup sauce), 339 cal/8 g fat	76 cal/13 g fat
sweet & sour pork (1 cup) with rice (1 cup), 817 cal/31 g fat	beef with broccoli (1 cup) with rice (1 cup), 563 cal/16 g fat	254 cal/15 g fat
beef, ground regular (3 oz, cooked), 244 cal/18 g fat	turkey, ground regular (3 oz, cooked), 200 cal/11 g fat	44 cal/7 g fat
bologna (1 slice), 88 cal/8 g fat	turkey pastrami (1 slice), 40 cal/2 g fat	48 cal/6 g fat
chicken breast (½), fried with skin 364 cal/18 g fat	chicken breast (½), with skin removed, dipped in bread crumbs and baked, 169 cal/3 g fat	196 cal/15 g fat
frankfurter, beef (1), 142 cal/13 g fat	frankfurter, chicken (1), 116 cal/9 g fat	26 cal/4 g fat
pork chop (3 oz, cooked), 218 cal/13 g fat	pork tenderloin (3 oz, cooked), 141 cal/4 g fat	77 cal/9 g fat

INSTEAD OF:	SWITCH TO:	SAVINGS:
sausage, Italian (1), 214 cal/17 g fat	Italian turkey sausage (1), 131 cal/8 g fat	83 cal/9 g fat
tuna, white meat in oil (6 oz), 316 cal/14 g fat	tuna, white meat in water (6 oz), 232 cal/4 g fat	84 cal/10 g fat
guacamole (2 Tbs), 50 cal/4 g fat	guacamole (2 Tbs) with mashed green peas replacing half the avocado, 31 cal/2 g fat	19 cal/2 g fat
popcorn, microwave (3 cups), 100 cal/6 g fat	popcorn, air-popped, plain (3 cups), 75 cal/0 g fat	25 cal/6 g fat
cream of mushroom, made with whole milk (1 cup), 203 cal/14 g fat	cream of mushroom, made with water (1 cup), 129 cal/9 g fat	74 cal/5 g fat
New England clam chowder (1 cup), 160 cal/7 g fat	Manhattan clam chowder (1 cup), 78 cal/2 g fat	82 cal/5 g fat
macaroni & cheese (¼ box) made using package instructions (whole milk and 4 Tbs margarine), 290 cal/13 g fat	macaroni & cheese (¼ box) made with low-fat milk (1%) and margarine (1 ½ Tbs), 235 cal/4 g fat	55 cal/9 g fat
potato, baked, with butter (1 tsp) and sour cream (1 Tbs), 209 cal/7 g fat	potato, baked, with diet margarine (1 tsp) and nonfat plain yogurt (1 Tbs), 170 cal/2 g fat	39 cal/5 g fat
potato salad (½ cup) made with mayonnaise, 180 cal/10 g fat	potato salad (½ cup) made with low-fat plain yogurt, 104 cal/0 g fat	76 cal/10 g fat
rice, fried (1 cup), 340 cal/12 g fat	brown rice, steamed (1 cup), 216 cal/2 g fat	124 cal/10 g fat
vegetables (1 cup) stir-fried in oil, 180 cal/7 g fat	vegetables (1 cup) stir-fried in nonstick pan with water or broth, 140 cal/2 g fat	40 cal/5 g fat
enchilada, cheese (1), 320 cal/19 g fat	soft taco, chicken (1) 213 cal/10 g fat	107 cal/9 g fat
bacon (¾ oz, before cooking), 36 cal/3 g fat	Canadian bacon (¾ oz, before cooking), 26 cal/1 g fat	10 cal/2 g fat
tortilla chips (1 oz), 142 cal/7 g fat	pretzels (1 oz), 113 cal/1 g fat	29 cal/6 g fat

Peggy Katalinich

MAINTENANCE MOTTO: Never skip breakfast.
FAVORITE FIND: Hidden Valley Fat Free French with Honey & Bacon Dressing: 2 tablespoons, 50 calories, 0 g fat; the bacon adds a haunting smoky flavor. Best with greens and mixed veggies.

"I never dreamed I would hear the sentence, 'Don't lose any more weight,'" says Peggy enthusiastically. As someone who struggled with an extra ten pounds since college, this is music to her ears. And an ongoing motivation to stay on track. "For me, one of the biggest changes was eating breakfast every morning. But having cereal in the A.M. carries me through to lunch, and I've continued this habit. Besides, the accompanying skim milk gives me more calcium, which is so important for women." Another tactic Peggy uses is to eat a huge salad virtually every evening. While she reaches for fat-free dressing most nights, she occasionally treats herself to a classic balsamic vinaigrette. "My new commitment is to the gym," she says. "I want to tone and strengthen and train for a race. Running is so much easier now that I'm not dragging around an extra 25-pound sack."

Diane Mogelever

MAINTENANCE MOTTO: Weigh in once a week.
FAVORITE FIND: Cozy Shack Tapioca Pudding: ½ cup, 130 calories, 3 g fat; refreshing, yet filling, old-fashioned comfort food.

"If I could make it through Christmas, followed by my daughter's wedding, I can make it through anything," exclaims Diane, who noted she actually lost a pound during the two weeks of celebrations. "And I did not deny myself. At the wedding, I enjoyed everything, just not a lot of everything." That said, one of Diane's prime challenges continues to be rice and pasta. "I have half a cup. Period. The End." This whole idea of portion control is key to Diane's success. "I even measured out snack sizes on a napkin, so I could visualize what the proper amounts would be. Now there's no excuse. I know what's appropriate and what's not." But when it comes to candy, there's no portion that's safe. "I just keep it out of the house," she says.

MAINTENANCE MOTTO: Cook ahead and portion it out.

FAVORITE FIND: Slim-Fast Chocolate Fudge Bar: 1 bar, 110 calories, 1.5 g fat; smooth and creamy with a nice chocolate flavor, surprised it was so low-cal!

Keeping a running tally of calories throughout the day helps Julie focus. "I shoot for a total of 1,800 or so," she says. "When I seem to be hungry, I reexamine my tally and try to satisfy my cravings with Diet 7-Up or a small bottle of water." She finds that proper hydration helps her feel full. In addition to the occasional fudge bar, several tools have helped Julie with her weight loss and into the maintenance period. "Since I live alone, I'm always dividing up and freezing uncooked portions. Weighing everything on a food scale allows me to measure out realistic portions," she states. And Ziploc individual storage containers are just the right size to hold dinners. "I wouldn't have made it through the diet without them!" she asserts. As for her fitness formula, Julie visits a personal trainer every so often. "I want to achieve a better muscle tone with targeted training," says Julie. "That way I can both stay motivated and show off the new shape I'm in!"

MAINTENANCE MOTTO: Celebrate what I've accomplished, but keep on going.

FAVORITE FIND: Miss Meringue Vanilla, Coconut, or Chocolate-Raspberry Meringue Cookies: 1 meringue, 20 calories, 0 g fat; irresistible, sweet but not cloying and one is enough; the flavors are pervasive yet subtle.

"I know it's going to be a slow process, but I want to continue to lose," says Donna, who is motivated by the progress she's already made. "Before the diet, going up the stairs at the subway I was huffing and puffing; now I don't feel as winded. Originally it took me 25 minutes to walk to the office; these days it's 15, and my progress depends on the number of people in my way!" Donna has made permanent changes not only in her exercise routine but in the way she snacks (those meringues really do it!) and cooks. "I eliminate a lot of the oil, cut back on cheese, and use turkey instead of ground beef. The switches are so small my family doesn't even notice." Another adjustment she has made is to eat nothing after dinner. "If I started, it would be all down hill," she fears. While she's lost and gained over the years, Donna believes this time it's for real. "Even when I was skinny before, I didn't eat correctly and it couldn't last. Now I feel I am losing the right way."

Michael Tyrrell

MAINTENANCE MOTTO: Get back to the gym.

FAVORITE FIND: Trader Joe's Fat Free Spicy Black Bean Dip: 2 tablespoons, 30 calories, 0 g fat; earthy rich flavor that fills you up before you consume too many calories.

Keeping breakfast and lunch modest, then relaxing his vigilance through dinner hour has helped Michael keep at his goal weight easily. "I don't feel the need to have more in the morning or at noon than I had on the diet plan," he explains. "So maintaining a lower calorie count is simple. Then at dinner, when I have more pasta or an extra glass of wine, I'm still on track because the whole day winds up around 2,000 calories." One change he has made is being very careful when going to friends' homes for dinners or parties. More often than not, he will invite them over and cook so he can control the food, including adding the bean dip to his appetizer array. Secure that he is in charge of his eating patterns, Michael's made a commitment to fitness. "I've started working out in the privacy of my apartment until I feel confident enough to venture out to the gym. The at-home workouts are already making a difference," he says.

Althea Needham

MAINTENANCE MOTTO: Don't give up; there's another 30 to go!

FAVORITE FIND: SmartOnes Chocolate Mousse Low-Fat Chocolate Ice Cream Bars: 1 bar, 40 calories, 1 g fat. The taste is just as good as regular ice cream so there's no temptation to cheat.

Paying strict attention to her meat consumption keeps Althea on the right path. "These days I stop at just one piece of chicken and that's it. I'm not even hungry for more," she says. Instead, she turns to big plates of salad for satisfaction. In addition to adding handfuls of shredded carrots and sliced cucumbers, she revs them up with jalapeño slices. This leaner eating pattern has become ingrained, so much so that a greasy hot dog or burger isn't even appealing. After minor surgery, Althea was disappointed when her doctor advised against strenuous resistance training. "I was surprised how much I missed working out. I know how much faster I can lose weight when I'm lifting weights!" Until she can get back in the gym, Althea has pumped up her walking to include a jaunt at lunchtime. Her willpower is revved not only from her successes thus far, but from the fact she wants to show off her trim, new body the next time she returns to her native Jamaica. "I'll be walking on the beach in a sleeveless dress," she says. "They won't believe their eyes!"

Supermarket Slimmers

We wandered the supermarket aisles in search of new products to keep us on the straight and narrow. These are items we turned to repeatedly not just because they were lower in calories and fat, but because they taste good, too!

Eggo Fat-Free Waffles: 2 waffles, 120 calories, 0 g fat; with a little real maple syrup, these are quite satisfying.

Ken's Steak House Lite Raspberry Walnut Vinaigrette: 2 tablespoons, 80 calories, 6 g fat; toss it with greens and toasted walnuts for an elegant salad—add a little goat cheese and it's almost a meal.

Lucini Gran Riserva Balsamico: 1 tablespoon, 20 calories, 0 g fat; well-priced, high-quality vinegar with lovely balance of sweet and tart, a little goes a long way; good on fruit as well as greens.

Cabot Jalapeño Light Cheddar Cheese: 1 ounce, 70 calories, 4.5 g fat; the full chile flavor makes you forget it's 50% less fat than the traditional version.

Quaker Quakes Rice Snacks, Cheddar Cheese flavor: 9 mini cakes, 70 calories, 2.5 g fat; a lot of munching for so few calories.

Smartfood Popcorn, White Cheddar Cheese Flavored, Reduced Fat: 3 cups, 140 calories, 0 g fat; salty and cheesy with lots of popcorn flavor.

Progresso Classics Soup, Hearty Tomato: 1 cup, 110 calories, 1 g fat; even if you finish the entire can (2 cups), this bold combo of chunky tomatoes and assertive herbs is still relatively low in calories and fat.

Nabisco SnackWell's Cracked Pepper Crackers: 5 crackers, 60 calories, 1.5 g fat; very peppery taste, great with cheese, also salsa; nice crumbled in soup or over a salad to add crunch.

New York Flatbreads: 1 piece, 50 calories, 1 g fat; crunchy, salty, crisp, and filling, serve with soups and salads.

Brummel & Brown Spread: 1 tablespoon, 45 calories, 5 g fat; half the calories and fat of butter or margarine, with a creamy yet tangy flavor reflecting its yogurt base; delectable on bread, crackers, or in mashed potatoes.

Remember Susan McQuillan's mantra, "It's all about the calories"? While much of that equation relates to taking in fewer calories—and that's what this book is all about—it also depends on burning off calories. You'll feel better and your dieting efforts will be much more effective if you devote as little as one hour a week to exercise. So drag yourself out of bed 15 minutes earlier for a series of simple strength-training moves. Or, do as most of us did and turn to walking to rev up your metabolism and shed pounds. Just do something! Our Calorie Burn-Off Counter, below, will give you ideas. Or, if our Top Ten Reasons to Walk inspire you, see Walk Off the Weight (page 242) for specifics on the easiest workout of all.

Calorie Burn-Off Counter

Check this chart of common activities to jumpstart your fitness level. These figures are based on 30 minutes of activity for a 150-pound adult. If you weigh more, you'll zap more calories in the same time; if you weigh less, you'll burn fewer.

Aerobic dance (medium intensity)	210	Raking	111
Basketball	282	Running (9-minute mile)	393
Bicycling		Shoveling snow	300
(5.5 mph)	132	Skiing	
(9.5 mph)	204	cross-country, walking speed	290
Badminton	195	downhill	201
Ballroom dancing	102	Swimming	
Bowling	120	slow crawl	261
Calisthenics	150	fast crawl	318
Climbing hills	246	Table tennis	138
with 9-pound load	261	Tennis (singles)	210
Climbing stairs	360	Volleyball	102
Golf	171	Walking	
Hoeing	183	(stroll, 1 mph)	60
Housework (light: dusting, etc.)	75	(brisk, 4 mph)	180
Jogging (6 mph)	330	(while pushing baby carriage)	100
Jumping rope	330	Washing windows	120
Mopping floors	126	Weeding	147
Mowing lawn	228	Weight training (circuit training)	180

10   It can help you live longer. Studies report that active people outlive inactive folk.

9   It helps you lose weight and lower blood pressure.

8   It tones your entire body. You'll add lean muscle and decrease your chance of injury.

7   It strengthens your heart, lungs, and bones. You gain stamina.

6   It prompts your brain to produce more feel-good chemicals.

5   It helps you sleep better, by both tiring and relaxing you.

4   It improves posture, as you stride with your chest and head up, shoulders back.

3   It's fun! Make it a date with your mate.

2   It's free (almost). Sturdy, well-padded shoes are all you need.

. . . and the number 1 reason to walk . . .

It's easy! You already know how to do it.

Walk Off the Weight

Hit the road! More than 70 million people participate in this, the most popular workout of them all. To follow our program, first find your fitness level in our chart and use the corresponding routine. (Consult your doctor before beginning.) Whether you're new to walking or a seasoned pro, these personalized plans will help you progress at a comfortable pace. No need to worry about boredom. Our special "Booster Shots" are guaranteed to keep your interest up. So lace your sneakers. It's time to walk your way to a better body.

To warm up: Walk a little slower than your normal exercise pace for about 5 to 8 minutes.

To cool down: Walk slower than your normal exercise pace for 3 to 5 minutes. Follow up with stretches.

BEGINNER

You currently have little to no regular physical activity, don't take part in any sports or exercise, and have a relatively inactive lifestyle or job.

Your goal: To create a daily walking habit. Initially, how far or how fast you walk matters much less than that you simply get out every day.

Sunday Walk for 15 minutes; after 4 weeks add Booster Shot 1.

Monday Walk for 10 minutes.

Tuesday Walk for 15 minutes.

Wednesday Walk for 20 minutes; after 4 weeks add Booster Shot 3.

Thursday Walk for 10 minutes.

Friday Walk for 15 minutes.

Saturday No walk today. Instead, do 30 minutes of an easy activity, say, gardening.

How to progress: Over next 8 weeks, add 5 minutes to every third day until you're walking 30 minutes most days of the week. Add pep to your step as you move on from week to week.

INTERMEDIATE

You participate in sporadic physical activity, are motivated to get exercise on occasion, and have a somewhat active lifestyle or job.

Your goal: To work up to a routine of regularly walking more than 30 minutes several days per week.

Sunday Walk for 40 minutes.

Monday Walk 20 minutes; do Booster Shot 1.

Tuesday Walk 30 minutes; do Booster Shot 3.

Wednesday Walk 25 minutes; do Booster Shot 4.

Thursday Walk for 35 minutes.

Friday Walk 30 minutes; do Booster Shot 5.

Saturday No walk today. Instead, do 45 minutes of a moderate activity, such as biking.

How to progress: Over next 8 weeks, add 5 minutes every other day until you're walking 45 to 60 minutes several days a week. Be certain to stride briskly during shorter outings.

ADVANCED

You already take part in a sport or exercise program, and have an active lifestyle or job.

Your goal: To focus on increasing the duration of some of your walks and the walking speed of others.

Sunday Walk for 60 minutes.

Monday Walk 20 minutes; do Booster Shot 1.

Tuesday Walk for 45 minutes; do Booster Shots 3 and 4.

Wednesday Walk for 35 minutes; do Booster Shot 2.

Thursday Walk for 50 minutes.

Friday Walk 30 minutes; do Booster Shot 5.

Saturday No walk today. Instead, do an hour of vigorous activity, for instance, aerobics.

How to progress: Over next 8 weeks, add 5 minutes to Sunday and/or Thursday walk; gradually speed up Monday, Wednesday, Friday walks to a very brisk pace (breathing hard, not panting or gasping).

BOOSTER SHOTS

These five add-on activities will give your walking workout a quick hit of adrenaline, helping you burn extra calories and build more strength with each step. Make sure you are at least 10 minutes into your walk before you do any of them.

1   **Burn Rubber** Walk as quickly as you can for 2 minutes and then cruise comfortably for 3 minutes. Repeat these speed bursts 3 to 6 times.

2   **Step It Up** Make sure your walking route takes you by stairs—for example, at a public building, near a bridge, or on bleachers at an athletic field. Dash up 10 to 40 steps, taking 2 at a time, then continue on your walk. Try to fit in 3 to 5 of these thigh- and buttock-firming forays during your outing.

3   **Lunge Forward** Do walking lunges for 30 seconds. Take a big step forward, bending both knees to 90° angles. As you come up, take another big step forward, and lunge again, bending knees to 90° angles. Repeat at least twice.

4   **Skip It** Walk forward 100 paces, then turn around and skip back to the starting point, driving your arms and raising your knees high and fast as you skip. Repeat at least twice.

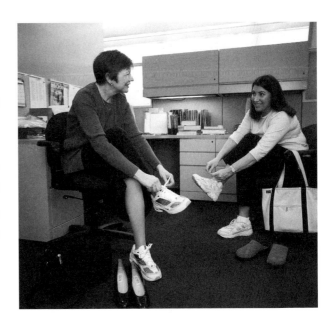

5   **Hop-to** Walk forward 100 paces, turn around and hop back to the starting point. Do 5 hops on one foot, and 5 on the other, alternating the whole way. Repeat at least twice.

DO'S AND DON'TS TO LIVE BY

Finally, take these tips to heart. We did. And if it worked for us, it can work for you!

- DO forgive any momentary lapses, then get back on track right away.

- DON'T banish favorite high-calorie foods; just eat them less often. (And share!)

- DO make everyday activities part of your workout.

- DON'T weigh in more than once a week.

- DO feel positive about who you are.

- DON'T skip meals. This can cause your blood sugar to dip; if you make it a habit, it slows down your metabolism.

- DO keep a sense of humor, especially about yourself.

NUTRITION DATA BACKGROUND

Nutrition analysis for the recipes in this book was completed using Food Processor for Windows, Nutrition Analysis & Fitness Software, Version 7.5, ESHA Research, Professional Nutrition Analysis Software & Databases.

All data presented in the recipe analyses were rounded to the nearest whole figure. The following list indicates the terminology and brands used in certain categories where the values vary. "Fat free" and "nonfat" are used interchangeably.

		CALORIES	FAT (GRAMS)
Mayonnaise			
Fat-Free (Kraft)	1 tablespoon	11.2 calories	0.4 g fat
Reduced-Fat Mayonnaise Dressing (Just 2 Good)	1 tablespoon	25	1
Light (Hellmanns/ Best Foods)	1 tablespoon	50	5
Frozen Nondairy Whipped Topping (all Kraft Cool Whip)			
Light	1 tablespoon	10	0.5
Fat-Free	1 tablespoon	7.5	0
Cream Cheese			
⅓-Less-Fat (Kraft Neufchatel)	1 tablespoon	35	3
Light (Weight Watchers)	1 tablespoon	20	1.3
Fat-Free (Kraft)	1 tablespoon	14.3	0
Sour Cream (all Land O' Lakes)			
Light	1 tablespoon	17.5	1
Fat-Free	1 tablespoon	15	0

ACKNOWLEDGMENTS

Thanks to the entire *Family Circle* food department for undertaking this project: Diane Mogelever, Julie Miltenberger, Donna Meadow, Michael Tyrrell, and Althea Needham. In addition, many thanks to David Ricketts for his careful recipe editing and Ana Dane for her support in all aspects of the book production. More kudos to Cheryl Solimini for her insightful interviews, executive editor Barbara Winkler for her care in editing and copywriting, and Susan McQuillan for her skill in designing the successful diet plan. Appreciation to art director David Wolf for his design insights, and editor-in-chief Susan Ungaro for her support. Thanks to regular *FC* contributors Andrew Schloss, Michael Krondl, Patty Santelli, Mindy Hermann, R.D., and photographic contributors Mark Ferri, Mark Thomas, Brian Hagiwara, Steve Cohen, Alan Richardson, Beatriz Da Costa, and Katrina De Leon. At ReganBooks, thanks to senior editor Cassie Jones for her speedy yet thoughtful read.

—*Peggy Katalinich*

INDEX